Compression (135)

How can you fit a quart of data into a pint pot of memory? Use a compressed representation to reduce the memory required.

TABLE COMPRESSION (143) How can you compress many short strings? Encode each element in a variable number of bits so that the more common elements require fewer bits.

DIFFERENCE CODING (153) How can you reduce the memory used by sequences of data? Represent sequences according to the differences between each item.

ADAPTIVE COMPRESSION (160) How can you reduce the memory needed to store a large amount of bulk data? Use an adaptive compression algorithm.

Small Data Structures (169)

How can you reduce the memory needed for your data? Choose the smallest structure that supports the operations you need.

PACKED DATA (174) How can you reduce the memory needed to store a data structure? Pack data items within the structure so that they occupy the minimum space.

SHARING (182) How can you avoid multiple copies of the same information? Store information once, and share it everywhere it is needed.

COPY-ON-WRITE (191) How can you change a shared object without affecting its other clients? Share the object until you need to change it, then copy it and use the copy in future.

EMBEDDED POINTERS (198) How can you reduce the space used by a collection of objects? Embed the pointers maintaining the collection into each object.

MULTIPLE REPRESENTATIONS (209) How can you support several different implementations of an object? Make each implementation satisfy a common interface.

Memory Allocation (219)

How do you allocate memory to store your data structures? Choose the simplest allocation technique that meets your need.

FIXED ALLOCATION (226) How can you ensure you will never run out of memory? Pre-allocate objects during initialization.

VARIABLE ALLOCATION (236) How can you avoid unused empty space? Allocate and deallocate variable-sized objects as and when you need them.

MEMORY DISCARD (244) How can you allocate temporary objects? Allocate objects from a temporary workspace and discard it on completion.

POOLED ALLOCATION (251) How can you allocate a large number of similar objects? Pre-allocate a pool of objects, and recycle unused objects.

COMPACTION (259) How do you recover memory lost to fragmentation? Move objects in memory to remove unused space between them.

REFERENCE COUNTING (268) How do you know when to delete a shared object? Keep a count of the references to each shared object, and delete each object when its count is zero.

GARBAGE COLLECTION (278) How do you know when to delete shared objects? Identify unreferenced objects, and deallocate them.

Katharine Tristaino
Marketing Specialist
Addison-Wesley
katharine.tristaino@aw.com
617.848.6532

SMALL
MEMORY
SOFTWARE

SMALL MEMORY SOFTWARE

Patterns for systems with limited memory

JAMES NOBLE and CHARLES WEIR

Illustrated by Duane Bibby

 Addison-Wesley

An imprint of **Pearson Education**

Harlow, England • London • New York • Reading, Massachusetts • San Francisco • Toronto

Don Mills, Ontario • Sydney • Tokyo • Singapore • Hong Kong • Seoul • Taipei • Cape Town

Madrid • Mexico City • Amsterdam • Munich • Paris • Milan

PEARSON EDUCATION LIMITED

Head Office:
Edinburgh Gate
Harlow CM20 2JE
Tel: +44 (0)1279 623623
Fax: +44 (0)1279 431059

London Office:
128 Long Acre
London WC2E 9AN
Tel: +44 (0)20 7447 2000
Fax: +44(0)20 7240 5771

Website: *www.aw.com/cseng*

First published in Great Britain 2001

ISBN 0 201 59607 5

British Library Cataloguing in Publication Data
A catalogue record for this book can be obtained from the British Library

Library of Congress Cataloging in Publication Data

Noble, James, 1967-
   Small memory software: patterns for systems with limited memory / James Noble and
Charles Weir.
      p. cm.
   Includes bibliographical references and index.
   ISBN 0-201-59607-5 (alk. paper)
      1. Memory management (Computer science) 2. Systems software. I. Weir, Charles,
1961- II. Title.

QA76.9.M45 N63 2000   00-061846
005.4'35–dc21

The programs in this book have been included for their instructional value. The publisher does not
offer any warranties or representations in respect of their fitness for a particular purpose,
nor does the publisher accept any liability for any loss or damage arising from their use.

Many of the designations used by manufacturers and sellers to distinguish their
products are claimed as trademarks. Pearson Education Limited has made every
attempt to supply trademark information about manufacturers and their products mentioned
in this book. A list of trademark designations and their owners appears on page vi.

10 9 8 7 6 5 4 3 2 1

Illustrated by Duane Bibby.
Typeset by M Rules.
Printed and bound in the United States of America.

The publishers' policy is to use paper manufactured from sustainable forests.

To Julia and to Katherine.

Who have suffered long and are kind.

TRADEMARK NOTICE

FOREWORD

It's downright silly to imply that personal computers are the only mass-market computing platform. According to Forrester Research, consumer spending on PCs peaked in 1999 even as spending on non-PC computing devices skyrocketed, with no end in sight. It's equally silly to claim that memory has ceased to be an important constraint in programming. 'If it's a problem, just buy more,' is the prevailing sentiment. But underneath all desktop applications, even the most memory-efficient ones, lurks a behemoth of software infrastructure with an appalling appetite for memory. Hundreds of megabytes — quantities that not long ago were used to describe the capacity of hard disks and tape drives — are now merely the price of admission, with 'large' memories measured exclusively in gigabytes. Just what is all that RAM storing, anyhow?

Some of the profligacy is for good reason. It may save the programmer time through code reuse, with implementation compromises causing redundancy at the binary level. It may be the result of trading space for time to make an application more responsive. It may reflect a truly challenging problem that is inherently memory-intensive. It may be all those things.

More often than not, though, high memory requirements come from sloppy programming, sloppy design, sloppy development methodology, and sloppy combinations thereof. Such causes can be avoided. The tragedy is that they're often not *worth* avoiding — at least not in the short term. Market realities and the 'worse is better' syndrome argue for getting the product out the door now and fixing it later. Sadly, memory problems are all too easily fixed ('Buy more!'), and 'later' never comes. Memory consumption is typically the last thing to be addressed, if it's addressed at all.

But a wondrous thing has been happening of late: the profusion of embedded systems and handheld digital devices — what we at IBM call 'pervasive computing'. These systems, with their limited computing horsepower dictated mostly by today's primitive battery technology, and with limited RAM as dictated by size or cost, have forced programmers to reexamine memory consumption as a developmental constraint. Eventually, one discovers that memory efficiency isn't something you hack in after the system's limping along; it must be *designed* in from the get-go. The hard part is figuring out how to do it.

For too long, these programmers have had to reinvent the tricks of the memory conservation trade, even though such tricks been around roughly as long as the von Neumann architecture. Indeed, conserving memory was the name of the game throughout computing's first quarter century, until virtual memory became widely available. Still, relentless miniaturization has always allowed for a class of computing devices with problematically small memories. The difference today is that such devices are quickly outstripping every other class of computers both in quantity and in diversity of applications.

That's what makes this book so significant. James and Charles offer a timesaver if not a lifesaver to the programmer of these devices. The authors have captured, in a succinct and potent form, most of the age-old yet essential and non-obvious memory-saving techniques of computerdom. These techniques have been described before, but never like this — as a catalogue of patterns woven into a synergistic whole, completely practical, technologically up-to-date, and immediately useful. I can scarcely overstate the book's potential impact on software development, be it software that runs on a PDA, a cell phone, a pager, or — most probably — an unsung embedded system. There's something here for everyone who writes small memory software. Even if you think you have memory to burn, these patterns will give you a healthy perspective on memory consumption, making your programs less prone to gluttony.

You can read the book cover to cover, but much of what you read will end up like water off a duck's back. The true benefits come from encountering a real problem, finding a relevant pattern, and applying it to solve the problem. Therefore I recommend you study and apply pattern(s) while you design and implement your code. As you do, invariably you'll find yourself bending a pattern to fit a problem. A good pattern will make that possible, if not easy, not by telling you the answer — which it could never do in detail, because no two problems are exactly the same — but by educating you about the problem. That's why you'll find the 'forces' sections so valuable: they reveal the constraints on how the problem is solved, whittling down the space of solutions to a much smaller (but probably still large) set of possibilities. Which one suits you best depends in part on the essential trade-offs you're willing and able to make, and the accidental constraints you have to work under. The rest depends on your creativity. Of course, a book like this can help you be creative, but creativity doesn't come in book form; it's entirely up to you.

Nevertheless, rest assured that if you're in the business of programming memory-constrained systems and you start using this book, it won't be long before you consider it a godsend.

John Vlissides
IBM, T.J. Watson Research

PREFACE

Once upon a time computer memory was one of the most expensive commodities on earth, and large amounts of human ingenuity were spent trying to simulate supernova explosions with nothing more than a future Nobel prize winner and a vast array of vacuum tubes. Nowadays many people have enough computer memory to simulate the destruction of most of the galaxy in any one of their hand-held phones, digital diaries, or microwave ovens.

But at least two things have remained constant throughout the history of computing. Software design remains hard (Gamma et al. 1995), and its functionality still expands to fill the memory available (Potter 1948). This book addresses both these issues. Patterns have proved a successful format to capture knowledge about software design; these patterns in particular tackle memory requirements.

As authors we had several additional aims in writing this book. As patterns researchers and writers we wanted to learn more about patterns and pattern writing, and as software designers and architects we wanted to study existing systems to learn from them. In particular:

- we wanted to gain and share an in-depth knowledge of portable small memory techniques; techniques that work in many different environments;
- we wanted to write a complete set of patterns dealing with one single force — in this case, memory requirements;
- we wanted to study the relationships between patterns, and to group and order the patterns based on these mutual relationships, and lastly
- we wanted an approachable book, one to skim for fun rather than to suffer as a penance.

This book is the result. It's written for software developers and architects, like ourselves, whether or not you happen to be facing memory constraints in your immediate work.

To make the book more approachable (and more fun to write) we've taken a light-hearted slant in most of our examples for the patterns and with Duane Bibby's cartoons. If frivolity doesn't appeal to you, please ignore the cartoons and the paragraphs describing the examples: the remaining text is as rigorous as we can make it.

This book is still a work in progress. We have incorporated the comments of many people, and we welcome more. You can contact us at our website, http://www.smallmemory.com/

ACKNOWLEDGEMENTS

No book can be the work of just its authors. First, we need to thank John Vlissides, our indefatigable series editor: we still have copies of the e-mail where he suggested this mad endeavour, and we're grateful for his many comments on our patterns, from the original EuroPLoP paper to the final drafts. Second, this book would not be the same without Duane Bibby's illustrations, and we hope you like them as much as we do.

We take the blame for this book's many weaknesses, but credit for most of its strengths goes to those members of the Memory Preservation Society (and fellow travellers) who took the time to read and comment on drafts of the patterns and the manuscript. These people include but are not limited to John Vlissides (again), Paul Dyson, Linda Rising, Klaus Marquardt, and Liping Zhao (EuroPLoP and KoalaPLoP shepherds for these patterns), Tim Bell, Jim Coplien, Frank Buschmann, Alan Dearle, Martine Devos, Martin Fowler, Nick Grattan, Neil Harrison, Benedict Heal, David Holmes, Ian Horrocks, Nick Healy, Dave Mery, Matt Millar, Alistair Moffat, Eliot Moss, Alan O'Callaghan, Will Ramsey, Michael Richmond, Hans Rohnert, Andreas Rüping, Peter Sommerlad, Laurence Vanhelsuwe, Malcolm Weir, and the Software Architecture Group at the University of Illinois and Urbana-Champaign, including: Federico Balaguer, John Brant, Alan Carrol, Ian Chai, Diego Fernandez, Brian Foote, Alejandra Garrido, John Han, Peter Hatch, Ralph Johnson, Apu Kapadia, Aaron Klish, An Le, Dragos-Anton Manolescu, Brian Marick, Reza Razavi, Don Roberts, Paul Rubel, Les Tyrrell, Roger Whitney, Weerasak Witthawaskul, Joseph W. Yoder, and Bosko Zivaljevic.

The team at Addison-Wesley UK (or Pearson Education, we forget which) have been great in dealing with two authors on opposite sides of the globe. We'd like to thank Sally Mortimore (for starting it all off), Allison Birtwell (for finishing it all up), and Katherin Ekstrom (for staying the distance). Credit goes also to two artists, George Platts for suggesting illustrations and Trevor Coard for creating many of them.

Finally, we must thank all the members of the patterns community, especially those who have attended the EuroPLoP conferences in Kloster Irsee. We are both admirers of the patterns 'literature' (in the same way one might be might be a fan of science fiction literature) and hope this collection of patterns will be a worthy contribution to the canon.

CONTENTS

Foreword   *vii*
Preface   *ix*
Acknowledgements   *xi*

Introduction   *1*

How to use this book   *3*
Introduction to small memory   *6*
Introduction to patterns   *11*
The patterns in this book   *18*

1 Small Architecture   *25*

Memory Limit   *32*
Small Interfaces   *38*
Partial Failure   *48*
Captain Oates   *57*
Read-Only Memory   *65*
Hooks   *72*

2 Secondary Storage   *79*

Application Switching   *84*
Data Files   *92*
Resource Files   *101*
Packages   *108*
Paging   *119*

3 Compression   135

Table Compression   143
Difference Coding   153
Adaptive Compression   160

4 Small Data Structures   169

Packed Data   174
Sharing   182
Copy-on-Write   191
Embedded Pointers   198
Multiple Representations   209

5 Memory Allocation   219

Fixed Allocation   226
Variable Allocation   236
Memory Discard   244
Pooled Allocation   251
Compaction   259
Reference Counting   268
Garbage Collection   278

Appendix: A Discussion of Forces   291

Forces in this book   292
Forces related to non-functional requirements   294
Architectural impact   302
Development process   305

References   310
Index   323

INTRODUCTION

How to use this book

Introduction to small memory

Introduction to patterns

The patterns in this book

INTRODUCTION

'Small is Beautiful'   E. F. SCHUMACHER

'You can never be too rich or too thin'   BARBARA HUTTON

Designing small software that can run efficiently in a limited memory space was, until recently, a dying art. PCs, workstations, and mainframes appeared to have exponentially increasing amounts of memory and processor speed, and it was becoming rare for programmers even to need to think about memory constraints.

At the turn of a new century, we're discovering an imminent market of hundreds of millions of mobile devices, demanding enormous amounts of high-specification software; physical size and power limitations mean these devices will have relatively limited memory. At the same time, the programmers of web and database servers are finding that their applications must be memory-efficient to support the hundreds of thousands of simultaneous users they need for profitability. Even PC and workstation programmers are finding that the demands of video and multimedia can challenge their system's memory capacities beyond reasonable limits. Small memory software is back!

But what is small memory software? Memory size, like riches or beauty, is always relative. Whether a particular amount of memory is small or large depends on the requirements the software should meet, on the underlying software and hardware architecture, and on much else. A weather-calculation program on a vast computer may be just as constrained by memory limits as a word-processor running on a mobile phone, or an embedded application on a smart card. Therefore:

> Small memory software is any software that doesn't have as much memory
> as you'd like!

This book is written for programmers, designers and architects of small memory software. You may be designing and implementing a new system, maintaining an existing one, or merely seeking to expand your knowledge of software design.

In this book we've described the most important programming techniques we've encountered in successful small memory systems. We've analysed the techniques as *patterns* — descriptions in a particular form of things already known to work (Alexander et al. 1977; 1979). Patterns are not invented, but are identified or *mined* from existing systems and practices. To produce the patterns in this book we've investigated the design of many successful systems that run on small machines. This book distils the essence of the techniques that seem most responsible for the systems' success.

The patterns in this book consider only limitations on memory: random access memory (RAM), and to a lesser extent read-only memory (ROM) and secondary storage, such as disk or battery-backed RAM. A practical system will have many other limitations; there may be constraints on graphics and output resources, network bandwidth, processing power, or real-time responsiveness, to name just a few. Although we focus on memory requirements, some of these patterns may help with these other constraints; others will be less appropriate: compression, for example, may be unsuitable where there are significant constraints on processor power; paging is unhelpful for real-time performance. We've indicated in the individual patterns how they may help or hinder supporting other constraints.

The rest of this chapter introduces the patterns in more detail. The sections are as follows:

How to use this book	Suggests how you might approach this book if you don't want to read every page.
Introduction to small memory	Describes the problem in detail, and contrasts typical kinds of memory-constrained software.
Introduction to patterns	Introduces patterns and explains the pattern format used in this book.
The patterns in this book	Suggests several different ways of locating, relating and contrasting all the patterns in the book.

How to use this book

You can, of course, start reading this book at page one and continue through to the end. But many people will prefer to use this book as a combination of several things:

- a programmer's introduction to small memory software;
- a quick overview of all the techniques you might want to use;
- a reference book to consult when you have a problem you need to solve;
- an implementation guide showing the tricks and pitfalls of using common — or less common — patterns.

The following sections explain how to use this book for each of the above, and also for other more specialized purposes:

- solving a particular strategic problem;
- academic study;
- keeping the boss happy.

A programmer's introduction to small memory software

Perhaps you're starting as a new developer on a memory-constrained project, and haven't worked on these kinds of projects before.

If so, you'll want to read about the programming and design-level patterns that will affect your daily work. Often your major design concern will initially be class design, so start with the straightforward PACKED DATA (174). You can then continue exploring several other SMALL DATA STRUCTURE (169) patterns used a lot in memory-limited systems: SHARING (182), COPY-ON-WRITE (191) and EMBEDDED POINTERS (198).

The immediate choices in coding are often how to allocate data structures, so next compare the three common forms of memory allocation: FIXED ALLOCATION (226), VARIABLE ALLOCATION (236) and MEMORY DISCARD (244). Equally important is how you'll have to handle running out of memory, so have a look at the important PARTIAL FAILURE (48) pattern, and perhaps also the simple MEMORY LIMIT (32) one.

Finally, most practical small memory systems will use the machine hardware in different ways to save memory. So explore the possibilities of READ-ONLY MEMORY (65), APPLICATION SWITCHING (84) and DATA FILES (92).

The description of each of these patterns discusses how other patterns complement them or provide alternatives, so by reading these patterns you can learn the most important techniques and get an overview of the rest of the book.

Quick overview of all the techniques

A crucial benefit of a collection of patterns is that it creates a shared *language* of pattern names to use when you're discussing the topic (Gamma et al. 1995; Coplien 1996). To learn this language, you can scan all the patterns quickly, reading the main substance but ignoring all the gritty details, code and implementation notes. We've structured this book to make this easy to do. Start at the first pattern SMALL ARCHITECTURE (25) and read through each pattern down to the first break:

This first part of the pattern provides all you really need to know about it: the problem, its context, a simple example, and the solution. Skimming all the patterns in this way takes a careful reader a couple of hours, and provides an overview of all the patterns with enough detail that you can begin to remember the names and basic ideas of the patterns.

Reference for problem solving

Perhaps you're already working on a project, in a desperate hurry, but faced with a thorny problem with no simple answer. In this case, first consult the brief summaries of patterns in the front cover. If one or more patterns look suitable, then turn to each one and read its bullet points and 'Therefore' paragraph to see if it's really what you're after.

If that approach doesn't produce a perfect match, then use the index to look for keywords related to your problem, and again scan the patterns to see which are suitable.

If none of the patterns you've found so far are quite what you want, then have a look at the summary pattern diagram in the back cover — there may be useful patterns related to the ones you've already checked. Check the 'See also' sections at the end of the patterns that seem most useful; perhaps one of the related patterns might address your problem.

Implementation guide

Perhaps you've already decided that one or more of the patterns are right for you. You may have known the technique all along, although you've not thought of it as a pattern, and you've decided — or been told — to use it to implement part of your system.

In this case you can consult the full text for each specific pattern you've chosen. Find the pattern using the summary in the front cover, and turn to the Implementation section for a discussion of many of the issues you'll come across in using the pattern, and some of the techniques other implementers have successfully used to solve them. If you prefer looking at specifics such as code, turn to the Example section first and then move back to the Implementation section.

You can also look at the Known uses section — perhaps the systems will be familiar and you can find out how they've implemented the pattern, and the See also section guides you to other patterns you may find useful.

Helping define a project strategy

If you're defining the overall strategy for a software project (Goldberg and Rubin 1995), you'll probably be concerned about many other issues in addition to memory restrictions. Maybe you're worried about time performance, real-time constraints, a hurried delivery schedule or a need for the system to last for several decades.

In this case turn to the discussion in the Appendix. These concerns are called *forces* (Alexander 1979). Scan the Appendix to identify the forces you're interested in; the sections on each force will tell you which patterns will best suit your needs.

Academic study

Of course many people still enjoy reading books from start to finish. We have written this book so that it can also be read in this traditional, second millennium style.

Each chapter starts with the simpler patterns that are easy to understand, and progresses towards the more sophisticated patterns; the patterns that come first in a chapter lead to the patterns that follow afterwards. The chapters make a similar progression, starting with the large-scale patterns you are most likely to need early in a project (SMALL ARCHITECTURE) and progressing to the most implementation-specific patterns (MEMORY ALLOCATION (219)).

Keeping the boss happy

Maybe you really don't care about this stuff at all, but your manager has bought this book for you and you want to retain your credibility. In this case, leave the book open face down on a radiator for three days. The book will then look as though you've read it, without any effort required on your part (Covey 1990).

Introduction to small memory

What makes a system small? We expect that the patterns in this book will be most useful for systems with memory capacities roughly between 50K and 10Mbytes total, although many of the patterns are frequently used with much smaller and even much larger systems.

Here are four different kinds of projects that can have difficulty meeting their memory requirements, and consequently can benefit from the patterns in this book:

1. Mobile computing

Palmtops, pagers, mobile phones, and similar devices are becoming increasingly important. Users of these mobile machines are demanding more complex and feature-ridden software, ultimately comparable to that on their desktops. But, compared to desktop systems, a portable device's hardware resources, particularly memory, are quite limited. Because of their ubiquitous nature (Norman 1998) these machines also need to be more robust than desktop machines — a digital diary with no hard disk cannot be restarted without losing its data.

Developments for such machines must take far more care with memory constraints than in similar applications for PCs and workstations. Virtually all the patterns in this book may be relevant to any given project.

2. Embedded systems

A second category of physically small device is embedded systems such as process control systems, medical systems and smart cards. When a posh new car can have more than a hundred microprocessors in it, and with predictions that we'll all have several embedded microprocessors in our bodies within the next decade, this is a very important area.

Embedded devices are limited by their memory, and have to be robust, but in addition they often have to meet hard real-time processing deadlines. If they are life critical or mission critical they must meet stringent quality control and auditing requirements too.

In systems with memory capacity much below about 50 Kbytes, the software must be tightly optimized for memory, and typically must make drastic trade-offs of functionality to fit into the available memory. In particular, the entire object-oriented paradigm, though possible, becomes less helpful as heap allocation becomes inappropriate. When implementing systems below 50Kbytes, the MEMORY ALLOCATION and DATA STRUCTURE (169) patterns are probably the most important.

3. Small slice of a big pie

Many ostensibly huge machines — mainframes, minicomputers or PC servers — can also face problems with memory capacity. These very large machines are most cost-effective when supporting hundreds, thousands, or even hundreds of thousands of simultaneous sessions. Even though they are physically very large, with huge physical memory capacities and communication bandwidths, their large workloads often leave relatively modest amounts of memory for each individual session.

For example, most Java virtual machines in 2000 require at least 10 Mbytes of memory to run. Yet a Java-based web server may need to support ten thousand simultaneous sessions. Naively replicating a single user virtual machine for each session would require a real hardware server with 100 Gigabytes of main memory, not counting the memory required for the application on each virtual machine. The patterns in this book, particularly the DATA STRUCTURE patterns, can increase the capacity of such servers to support large numbers of users.

4. Big problems on big machines

In single-user systems with a memory capacity greater than 10 Mbytes, memory is rarely the major concern for most applications, but general-purpose computers can still suffer from limited memory capacity.

For example, organizations may have a large investment in particular hardware with a set memory capacity that it is not feasible to increase. What happens if you're a bank with twenty thousand three-year-old PCs sitting on your tellers' desks and would like to upgrade the software? What happens if you bought a new 1 Gigabyte server last year, can't afford this year's model, but need to process 2 Gigabytes this year? Even if you could afford to upgrade the machines, other demands (such as your staff bonus) may have higher priority.

Alternatively, you may be working on an application that must handle very large amounts of data, such as multimedia editing, video processing, pattern recognition, weather prediction, or maintaining a collection of detailed bitmap images of the entire world. Any such application could easily exhaust the RAM in even a large system, so you'll need careful design to limit its memory use. For such applications, the SECONDARY STORAGE (79) and COMPRESSION (135) patterns are particularly important.

Ultimately, no computer can ever have enough memory. Users can always run more simultaneous tasks, process larger data sets, or simply choose a less expensive machine with a lower physical memory capacity. In a small way, every machine has a small memory.

Types of memory constraint

Imagine you're just starting a new project in a new environment. How can you determine which memory constraints are likely to be a problem, and what types of constraint will give the most trouble?

Hardware constraints

Depending on your system, you may have constraints on one or more of the following types of memory:

RAM memory | Used for executing code, execution stacks, transient data and persistent data.

ROM memory | Used for executing code and read-only data.

Secondary storage | Used for code storage, read-only data, and persistent data.

You may also have more specific constraints: for example, stack size may be limited, or you may have both dynamic RAM, which is fast but requires power to keep its data, and static RAM, which is slower but will keep data with very little power.

RAM is usually the most expensive form of memory, so many types of system keep code on secondary storage and load it into RAM memory only when it's needed; they may also share the loaded code between different users or applications.

Software constraints

Most software environments don't represent their memory use in terms of main memory, ROM and secondary storage. Instead, as a designer, you'll usually find yourself dealing with heap, stack and file sizes. Table I.1 below shows typical attributes of software and how each maps to the types of physical memory discussed above.

Table I.1   Mapping software attributes to physical memory

Attribute	Where it lives
Persistent data	Secondary storage or RAM
Heap and static data	RAM
Code storage	Secondary storage or ROM
Executing code	RAM or ROM
Stack	RAM

Different types of memory-constrained system

Different kinds of systems have different resources and different constraints. Table I.2 describes four typical kinds of system: embedded systems, mobile phones or digital assistants, PCs or workstations, and large mainframe servers. This table is intended to be a general guide, and few practical systems will match it exactly. An embedded system for a network card will most certainly have network support, for example; many mainframes may provide GUI terminals; a games console might lie somewhere between an embedded system and a PDA.

Table I.2   Comparison of different kinds of system

	Embedded system	Mobile phone, PDA	PC, workstation	Mainframe or server farm
Typical applications	Device control, protocol conversion, etc.	Diary, address book, phone, e-mail	Word processing, spreadsheet, small database, accounting	E-commerce, large database applications, accounting, stock control
UI	None	GUI, libraries in ROM	GUI, with several possible libraries as DLLs on disk	Implemented by clients, browsers, or terminals
Network	None, serial connection, or industrial LAN	TCP/IP over a wireless connection	10 MBps LAN	100 MBps LAN
Other IO	As needed – often the main purpose of device	Serial connections	Serial and parallel ports, modem, etc.	Any, accessed via LAN

All these environments will normally keep transient program and stack data in RAM, but differ considerably in their other memory use. Table I.3 shows how each of these kinds of system typically implements each kind of software memory.

Table I.3   Memory use on each type of system

	Embedded system	Mobile phone, PDA	PC, workstation	Mainframe or server farm
Vendor-supplied code	ROM	ROM	Disk, loaded to RAM	Disk, loaded to RAM
Third-party code	None	Loaded to RAM from flash memory	As vendor-supplied code	As vendor-supplied code
Shared code	None	DLLs shared between multiple applications	DLLs shared between multiple applications	DLL and application code shared between multiple users
Persistent data	None, or RAM	RAM or flash memory	Local hard disk or network server	Secondary disk devices

Note how mobile phones and PDAs treat third-party code differently from vendor-supplied code, since the former cannot live in ROM.

Relative importance of memory constraints

Table I.4 shows the importance of the different constraints on memory for typical applications on each kind of system discussed above. Three diamonds mean that the constraint is usually the chief driver for a typical project architecture; two diamonds mean that it is an important design consideration. One diamond means that the constraint may need some effort from programmers but probably won't affect the architecture significantly; and no stars mean that it's virtually irrelevant to development.

Table I.4   Importance of memory constraints

	Embedded system	Wireless PDA	PC, workstation	Mainframe or server farm
Code storage	❖ ❖	❖ ❖		
Code working set		❖ ❖	❖	
Heap and stack	❖ ❖ ❖	❖ ❖	❖	❖
Persistent data	❖ ❖ ❖	❖		

In practice, every development is different; there will be some smart card applications that can virtually ignore the restrictions on heap and stack memory, just as there will be some mainframe applications where the main constraint is on persistent storage.

Introduction to patterns

What, then, actually *is* a pattern? The short answer is that a pattern is a *'solution to a problem in a context'* (Alexander et al. 1977; Coplien 1996). This focus on context is important, because with a large number of patterns it can be difficult to identify the best patterns to use. All the patterns in this book, for example, solve the same problem — too little memory — but they solve it in many different ways.

A pattern is not just a particular solution to a particular problem. One of the reasons programming is hard is that no two programming problems are exactly alike, so a technique that solves one very specific problem is not much use in general (Jackson 1995). Instead, a pattern is a generalized description of a solution that solves a general class of problems — just as an algorithm is a generalized description of a computation, and a program is a particular implementation of an algorithm. Because patterns are general descriptions, and because they are higher-level than algorithms, you should not expect the implementation to be the same every time they are used. You can't just cut out some sample code describing a pattern in this book, paste it into your program and expect it to work. Rather, you need to understand the general idea of the pattern, and to apply that in the context of the particular problem you face.

How can you trust a pattern? For a pattern to be useful, it must be known to work. To enforce this, we've made sure each pattern follows the so-called Rule of Three: we've found at least three known uses of the solution in practical systems. The more times a pattern has been used, the better, as it then describes a better proven solution. Good patterns are not invented; rather they are identified or *mined* from existing systems and practices. To produce the patterns in this book we've investigated the design of many successful systems that run on small machines. This book distils the essence of the techniques that seem most responsible for the systems' success.

Forces

A good pattern should be intellectually rigorous. It should present a convincing argument that its solution actually solves its problem, by explaining the logic that leads from problem to solution. To do this, a good pattern will enumerate all the important *forces* in the context and enumerate the positive and negative *consequences* of the solution. A force is *'any aspect of the problem that should be considered when solving it'* (Buschmann et al. 1996), such as a requirement the solution must meet, a constraint the solution must overcome, or a desirable property that the solution should have.

The most important forces the patterns in this book address are: *memory requirements*, the amount of memory a system occupies; and *memory predictability*, or whether this amount can be determined in advance. These patterns also address many other forces, however, from real-time performance to usability. A good pattern describes both its benefits (the forces it *resolves*), and its disadvantages (the forces it *exposes*). If you use a pattern you may have to address its disadvantages by applying another pattern (Meszaros and Doble 1998).

The Appendix discusses the major forces addressed by the patterns in this collection, and describes the main patterns that can resolve or expose each force. There's also a summary in the table printed inside the back cover.

Collections of patterns

Some patterns may stand alone, describing all you need to do, but many are *compound patterns* (Vlissides 1998; Riehle 1997) and present their solution partially in terms of other patterns. Applying one pattern resolves some forces completely, more forces partially, and also exposes some forces that were not yet considered. Other, usually smaller-scale, patterns can address problems left by the first pattern, resolving forces the first pattern exposes.

Alexander organized his patterns into a *pattern language*, a sequence of patterns from the highest level to the lowest, where each pattern explicitly directed the reader to subsequent patterns. By working through the sequence of patterns in the language, an architect could produce a complete design for a whole room, building, or city (Alexander 1977).

The patterns in this book are not a pattern language in that sense, and we certainly have not set out to describe every programming technique required to build a complete system! Where practical, however, we have described how the patterns are related, and how using one pattern can lead you to consider using other patterns. The most important of these relationships are illustrated in the diagram printed inside the back cover.

A brief history of patterns

Patterns did not originate within programming. Christopher Alexander, an architect, developed the pattern form as a tool for recording knowledge of successful building practices (architectural folklore) (Alexander et al. 1977; Alexander 1979). Kent Beck and Ward Cunningham adapted patterns to software, writing a few patterns that were used to design user interfaces at Textronix. The 'Hillside Group' of software engineers developed techniques to improve pattern writing, leading to the PLoP series of conferences.

Gamma et al. developed patterns for object-oriented frameworks in their 1995 book *Design Patterns*. Many other valuable pattern books have followed, particularly *Patterns of Software Architecture* (Buschmann et al. 1996), *Analysis Patterns* (Fowler 1997), the Addison-Wesley *Pattern Languages of Program Design* series, and more specialist books, such as the *Smalltalk Companion to Design Patterns* (Alpert et al. 1998), etc. You can now find patterns on virtually any aspect of software development using the *Patterns Almanac* (Rising 2000).

How we wrote this book

To produce this particular collection of patterns, we built up a comprehensive list of memory-saving techniques that we'd seen in software, been told about, seen on the web, or just known about all along. We then pruned out any techniques that seemed related but that didn't actually save memory (such as bank switching or power management), and any techniques outside the scope of this book (UI design, project management). The result was several hundred different ideas, known uses and examples.

We then grouped them together, looking for a number of underlying themes or ideas that provided a set of underlying techniques. Each technique formed the basis for a pattern, and we wrote them up as a draft that was presented at a pattern writers' workshop in 1998 (Noble and Weir 1998, 2000). As we built up a set of draft patterns, and received comments, criticism and suggestions, we 'refactored' (Fowler 1999) the patterns to give a more complete picture, expanding the scope of one pattern and reducing or changing the thrust of another. We analysed the major forces addressed by each pattern, and the relationships between the patterns, to find a good way to arrange the patterns into a coherent collection. The result is what you're reading now.

Like any story after the fact, this step-by-step approach wasn't exactly what happened in practice. The reality was much more organic and creative; it took place over several years, and most of the steps happened in parallel throughout that time: but in principle it's accurate.

Our pattern format

All the patterns in this book use the same format. Consider the example shown in Figure I.1, an abbreviated version of one of the data structure patterns. The full pattern is on page 174.

Packed Data

Also known as: Bit Packing

How can you reduce the memory needed to store a data structure?

- You have a data structure (a collection of objects) that has significant memory requirements.
- You need fast random access to every part of every object in the structure . . .

No matter what else you do in your system, sooner or later you end up having to design low-level data structures to hold the information your program needs . . .

For example, the Strap-It-On's Insanity-Phone application needs to store all of the names and numbers in an entire local telephone directory (200,000 personal subscribers) . . . .

Because these objects (or data structures) are the core of your program, they need to be easily accessible as your program runs . . .

Therefore: Pack data items within the structure so that they occupy the minimum space.

There are two ways to reduce the amount of memory occupied by an object . . .

Consider each individual field in turn, and consider how much information that field really needs to store. Then, choose the smallest possible language-level data type that can store that information, so that the compiler (or assembler) can encode it in the minimum amount of memory space . . .

Considering the Insanity-Phone again, the designers realized that local phone books never cover more than 32 area codes — so each entry requires only 5 bits to store the area code . . .

Consequences

Each instance occupies less memory, reducing the total *memory requirements* of the system, even though the same amount of data can be stored, updated, and accessed randomly . . .

However: The time performance of a system suffers, because CPUs are slower at accessing unaligned data . . .

❖   ❖   ❖

Figure I.1 Excerpt from a pattern

The example shows the sections of the pattern, which are as follows:

Pattern name   Every pattern has a unique name, which should also be memorable

Cartoon   A cartoon provides a visual representation of the solution.

Also known as   Any other common names for the pattern, or for variants of the pattern.

Problem statement   A single sentence summarizes the main problem this pattern solves.

Context summary	Bullet points summarize each main force involved in the problem, giving an at-a-glance answer to 'is this pattern suitable for my particular problem?'
Context discussion	Longer paragraphs expand on the bullet points: when might this pattern apply; and what makes it a particularly interesting or difficult problem? This section also introduces a simple example problem — often fanciful or absurd — as an illustration.
Solution	**Therefore:** A single sentence summarizes the solution.
Solution description	Further paragraphs describe the solution in detail, sometimes providing illustrations and diagrams. This section also shows how the solution solves the example problem.
Consequences	This section identifies the typical consequences of using the pattern, both advantages and disadvantages. To distinguish the two, the positive benefits are first, and the negative liabilities second, partitioned by the word '**However:**'. In this discussion, the important forces are shown in *italic*; these forces are cross-referenced in the discussion in the Appendix.
Separator	Three '❖' symbols indicate the end of the pattern description.

Throughout the text we refer to other patterns using SMALL CAPITALS: thus 'PACKED DATA'.

This is all you need to read for a basic knowledge of each pattern. For a more detailed understanding — for example, if you need to apply the pattern — every pattern also provides much more information, in the following sections:

Implementation	A collection of 'implementation notes' discuss the practical details of implementing the pattern in a real system. This is usually the longest section, extending to several pages.
	The instructions in the implementation notes are not obligatory; you may find alternative, and better, ways to implement the pattern in a particular context. The notes capture valuable experience and it's worth reading them carefully before starting an implementation.
Example	This section provides code samples from a particular, usually fairly simple, implementation, together with a detailed discussion of what the code does and why. We recommend reading this section in conjunction with the Implementation section.
	Our website (www.smallmemory.com) provides the full source for most of the samples.
Known uses	This section describes several successful existing systems that use this pattern. This section validates our assertion that the pattern is useful and effective, and it also suggests places where you might look for further information.

See also   This section points the reader to other related patterns in this book or elsewhere. This section may also refer you to books and web pages with more information on the subject or to help further with implementation.

Major techniques and pattern relationships

We've grouped the patterns in this book into five chapters. Each chapter presents a major technique for designing small memory software: SMALL ARCHITECTURE, SECONDARY STORAGE, COMPRESSION, SMALL DATA STRUCTURES, and MEMORY ALLOCATION.

Each major technique is, itself, a pattern, though more abstract than the patterns it contains. We've acknowledged that by using a variant of the same pattern format for major techniques as for the normal patterns.

In each major technique, a Specialized patterns section summarizes each pattern in the chapter, replacing the Example section (see Figure I.2).

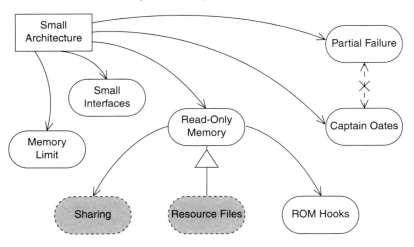

Specialized patterns

The following sections describe six specialized patterns that describe ways architectural decisions can reduce RAM memory use. The figure below shows how they interrelate . . .

The patterns in this chapter are as follows:

SMALL INTERFACES (38)   Design the interfaces between components to manage memory explicitly, minimizing the memory required for their implementation . . .

Figure I.2   Excerpt from a major technique

This diagram illustrates the relationships between the patterns in the chapter. In the diagram, the rectangle represents the major technique pattern; white ovals represent patterns in the chapter; and grey ovals represent patterns in other chapters. The relationships between the patterns are shown as follows (Noble 1998):

(arrow)	*Uses*	If you're using the left-hand pattern, you should also consider using the right-hand one. The smaller-scale pattern on the right resolves forces exposed by the larger pattern on the left. For example, if you are using the READ-ONLY MEMORY pattern, you should consider using the HOOKS pattern.
(arrow)	*Specializes*	If you are using the left-hand pattern, you may want the right-hand pattern in particular situations. The right-hand pattern is a more specialized version of the left-hand one, resolving similar *forces* in more particular ways. For example, RESOURCE FILES are a special kind of READ-ONLY MEMORY.
<-✕->	*Conflicts*	Both patterns provide alternative solutions to the same problem. They resolve similar *forces* in incompatible ways. For example, PARTIAL FAILURE and CAPTAIN OATES both describe how a component can deal with memory exhaustion; either by providing a reduced quality of service, or by terminating another component.

Figure I.3   Relationships between patterns

The running example

We've illustrated many of the patterns with examples taken from a particularly memory-challenged system, the unique Strap-It-On wrist-mounted PC from the well-known company StrapItOn (Figure I.4). This product includes the famous Word-O-Matic word processor, with its innovative Morse Code keypad and Voice User Interface (VUI).

Figure I.4   The Strap-It-On

If you're foolish enough to implement any of the applications we suggest, and make money out of it, well, good luck to you!

The patterns in this book

We've chosen a particular order for the patterns in this book (see the table in the front inside cover). This order makes the patterns easy to learn, working top-down so that the first patterns set the scene for the patterns in later chapters.

There are many other valid ways to arrange or discuss the list of patterns. This section examines it from several different perspectives: the list of major techniques, the forces addressed by each technique, different approaches to saving memory, and via case studies. You may also like to consult the discussion in the Appendix, which recommends patterns according to the types of small software involved.

The major techniques

The patterns are organized into five major techniques, summarized in Table I.5.

Table I.5 The five major techniques

Small Architecture	Memory-saving techniques that require co-operation between several components in a system.
Secondary Storage	Using disk, or equivalent, as an adjunct to RAM.
Compression	Processing-based techniques to reduce data sizes by automatically compressing data.
Small Data Structures	Defining data structures and algorithms that contrive to reduce memory use.
Memory Allocation	Mechanisms to create a data structure from the 'primordial soup' of unstructured available memory, and to return it again when no longer required by the program.

The forces addressed by the patterns

Another way to look at the patterns is to compare the forces addressed by each pattern.

The Appendix discusses the forces in detail, and discusses which patterns address each force. Meanwhile, the following two tables provide a partial summary of the Appendix. Table I.6 summarizes ten of the forces we consider most important, and Table I.7 shows how the patterns address each one.

Table I.6   Ten important forces

Memory requirements	Does the pattern reduce the absolute amount of memory required to run the system?
Memory predictability	Does the pattern make it easier to predict the amount of memory a system will require in advance?
Time performance	Does the pattern tend to improve the runtime speed of the system?
Real-time response	Does the pattern decrease the latency of the program's response to events, usually by making the runtime performance of the program predictable?
Start-up time	Does the pattern reduce the time between the system receiving a request to start the program, and the program beginning to run?
Local vs. global	Does the pattern tend to help encapsulate different parts of the application, keeping them more independent of each other?
Secondary storage	Does the pattern tend to shift memory use towards cheaper secondary storage in preference to more expensive RAM?
Maintainability	Does the pattern encourage better design quality? Will it be easier to make changes to the system later on?
Programmer effort	Does the pattern reduce the total programmer effort to produce a given system?
Testing cost	Does the pattern reduce the total testing effort for the application development?

Table I.7 shows how each pattern addresses these forces. If the pattern generally benefits you as far as this force is concerned (resolves the force), it's shown with a '☺'. If it's generally a disadvantage (exposes the force), that's shown with an '☹'. The Appendix explores these forces in much more detail.

Reduce, reuse, recycle

Environmentalists have identified three strategies to reduce the impact of human civilization on the natural environment:

- Reduce consumption of manufactured products and the production of waste products.
- Reuse products for uses other than that for which they were intended.
- Recycle the raw material of products to make other products.

Of these, reduction is the most effective; if you reduce the amount of waste pro-

Table I.7   How patterns address the forces

	Time performance	Real-time	Start-up time	Local vs. global	Predictability	Quality and maintainability	Programmer effort	Testing cost	Usability
Architecture				☺	☺	☺	😐		☺
Memory Limit				☺	☺			😐	
Small Interfaces	☹	☺		☺	☺	☺	😐	😐	
Partial Failure				☹	☺	☺	☹	☹	☺
Captain Oates	☹			☺	😐		☹	☹	☺
Read-only Memory		☺	☺	😐		☹	☹	☺	
Hooks	☹					☺	☺	☹	
Secondary Storage		☹		☹			☹		☹
Application Switching	☹	☺	☺	😐	☺	☺	😐	☺	☹
Data Files	☹		☹	😐	☺		☹	☺	☹
Resource Files	☹		☹			☺	😐		
Packages		☹	☺			☺	☹	☹	😐
Paging	☹	☹		☺		☺	☺	☺	☺
Compression	☹	😐			☹	☹	☹	☹	
Table Compression	😐							☹	
Difference Coding	😐	☺			☺			☹	
Adaptive Compression	☹	☹					☹	☹	
Data Structures		😐		☺	😐	☺	☹	😐	☺
Packed Data	☹			☺		☹	☹		
Sharing	☺		☺	☹		😐	☹	☹	
Copy-on-Write	😐	☹	☺		☹		☹	☹	
Embedded Pointers	☺	☺		☹	☺	☹	☹		
Multiple Representations	☺			☺	☹	☺	😐	☹	
Allocation	😐	😐	😐	😐	☺				
Fixed Allocation	☺	☺	☹		☺		😐	☺	☹
Variable Allocation	☹	☹	☺	☹	☹	☺	☺	☹	
Memory Discard	☺	☺	☺	☺	☺		☺	☹	
Pooled Allocation	☺	☺	☹		☺			☹	
Compaction	☹	☹					☹	☹	
Reference Counting	☹	☺		☺		☺			
Garbage Collection	☺	☹		☺	☹	☺	☺		

duced you don't have to worry about how to handle it. Recycling is the least effective; it requires a large expenditure of energy and effort to produce new finished products from old waste. The patterns we have described can be grouped in a similar way. They can:

- **reduce** a program's memory requirements. Patterns such as PACKED DATA (174), SHARING (182) and COMPRESSION (135) reduce the amount of absolute memory required, by reducing data sizes and removing redundancy. In addition the SECONDARY STORAGE (79) and READ-ONLY MEMORY (65) patterns reduce RAM memory requirements by using alternative storage.

- **reuse** memory for a different purpose. Memory used within a FIXED ALLOCATION (226) or in POOLED ALLOCATION (251) is generally (re)used to store a number of different objects of roughly the same type, one after another. HOOKS (72) allow software to reuse existing read-only code rather than replacing it.

- **recycle** memory for different uses at different times. VARIABLE ALLOCATION (236), REFERENCE COUNTING (268), COMPACTION (259), GARBAGE COLLECTION (278) and CAPTAIN OATES (57) all help a program to make vastly different uses of the same memory over time.

Case studies

This section looks at three simple case studies, and describes the patterns you might use to deliver a successful implementation in each case.

1. Hand-held application

Consider working on an application for a hand-held device such as Windows CE, PalmOs or an EPOC smart-phone.

The application will have a GUI, and will need much of the basic functionality you'd expect of a full-scale PC application. Memory is, however, more limited than for a PC; acceptable maximums might be 2 Mb of working set in RAM, 700 Kb of (non-library) code, and a couple of Mb or so of persistent data according to the needs of each particular user.

Memory is limited for all applications on the device, including your own. The SMALL INTERFACES (38), architectural pattern is ubiquitous and vital. Applications will use RESOURCE FILES (101), as dictated by the operating system style guide, and to keep code sizes and testing to a minimum you'll want to access the vendor-supplied libraries in READ-ONLY MEMORY (65) using the libraries' HOOKS (72). Since the environment supports many processes and yours won't be running all the time, you'll need persistent data stored in DATA FILES (92).

The environment may mandate other architectural patterns: PalmOs requires APPLICATION SWITCHING (84); CE expects CAPTAIN OATES (57); and EPOC expects PARTIAL FAILURE (48). If you're not working for the system vendor then yours will be a 'third-party' application loaded from secondary storage, so you may use PACKAGES (108) to reduce the code's memory requirements.

Most of your application's objects will use VARIABLE ALLOCATION (236) or MEMORY DISCARD (244). Components where real-time performance is important — a communications driver, for example — will use FIXED ALLOCATION (226) and EMBEDDED POINTERS (198).

Classes that have many instances may use PACKED DATA (174), MULTIPLE REPRESENTATIONS (209), SHARING (182) or COPY-ON-WRITE (191) to reduce their total memory footprint. Objects shared by several components may use REFERENCE COUNTING (268).

2. Smart card project

Alternatively, consider working on a project to produce the software for a smart card — say a PCMCIA card modem to fit in a PC. Code will live in ROM (actually flash RAM used as ROM), and there's about 2 Mb of ROM in total; however, there's only some 500K of RAM. The only user interface is the Hayes 'AT' command set available via the serial link to the PC; the modem is also connected to a phone cable.

The system code will be stored in the READ-ONLY MEMORY (65), along with static tables required by the modem protocols. You'll only need a single thread of control and a single, say 50K, stack.

The real-time performance of a modem is paramount, so most long-lived objects will use FIXED ALLOCATION (226). Transient data will use MEMORY DISCARD (244), being stored on the stack. The system will need lots of buffers for input and output, and these can use POOLED ALLOCATION (251); you may also need REFERENCE COUNTING (268) if the buffers are shared between components.

Much of the main processing of the modem is COMPRESSION (135) of the data sent on the phone line. Simple modem protocols may use DIFFERENCE CODING (153); more complicated protocols will use TABLE COMPRESSION (143) and ADAPTIVE COMPRESSION (160). To implement these more complicated protocols you'll require large and complicated data structures built up in RAM. To minimize the memory they use and improve performance, you can implement them with PACKED DATA and EMBEDDED POINTERS (198).

3. Large web server project

Finally you might be working on a Java web server, which will provide an e-commerce web and WAP interface to allow users to buy products or services. The server will connect to internal computers managing the pricing and stock control and to a database containing the details of individual users, via a local area network.

RAM memory is relatively cheap compared with development costs, but there are physical limits to the amounts of RAM a server can support. The sever's operating system provides PAGING (119) to increase the apparent memory available to the applications, but since most transactions take a relatively short time you won't want to have much of the memory paged out at any time. There will be many thousands of simultaneous users, so you can't afford simply to assign dozens of megabytes to each one.

You can use **SHARING** (182) so that all the users share just one, or perhaps just a few Java virtual machine instances. Where possible data will be **READ-ONLY** (65), to make it easy to share. If the transaction with each user can involve arbitrarily complex data structures you can enforce a **MEMORY LIMIT** (32) for each user. Maintainability and ease of programming are important so virtually all objects use **VARIABLE ALLOCATION** (236) and **GARBAGE COLLECTION** (278).

The internet connections to each user are a significant bottleneck, so you'll use **ADAPTIVE COMPRESSION** (160) to send out the data, wherever the web or WAP protocols support it. Finally, you may need to support different languages and page layouts for different users via **RESOURCE FILES** (101).

SMALL ARCHITECTURE

Memory Limit

Small Interfaces

Partial Failure

Captain Oates

Read-Only Memory

Hooks

1

SMALL ARCHITECTURE

- Memory limitations restrict entire systems.
- Systems are made up of many components.
- Each component can be fabricated by a different team.
- Components' memory requirements can change dynamically.

A system's memory consumption is a global concern. Working well in limited memory isn't a feature that you can incorporate into your program in isolation: you can't ask a separate team of programmers to add code to your system hoping to reduce its memory requirements. Rather, memory constraints cross-cut the design of your system, affecting every part of it. This is why designing software systems for limited memory is difficult (Buschmann et al. 1996; Shaw and Garlan 1996; Bass et al. 1998; Bosch 2000).

For example, the Strap-It-On wrist-top PC has an e-mail application supporting text in a variety of fonts. Unfortunately in early implementations it cached every font it ever loaded, to improve performance; but it stored every e-mail compressed, threw away attachments and crashed if memory ran out loading a font, giving poor performance and awful usability. There's no sense in one function limiting its memory use to a few hundred bytes when another part of the program wastes megabytes, and then brings the system down when it fails to receive them.

You could simply design your system as a monolithic single component: a 'big ball of mud' (Foote and Yoder 2000). Tempting though this approach might be, it tends to be unsatisfactory for any but the simplest systems, for several reasons: it's difficult to split the development of such a system between different programmers, or different programming teams; the resulting system will be difficult to understand and maintain, since every part of the system can affect every other part; and you lose any possibility of buying in existing reusable components.

To keep control over your system, you can construct it from components that you can design, build, and test independently. Components can be reused from earlier systems, purchased from external suppliers, or built new; some may need specialized skills to develop; some may even be commercially viable in their own right. Each component can be assigned to a single team, to avoid several teams working on the same code (Szyperski 1999).

These components may be of many different kinds, and interact in many different ways: source libraries to compile into the system; object libraries that must be compiled into an executable; dynamic-linked libraries to load at runtime; runtime objects in separate address-spaces using frameworks like CORBA, Java Beans or ActiveX; or simply separate executables running in their own independent process. All are logically separate components, and communicate, if they communicate at all, through interfaces.

Unfortunately, separating a program into components doesn't reduce its memory use. The whole system's memory requirements will be the sum of the memory required by each component. Furthermore, the memory requirements for each component, and so for the whole system, will change dynamically as the system runs. Even though memory consumption affects the architecture globally, it is still important that components can be treated separately as much as possible. How can you make the system use memory effectively, and give the best service to its users, if a system is divided into components?

Therefore: **Make every component responsible for its own memory use.**

A system's architecture is more than just the design of its high-level components and their interconnections; it also defines the system's *architectural strategies* — the policies, standards and assumptions common to every component (Bass et al. 1998; Brooks 1982). The architecture for a system for limited memory must describe policies for memory management and ensure that each component's allocations are feasible in the context of the system as a whole.

In a system for limited memory, this means that each individual component must take explicit responsibility for implementing this policy: for managing its own memory use. In particular, you should take care to design SMALL DATA STRUCTURES (169) that require the minimum memory to store the information your system needs.

Taking responsibility for memory is quite easy where a component allocates memory statically (FIXED ALLOCATION (226)); a component simply owns all the memory that is fixed inside it. Where a component allocates memory dynamically from a heap (VARIABLE ALLOCATION (236)) it is more difficult to assign responsibility; the heap is a global resource. A good start is to aim to make every dynamically allocated object or record be owned by one component at all times (Cargill 1996). You may need to implement a MEMORY LIMIT (32) or allocate objects using POOLED ALLOCATION (251) for a component to control its dynamic memory allocation. Where components exchange objects, you can use SMALL INTERFACES (38) to ensure that some component always takes responsibility for the memory required for the exchange.

A system architecture also needs to set policies for mediating between components' competing memory demands, especially when there is little or no unallocated memory. You should ensure that components suffer only PARTIAL FAILURE (48) when their memory demands cannot be met, perhaps by sacrificing memory from low-priority components (CAPTAIN OATES (57)) so that the system can continue to operate until more memory becomes available.

For example, the software architecture for the Strap-It-On PC defines the Font Manager and the E-mail Display as separate components. The software architecture also defines a memory budget constraining reasonable memory use for each component. The designers of the Font Manager implemented a MEMORY LIMIT to reduce their font cache to a reasonable size, and the designers of the E-mail Display component discovered they could get much better performance and functionality than they had thought. When the E-mail application displays a large e-mail, it uses the SMALL INTERFACE of the Font Manager to reduce the size of the font cache. Similarly, when the system is running short of memory the font cache discards any unused items (CAPTAIN OATES).

Consequences

Handling memory issues explicitly in a program's architecture can reduce the program's *memory requirements,* increase the *predictability* of its memory use, and may make the program more *scalable* and more *usable.*

A consistent approach to handling memory reduces the *programmer effort* required since the memory policies do not have to be re-determined for each component. Individual modules and teams can co-ordinate smoothly to provide a consistent *global* effect, so users can anticipate the final system's behaviour when memory is low, increasing *usability.*

In general, explicitly describing a system's architecture increases its *design quality,* improving *maintainability.*

However: Designing a small architecture takes programmer effort, and then ensuring that components are designed according to the architecture's rules takes programmer discipline. Making memory an architectural concern moves it from being a local issue for individual components and teams to a global concern, involving the whole project. For example, developers may try to minimize their component's memory requirements at the expense of other components produced by other teams.

Incorporating external components can require large amounts of *programmer effort* if they do not meet the standards set by the system architecture — you may have to reimplement components that cannot be adapted.

Designing an architecture to suit limited memory situations can restrict a program's *scalability* by imposing unnecessary restrictions should more memory become available.

❖   ❖   ❖

Implementation

The main ideas behind this pattern are 'consistency' and 'responsibility'. By splitting up your system into separate components you can design and build the system piece by piece; by having a common memory policy you ensure that the resulting pieces work together effectively.

The actual programming mechanism used to represent components is not particularly important. A component may be a class, a package or a namespace, a separate executable or operating system process, a component provided by middleware like COM or CORBA, or an ad-hoc collection of objects, data structures, functions, and procedures. In an object-oriented system a component will generally contain many different objects, often instances of different classes, with one or more objects acting as FACADES (Gamma et al. 1995) to provide an interface to the whole component.

Here are two further issues to consider when designing interfaces for components in small systems.

1. Tailorability

Different clients vary in the memory requirements they place on other components that they use. This is especially the case for components that are designed to be reusable; such components will be used in many different contexts, and those contexts may have quite different memory requirements.

A component can address this by including parameters to tailor its memory use in its interface. Clients can adjust these parameters to adapt the component to fit its context. Components using FIXED ALLOCATION (226), for example, have to provide creation-time parameters to choose the number of items they can store. Similarly, components using VARIABLE ALLOCATION (236) can provide parameters to tune their memory use, such as maximum capacity, initial allocation, or even the amount of free space (in a hash table, for example, leaving free space can increase lookup performance). Components can also support operations to control their behaviour directly, such as requesting a database to compact itself, or a cache to empty itself.

For example, the Java vector class has several methods that control its memory use. Vectors can be created with sufficient memory to hold a given number of items (say 10):

```
Vector v = new Vector(10);
```

This capacity can be increased dynamically (say to store 20 items):

```
v.ensureCapacity(20);
```

The capacity can also be reduced to provide only enough memory for the number of elements in the container, in this case one object:

```
v.addElement( new Object() );
v.trimToSize();
```

Allocating correctly sized structures can save a surprisingly large amount of memory and reduce the load a component places on a low-level memory allocator or garbage collector. For example, imagine a vector that will be used to store 520 items inserted one at a time. The vector class initially allocates enough space for 8 elements; when that is exhausted, it allocates twice as much space as it is currently using, copies its current elements into the new space, and deallocates the old space. To store 520 elements, the vector will resize itself seven times, finally allocating almost twice the required memory, and having allocated about four times as much memory in total. In contrast, initializing the vector with 520 elements would have required one call to the memory system and allocated only as much memory as required (Soukup 1994).

2. Make clients responsible for components' memory allocation

Sometimes a component needs to support several radically different policies for allocating memory — some clients might want to use POOLED ALLOCATION (251) for each object allocated dynamically within the package; others might prefer a MEMORY LIMIT (32) or to use MEMORY DISCARD (244); and still others might want the simplicity of allocating objects directly from the system heap. How can you cater for all of these with a single implementation of the component?

2.1. Callbacks to manage memory.   A simple approach is to require the component to call memory management functions provided by the client. In non-OO environments, for example, you can make the component call a function supplied by its client, and link the client and component together. In C, you might use function pointers, or make the component declare a function prototype to be implemented by the library environment. For example, the Xt Window System Toolkit for the X Window System supports a callback function, the XAlloc function hook; clients may provide a function to do the memory allocation and another function to do the memory freeing (Gilly and O'Reilly 1990).

2.2. Memory strategy.   In an object-oriented environment, you can apply the STRATEGY pattern (Gamma et al. 1995): define an interface to a family of allocation algorithms, and then supply the component with the algorithm appropriate for the context of use. For example, in C++ a strategy class can simply provide operations to allocate and free memory:

```
class MemoryStrategy {
    virtual char* Alloc(size_t nBytes) = 0; // returns null when exhausted.
    virtual void Free(char* anItem;) = 0;
}
```

Particular implementations of the MemoryStrategy class then implement a particular strategy: a PooledStrategy implements POOLED ALLOCATION; a LimitStrategy applies a MEMORY LIMIT; a TemporaryHeapStrategy implements MEMORY DISCARD; and a HeapStrategy simply delegates the Alloc and Free operations straight to the system malloc and free functions.

An alternative C++ design uses compile-time template parameters rather than runtime objects. The C++ STL collection and string templates accept a class parameter (called Allocator) that provides allocation and freeing functions

(Stroustrup 1997). They also provide a default implementation of the `allocator` that uses normal heap operations. So the definition of the STL **SET** template class is:

```
template <class Key, class Compare = less<Key>,
          class Allocator = allocator> class set;
```

Note how the `Allocator` template parameter defaults to `allocator`, the strategy class that uses normal heap allocation.

❖   ❖   ❖

Specialized patterns

The following sections describe six specialized patterns that describe ways architectural decisions can reduce RAM memory use. Figure 1.1 shows how they interrelate. Several other patterns in this book are closely related to the patterns in this chapter, and these patterns are shown in grey.

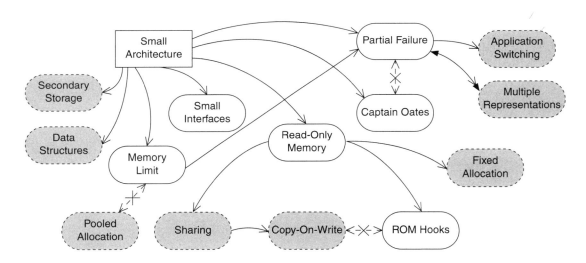

Figure 1.1   Relationships between patterns

This chapter contains the following patterns:

MEMORY LIMIT (32) enforces a fixed upper bound on the amount of memory a component can allocate.

SMALL INTERFACES (38) between components are designed to manage memory explicitly, minimizing the memory required for their implementation.

PARTIAL FAILURE (48) ensures that a component can continue in a 'degraded mode', without stopping its process or losing existing data, when it cannot allocate memory.

CAPTAIN OATES (57) improves the overall performance of a system by surrendering memory used by less important components when the system is running low on memory.

READ-ONLY MEMORY (65) can be used to store components that do not need to be modified, in preference to more constrained and expensive main memory.

HOOKS (72) allow information stored in READ-ONLY MEMORY (or shared between components) to appear to be changed.

❖   ❖   ❖

Known uses

Object-oriented APIs designed to support different memory strategies include the C++ standard template library (Stroustrup 1997) and the Booch components (Booch 1987). These libraries, and to a lesser extent the standard Java and Smalltalk collection classes, also provide parameters that adjust components' strategies, for example, by preallocating the correct amount of memory to hold an entire structure.

See also

Many small architectures take advantage of SECONDARY STORAGE (79) to reduce requirements for main memory. Architectures can also design SMALL DATA STRUCTURES (169) to minimize their memory use, and encourage SHARING (182) of code and data between components.

Tom Cargill's patterns for *Localized Ownership* (Cargill 1996) describe how you can ensure that every object is the responsibility of precisely one component at all times. The HYPOTH-A-SIZED COLLECTION pattern (Auer and Beck 1996) describes how collections should be created with sufficient capacity to meet their clients' needs without extra allocations.

Software Requirements & Specifications (Jackson 1995) and *Software Architecture* (Shaw and Garlan 1996) describe ways to keep a coherent architecture while dividing an entire system into components. *Software Architecture in Practice* (Bass et al. 1998) describes much about software architecture; *Design and Use of Software Architectures* (Bosch 2000) is a newer book that focuses in particular on producing product-lines of similar software systems. *Patterns in Software Architecture* has a number of architecture-level patterns to help design whole systems and is well worth reading (Buschmann et al. 1996).

The *Practice of Programming* (Kernighan and Pike 1999), the *Pragmatic Programmer* (Hunt and Thomas 2000) and *High-Level and Process Patterns from the Memory Preservation Society* (Noble and Weir 2000) describe techniques for estimating the memory consumption of a system's components, and managing those estimates throughout a development project.

Memory limit

Also known as: Fixed-sized Heap, Memory Partitions

How can you share out memory between multiple competing components?

- Your system contains many components, each with its own demands on memory.
- Components' memory requirements change dynamically as the program runs.
- If one component hogs too much memory, it will prevent others from functioning.
- You can define reasonable upper bounds on the memory required for each task.

As part of designing a **SMALL ARCHITECTURE** (25), you will have divided up your system into architectural components, and made each component responsible for its own memory use. Each component's memory demands will change as the program runs, depending on the overall kind of load being placed on the system. If access to memory is unrestricted, then each component will try to allocate as much memory as it might need, irrespective of the needs of other components. As other components also allocate memory to tackle their work, the system as a whole may end up running out of memory.

For example, the Strap-It-On's Virtual Reality 'Stair Wars' game has several components: virtual reality display, voice output, music overview, and voice recognition, not to mention the artificial intelligence brain co-ordinating the entire game plan. Each of these tasks is capable of using as much memory as it receives, but if every component tries to allocate a large amount of memory there will not be enough to go round. You must apportion the available memory sensibly between each component.

You could consider implementing the **CAPTAIN OATES** (57) pattern, allowing components low on memory to steal it from components with abundant allocations. Captain Oates relies on the goodwill of component programmers to release memory, however, and can be difficult and complex to implement.

You could also consider budgeting components' memory use in advance. Just planning memory consumption is also insufficient, however, unless there is some way to be sure that components will obey the budget. This is trivial for components that use **FIXED ALLOCATION** (226) exclusively, but for others it can be difficult to model their dynamic behaviour to be sure they will not disrupt your plans.

Therefore: **Set a limit for each component and fail allocations that exceed the limit.**

There are three steps to applying the memory limit pattern.

1. Keep an account of the memory currently allocated by each component. For example, you might modify a component's memory allocation routine to increase a memory counter when allocating memory, and decrease the counter when deallocating memory.

2. Ensure that components cannot allocate more memory than an allotted limit. Allocation operations that would make a component exceed its limit should fail in exactly the same way that they would fail if there were no more memory available in the system. Components should support PARTIAL FAILURE (48) so that they can continue running even when they are at the limit.

3. Set the limits for each component, ideally by experimenting with the program and examining the memory use counters for each component. Setting the limits last may seem to be doing things backwards, but in practice you will have to revise limits during development, or alternatively allow users to adjust them to suit their work. So, build the accounting mechanisms first, experiment, gathering usage information, and then set the memory use policies that you want enforced.

Should the sum of the limits for each component be equal to or greater than the total available? The answer depends on whether all the tasks are likely to be using their maximum memory limit simultaneously. This is unlikely in practice, and the main purpose of the MEMORY LIMIT (32) pattern is to prevent a single component from hogging all the memory. It is generally sufficient to ensure that the limit on each task is a reasonable fraction of the total memory available.

Note that it's only worth implementing a limit for components that make variable demands on memory. A memory limit provides little benefits for components where most data structures use FIXED ALLOCATION (226) and the memory use doesn't vary significantly with time.

In the Stair Wars program, for example, the artificial intelligence brain component uses memory roughly in proportion to the number of hostile and friendly entities supported. By experimenting with the game, the developers determined a maximum number of such entities, and then adjusted the brain component's memory limit to provide enough memory to support the maximum. On the other hand, the screen display component allocates a fixed amount of memory, so Stair Wars doesn't apply an extra memory limit for this component.

Consequences

Because there are guaranteed limits on the memory use of each component, you can *test* each one separately, while remaining sure that it will continue to work in the same way in the final system. This increases the *predictability* of the system.

By examining the values of the memory counters, it's easy to identify problem areas, and to see which components are failing due to insufficient memory at runtime, increasing the *localization* of the system.

Implementing a simple memory counter takes only a small amount of *programmer effort.*

However: Some tasks may fail due to lack of memory while others are still continuing normally; if the tasks interact significantly this may lead to unusual error situations which are difficult to reproduce and *test.* A component can fail because it's reached its memory limit even when there is plenty of memory in the system; thus the pattern can be wasteful of memory. Most simple memory counter mechanisms don't account for extra wastage due to *fragmentation* (see the MEMORY ALLOCATION (219) chapter). On the other hand, more complex operating system mechanisms such as separate heaps for each component tend to increase this same *fragmentation* wastage.

❖   ❖   ❖

Implementation

There are several alternative approaches to implementing memory limits.

1. Intercepting memory management operations

In many programming languages, you quite simply can intercept all operations that allocate and release memory, and modify them to track the amount of memory currently allocated. When the count reaches the limit, further memory allocations can fail until deallocations return the count below the limit. In C++, for example, you can limit the total memory for a process by overriding the four global new and delete operators (Stroustrup 1995).

A memory counter doesn't need to be particularly accurate for this pattern to work. It can be sufficient to implement a count only of the major memory allocations: large buffers, for example. If smaller items of allocated memory are allocated in proportion to these larger items, then this limit indirectly governs the total memory used by the task. For example, the different entities in the Stair Wars program each use varying amounts of memory, but the overall memory use is roughly proportional to the total number of entities, so limiting them implemented an effective memory limit.

In C++ you can implement a more localized memory limit by overriding the new and delete operators for a single class — and thus for its derived classes. This approach also has the advantage that different parts of the same program can have different memory limits, even when memory is allocated from a single heap (Stroupstrup 1997).

2. Separate heaps

You can make each component use a separate memory heap, and manage each heap separately, restricting their maximum size. Many operating systems provide support for separate heaps notably Windows and Windows CE (Microsoft 1997a, Boling 1998).

3. Separate processes

You can make each component an individual process, and use operating system or virtual machine mechanisms to limit each component's memory use. EPOC and most versions of UNIX allow you to specify a memory limit for each process, and the system prevents processes from exceeding these limits. Using these limits requires little *programmer effort,* especially as the operating systems also provide tools that can monitor processes' memory use so that you can determine appropriate limits for each process. Of course, you have to design your whole system so that separate components can be separate processes — depending on your system, this can be trivial or very complex.

Many operating systems implement heap limits using virtual memory. They allocate the full size heap in the virtual memory address space (see the PAGING (119) pattern); the memory manager maps this to real memory only when the process chooses to access each memory block. Thus the heap size is fixed in virtual memory, but until it is used there's no real memory cost at all. The disadvantage of this approach is that very few virtual memory systems can detect free memory in the heap and restore the unused blocks to the system. So in most VM systems a process that uses its full heap will keep the entire heap allocated from then on.

Examples

The following C++ code restricts the total memory used by a `MemoryResrictedClass` and its subclasses. Exceeding the limit triggers the standard C++ out-of-memory exception, `bad_alloc`. Here the total limit is specified at compile time, as `LIMIT_IN_BYTES`:

```
class MemoryRestrictedClass {
public:
    enum { LIMIT_IN_BYTES = 10000 };
    static size_t totalMemoryCount;

    void* operator new(size_t aSize);
    void operator delete(void* anItem, size_t aSize);
};
size_t MemoryRestrictedClass::totalMemoryCount = 0;
```

The class must implement an `operator new` that checks the limit and throws an exception:

```
void* MemoryRestrictedClass::operator new(size_t aSize) {
    if (totalMemoryCount + aSize > LIMIT_IN_BYTES)
        throw (bad_alloc());
```

```
        totalMemoryCount += aSize;
        return malloc(aSize);
    }
```

And of course the corresponding `delete` operator must reduce the memory count again:

```
void MemoryRestrictedClass::operator delete(void* anItem, size_t aSize) {
    totalMemoryCount -= aSize;
    free((char*)anItem);
}
```

For a complete implementation we'd also need similar implementations for the array versions of the operators (Stroustrup 1995).

In contrast, Java does not provides allocation and deletion operations in the language. It is possible, however, to limit the number of instances of a given class by keeping a static count of the number of instances created. Java has no simple deallocation call, but we can use finalization to intercept deallocation. Note that many Java virtual machines do not implement finalization efficiently (if at all), so you should consider this code as an example of one possible approach, rather than as recommended good practice (Gosling et al. 1996).

The following class permits only a limited number of instances. The class counts the number of its instances, increasing the count when a new object is constructed, and decreasing the count when it is finalized by the garbage collector. Now, since objects can only be finalized when the garbage collector runs, at any given time there may be some garbage objects that have not yet been finalized. To ensure we don't fail allocation unnecessarily, the constructor does an explicit garbage collection before throwing an exception if we are close to the limit.

```
class RestrictedClass
{
    static final int maxNumberOfInstances = 5;
    static int numberOfInstances = 0;

    public RestrictedClass() {
      numberOfInstances++;
      if (numberOfInstances > maxNumberOfInstances) {
        System.gc();
      }
      if (numberOfInstances > maxNumberOfInstances) {
          throw new OutOfMemoryError("RestrictedClass can only have" +
                              maxNumberOfInstances + "instances");
      }
    }
}
```

There's a slight issue with checking for memory in the constructor: even if we throw an exception, the object is still created. This is not a problem in general, because the object will eventually be finalized unless one of the superclass constructors stores a reference to the object.

The actual finalization code is trivial:

```
public void finalize() {
    --numberOfInstances;
}
};
```

❖   ❖   ❖

Known uses

By default, UNIX operating systems put a memory limit on each user process (Card et al. 1998). This limit prevents any one process from hogging all the system memory, as only processes with system privileges can override this limit. The most common reason for a process to reach the limit is a continuous memory leak: after a process has run for a long time a memory request will fail, and the process will terminate and be restarted.

EPOC associates a heap with each thread, and defines a maximum size for each heap. There is a default, very large, limit for applications, but server threads (daemons) are typically created with rather smaller limits using an overloaded version of the thread creation function Rthread::Create (Symbian 1999b). The EPOC culture places great importance on avoiding memory leaks, so the limit serves to limit the resources used by a particular part of the system. EPOC servers are often invisible to users of the system, so it is important to prevent them from growing too large. If a server does reach the memory limit it will do a PARTIAL FAILURE (48), abandoning the particular request or client session that discovered the problem rather than crashing the whole server (Tasker et al. 2000).

Microsoft Windows CE and Acorn Archimedes RICS OS allow users to adjust the memory limits of system components at runtime. Windows CE imposes a limit on the amount of memory used for programs, as against data, and RISC OS imposes individual limits on every component of the operating system (Boling 1998; RISC OS 2000).

Java virtual machines typically provide runtime flags to limit the total heap size, so you can restrict the size of a Java process (Lindholm and Yellin 1999). The Real-Time Specification for Java will support limits on the allocation of memory within the heap (Bollella et al. 2000).

See also

Since it's reasonably likely that a typical process will reach the limit, it's better to suffer a PARTIAL FAILURE rather than failing the whole process. Using only FIXED ALLOCATION (or POOLED ALLOCATION) is a simpler, but less flexible, technique to apportion memory among competing components.

Small Interfaces

- You are designing a SMALL ARCHITECTURE where every component takes responsibility for its own memory use.

- Your system has several components, which communicate via explicit interfaces.

- Interface designs can force components or their clients to allocate extra memory, solely for inter-component communication.

- Reusable components require generic interfaces, which risk needing more memory than would be necessary for a specific example.

You are designing a SMALL ARCHITECTURE, and have divided your system into components with each component responsible for its own memory use. The components collaborate via their interfaces. Unfortunately the interfaces themselves require temporary memory to store arguments and results. Sending a large amount of information between components can require a correspondingly large amount of memory.

For example, the Strap-It-On 'Spookivity' ghost hunter's support application uses a compressed database in ROM with details of every known ghost matching given specifications. Early versions of the database component were designed for much smaller RAM databases, so they implemented a 'search' operation that simply returned a variable-sized array of structures containing copies of full details of all the matching ghosts. Though functionally correct, this interface design meant that Spookivity required a temporary memory allocation of several Mbytes to answer common queries — such as 'find ghosts that are transparent, whitish, floating and dead' — an amount of memory simply not available on the Strap-It-On.

Interfaces can also cause problems for a SMALL ARCHITECTURE by removing the control each component has over memory allocation. If an object is allocated in one component, used by another and finally deleted by a third, then no single component can be responsible for the memory occupied. In the Spookivity application, although the array of ghost detail structures was allocated by the database component, it somehow became the responsibility of the client.

Reusable components can make it even more difficult to control memory use. The designer of a reusable component often faces questions about the trade-offs between memory use and other factors, such as execution speed or failure modes. For example, a component might pre-allocate some memory buffers to support fast response during normal processing: how much memory should it allocate? The answers to such questions depend critically on the system environment; they may also depend on which client is using the component, or even on what the client happens to be doing at the time. The common approach — for the designer to use some idea of an 'average' application to answer such questions — is unlikely to give satisfactory results in a memory-limited system.

Therefore: **Design interfaces so that clients control data transfer.**

There are two main steps to designing component interfaces:

1. *Minimize the amount of data transferred across interfaces.* The principles of 'small interfaces' (Meyer 1997) and 'strong design' (Coplien 1994) say that an interface should present only the minimum data and behaviour to its client. A small interface should not transmit spurious information that most components or most clients will not need. You can reduce the amount of memory overhead imposed by interfaces by reducing the amount of data that you need to transfer across them.

2. *Determine how best to transfer the data.* Once you have identified the data you need to pass between components, you can determine how best to transfer it. There are many different mechanisms for passing data across interfaces, and we discuss the most important of them in the Implementation section.

For example, later versions of the Spookivity Database 'search' method returned a database ITERATOR object (Gamma et al. 1995). The iterator's getNext function returned a reference to a GhostDetails result object, which provided methods to return the data of each ghost in turn. This also allowed the implementers of the database component to reuse the same GhostDetails object each time; their implementation contained only a database ID, which they changed on each call. The GhostDetails methods accessed their data directly from the high-speed database. The revised interface required only a few bytes of RAM to support, and since the database is itself designed to use iterators there was no cost in performance.

Consequences

By considering the memory requirements for each component's interface explicitly, you can reduce the *memory requirements* for exchanging information across interfaces, and thus for the system as a whole. Because much of the memory used to pass information across interfaces is transient, eliminating or reducing interface's memory overheads can make your program's memory use more *predictable*, and support better *real-time* behaviour. Reducing inter-component interface memory requirements reduces the overheads of using more components in a design, increasing *locality* and *design quality* and *maintainability*.

However: Designing small interfaces requires *programmer discipline,* and increases team co-ordination overheads. A memory-efficient interface can be more *complex,* and so require more code and *programmer effort* and increase *testing costs.* As with all designs that save memory, designing small interfaces may increase *time performance.*

❖   ❖   ❖

Implementation

There are a number of issues and alternatives to consider when designing interfaces between components in small systems. The same techniques can be used whether information is passing 'inward' from a client to a server, in the same direction as control flow, or 'outward' from component to client.

1. Passing data by value vs. by reference

Data can be passed and returned either by value (copying the data) or by reference (passing a pointer to the data). Passing data by reference usually requires less memory than by value, and saves copying time. Java and Smalltalk programs usually pass objects by reference. Passing references does mean that the components are now SHARING (182) the data, so the two components need to co-operate somehow to manage the responsibility for their memory. On the other hand, in pass-by-value the receiving component must manage the responsibility for the temporary memory receiving the value. Pass-by-value is common in C++, which can DISCARD (244) stack memory.

2. Exchanging memory across interfaces

There are three common strategies for a client to transfer memory across a component interface:

- **Lending** — some client memory is lent to the supplier component for the duration of the client's call to the supplier (or longer).
- **Borrowing** — the client gets access to an object owned by the supplier component.
- **Stealing** — the client receives an object allocated by the supplier, and is responsible for its deallocation.

When information is passed inward the client can often *lend* memory to the component for the duration of the call. Returning information 'outward' from component to client is more difficult. Although clients can *lend* memory to a supplier, it is often easier for the client to *borrow* a result object from the server, and easier still for the client to *steal* a result object and use it without constraint.

The following sections describe and contrast each of these three approaches. For convenience, we describe a component that returns a single result object; but the same sub-patterns apply when a number of objects are returned.

2.1 Lending. The client passes an object into the component method, and the component uses methods on the object to access its data (Figure 1.2). If the client keeps a reference to the result object it can access the data directly, or the

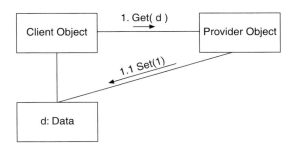

Figure 1.2 Lending

component can pass it back to the client. For example, the following Java code sketches how an object using a word processor component could create a new document properties object, and pass it to the word processor, which initializes it to describe the properties of the current document.

```
DocumentProperties d = new DocumentProperties();
wordProcessor.getCurrentDocumentProperties(d);
```

The client can then manipulate the document properties object:

```
long docsize = d.getSize();
long doctime = d.getEditTime();
```

The client must also release the document properties object when it is no longer useful:

```
d = null;
```

because it has kept the responsibility for the document properties object's memory. When lending memory to a component, the client manages the allocation and lifetime of the data object (the document properties, in this case), which may be allocated statically, or on the heap or the stack.

Consider using lending to pass arguments across interfaces when you expect the client to have already allocated all the argument objects, and when you are sure they will need all the results returned. Making the client own a result object obviously gives a fair amount of power and flexibility to the client. It does require the client to allocate a new object to accept the results, and to take care to delete the object when it is no longer needed, requiring *programmer discipline*. The component must calculate all the result properties, whether the client needs them or not.

In C++ libraries a common form of this technique is to return the result by value, copying from temporary stack memory in the component to memory lent by the client.

Another example of lending is where the client passes in a buffer for the component to use. For example in the **BUFFER SWAP** (Sane and Campbell 1996) pattern, a component needs to record a collection of objects (e.g. sound samples) in real time and return them to the client. The client begins by providing a single buffer to the main component, and then provides a new empty buffer every time it receives a filled one back.

2.2 Borrowing.   The component owns a simple or composite object, and returns a reference to that object to the client. The client uses methods on the object to access its data, then signals to the component when it no longer needs the object (Figure 1.3).

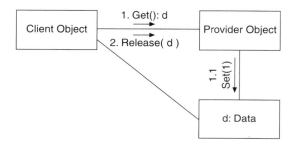

Figure 1.3   Borrowing

For example, the word processor component could let its client borrow an object representing the properties of the current document:

```
DocumentProperties d = wordProcessor.getDocumentProperties();
```

The client can then manipulate the document properties object:

```
long docsize = d.getSize();
long doctime = d.getEditTime();
```

but must tell the word processor when the properties object is no longer required.

```
wordProcessor.releaseDocumentProperties(d);
```

Like lending, borrowing can be used to transfer data both into and out of a component. Having the component own the result object gives maximum flexibility to the component returning the result. The component can allocate a new data object each time (**VARIABLE ALLOCATION** (236)), or it can hold one or more instances permanently (**FIXED ALLOCATION** (226)), or some combination of the two.

On the other hand, the component now has to manage the lifetime of the result object, which is difficult if there are several clients or several data objects needed at a time. Alternatively, the component can allocate only one result object statically, and recycle it for each invocation. This requires the client to copy the information immediately it is returned. A static result object also cannot handle concurrent accesses, but this is fine as long as you are sure there will only ever be one client at a time.

Alternatively, the component interface can provide an explicit 'release' method to delete the result object. This is rarer in Java and Smalltalk, as these languages make it clumsy to ensure that the release method is called when an exception is thrown. But it is quite common in C++ interfaces, as it allows the component to implement REFERENCE COUNTING (268) on the object, or just to do `delete this` in the implementation of the `Release` function. For example, the EPOC coding style (Tasker et al. 2000) is that all interfaces ('R classes') must provide a `Release` function rather than a destructor.

Consider using borrowing when components need to create or to provide large objects for their clients, and clients are unlikely to retain the objects for long periods of time.

2.3 Stealing.   The component allocates a simple or composite object, and transfers responsibility for it to the client. The client uses methods on the object to get data, then frees it (C++) or relies on garbage collection to release the memory (Figure 1.4).

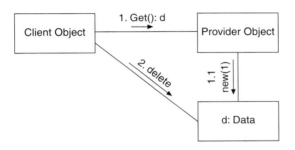

Figure 1.4   Stealing

For example, the word processor can let its client steal a document properties object:

```
DocumentProperties d = wordProcessor.getDocumentProperties();
```

allowing the client to use it as necessary,

```
long docsize = d.getSize();
long doctime = d.getEditTime();
```

but the client now has the responsibility for managing or deleting the object:

```
d = null;
```

This example shows a client stealing an object originally belonging to a component; however, components can also steal objects belonging to their clients when data is flowing from clients to components. Transferring responsibility for objects (or ownership of objects) is simple to program, and is particularly common in languages such as Java and Smalltalk that support garbage collection and don't need an explicit `delete` operation. In C++ it's most suitable for variable size structures, such as unbounded strings. However, in systems without garbage collection, this technique can cause memory leaks unless great *programmer discipline* is used to delete every single returned object. Ownership transfer forces the server to allocate a new object to return, and this object needs memory. The server must calculate all the properties of the returned object, whether the client needs them or not, wasting *processing time* and memory.

Consider using stealing when components need to provide large objects that their clients will retain for some time after receiving them.

3. Incremental interfaces

It is particularly difficult to pass a sequence or collection of data items across an interface. In systems with limited memory, or where memory is often fragmented, there may not be enough memory available to store the entire collection. In these cases, the interface needs to be made *incremental* — that is, information is transferred using more than one call from the client to a component, each call transferring only a small amount of information. Incremental interfaces can be used for both inward and outward data transfer. Clients can either make multiple calls directly to a component, or can use an ITERATOR (Gamma et al. 1995) as an intermediate object.

3.1 Client makes multiple calls.   The client makes several method calls to the component, each call *loaning* a single object for the duration of the call. When all the objects are passed, the client makes a further call to indicate to the component that it's got the entire collection, so it can get on with processing (Figure 1.5).

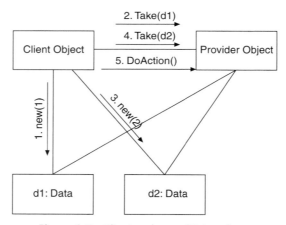

Figure 1.5   Client makes multiple calls

For example, a client can insert a number of paragraphs into a word processor, calling addParagraph to ask the word processor to take each paragraph, and then processAddedParagraphs to process and format all the new paragraphs.

```
for (int i = 0; i < num_new_paras; i++) {
    wordProcessor.addParagraph(paras[i]);
};
wordProcessor.processAddedParagraphs();
```

The client making multiple calls is easy to understand, and so is often the approach chosen by novice programmers or used in non-OO languages. However, it forces the component either to find a way of processing the data incrementally (see DATA FILES (92)), or to create its own collection of the objects passed in, requiring further allocated memory. Alternatively the client can *loan* the objects for the duration of the processing rather than for each call, but this forces the client to keep all the data allocated until the DoAction operation completes.

To return information from a component incrementally, the client again makes multiple calls, but the component signals the end of the data stream using a return value or similar.

```
spookivity.findGhosts("transparent|dead");
while (spookivity.moreGhostsToProcess()) {
    ghostScreen.addDisplay(spookivity.getNextGhost());
};
```

3.2 Passing data via an iterator. Rather than make multiple calls, the client may *lend* an iterator to the component. The component then accesses further *loaned* objects via the iterator. For example, the client can pass an iterator to one of its internal collections:

```
ghostScreen.displayAllGhosts(Spookivity.ghostIterator());
```

and the component can use this iterator to access the information from the client:

```
void displayAllGhosts(Iterator it) {
    while (it.hasNext()) {
        displayGhost((Ghost) it.next());
    }
}
```

Passing in an iterator reverses the control flow, so the component is now invoking messages on the client.

Using an iterator is generally more flexible than making multiple calls to a special interface. The component doesn't have to store its own collection of objects, since it can access them through the iterator. It's important that the interface uses an abstract iterator or abstract collection class a common interface design error is to use a specific collection class instead, which constrains the implementation of the client.

3.3 Returning data with a writable iterator. A *writable iterator* is an iterator that inserts elements into a collection, rather than simply traverses a collection. A writable iterator produced by the client can be used to implement outward flows from component to client, in just the same way that a normal iterator implements inward flows.

```
Vector retrievedGhosts = new Vector();
spookivity.findGhosts("transparent|dead");
spookivity.returnAllGhosts(retrievedGhosts.writeableIterator());
```

Note that at the time of writing, the Java library does not include writable iterators.

3.4 Returning data by returning an iterator.   Alternatively, the client may *borrow* or *steal* an iterator object from the component, and access returned values through that:

```
Iterator it = spookivity.findGhostsIterator("transparent|dead");
while (it.hasNext()) {
    ghostScreen.displayGhost((Ghost) it.next());
}
```

Returning an iterator keeps the control flow from the client to the component, allowing the iterator to be manipulated by client code or passed to other client components.

❖   ❖   ❖

Known uses

Interfaces are everywhere. For good examples of interfaces suitable for limited-memory systems, look at the API documentation for the EPOC or PalmOs operating systems (Symbian 1999b, Palm 2000).

Operating system file IO calls have to pass large amounts of information between the system and user applications. Typically they require buffer memory to be loaned by the client, and then read or write directly into their client-side buffers. For example, the classic UNIX (Ritchie and Thompson 1978) file system call:

```
read(int fid, char *buf, int nchars);
```

reads up to nchars characters from file fid into the buffer starting at buf. The buffer is simply a chunk of raw memory.

EPOC client–server interfaces always use lending, since the server is in a different memory space to its client, and can only return output by copying it into memory set aside for it within the client. This ensures that memory demand is typically small, and that the client's memory requirements can be fixed.

Many standard interfaces use iterators. For example, the C++ iostreams library uses them almost exclusively for access to container classes (Stroustrup 1997), and Java's Zlib compression library uses iterators (streams) for both input and output.

See also

Interfaces have to support the overall memory strategy of the system, and therefore many other memory patterns may be reflected in the interfaces between components.

Interfaces can supply methods to set up simulating a memory failure in the component to allow EXHAUSTION TESTING (Noble and Weir 2000) of both client and component. Interfaces that return references to objects owned by the component may SHARE (182) these objects, and may use REFERENCE COUNTING (268) or COPY-ON-WRITE (191).

Interfaces, particularly in C++, can enforce constant parameters that refer to READ-ONLY MEMORY (65) and thus may not be changed. In other languages, such enforcement is part of the interface documentation. Where components use RESOURCE FILES (101), interfaces often specify strings or resources as resource IDs rather than structures. As well as reducing the amount of information passing across the interface, the memory costs of the resource can be charged to the component that actually instantiates and uses it.

If the component (or the programming environment) supports COMPACTION (259) using handles, then the interface may use handles rather than object references to specify objects in the component.

The patterns for *Arguments and Results* (Noble 2000) and *Pattern Languages of Program Design 4* (Pryce 2000) describe how objects can be introduced to help design interfaces between components. Meyers' *Effective C++* (1998) and Sutter's *Exceptional C++* (2000) describe good C++ interface design. Tony Simons has described some options using borrowing, copying and stealing for designing C++ classes (Simons 1998).

Partial Failure

Also known as: Graceful Degradation; Feast and Famine

How can you deal with unpredictable demands for memory?

- No matter how much you reduce a program's *memory requirements,* you can still run out of memory.

- It is better to fail at a trivial task than to rashly abandon a critical task.

- It is more important to keep running than to run perfectly all the time . . .

- . . . and much more important to keep running rather than to crash.

- The amount of memory available to a system varies wildly over time.

No matter how much you do to reduce the *memory requirements* of your program, it can always run out of memory. You can silently discard data you do not have room to store, terminate processing with a rude error message, or continue as if you had received the memory you requested so that your program crashes in unpredictable ways, but you can't avoid the problem. Implicitly or explicitly, you have to deal with running out of memory. In a 'traditional' system, low-memory conditions are sufficiently rare that it is not really worth spending programmer effort dealing with the situation of running out of memory. The default, letting the program crash, is usually acceptable. After all, there are lots of other reasons why programs may crash, and users will hardly notice one or two more! However, in a memory-limited system, low-memory situations happen sufficiently often that this approach would seriously affect the usability of the system, or even make it unusable.

For example, the Word-O-Matic word processor provides voice output for each paragraph; adds flashing colours on the screen to highlight errors in spelling, grammar and political correctness; and provides a floating window that continuously suggests sentence endings and possible rephrasing. All this takes a great deal of memory, and frequently uses up all the available RAM memory in the system.

There is some good news, however. First, some system requirements are more important than others — so if you have to fail something, some things are better to fail at than others. Second, provided your system can keep running, failing to meet one requirement does not have to mean that you will fail subsequent ones. Finally, you are unlikely to remain short of memory indefinitely. When a system is idle, its demands on memory will be less than when it is heavily loaded.

In the Strap-It-On PC, for example, it's more important that the system keeps running, and keeps its watch and alarm timers up to date, than that any fancy editing function actually works. Within Word-O-Matic, retaining the text users have laboriously entered with the two-finger keypad is more important even than displaying that text, and much more important than spelling or grammar checking and suggesting rephrasing.

Therefore: **Ensure that running out of memory always leaves the system in a safe state.**

Ensure that for every memory allocation there is a strategy for dealing with failure before it propagates through your program.

When a program detects that its memory allocation has failed, its first priority must be to get back to a safe, stable state as soon as possible, and clean up any inconsistencies caused by the failure. As far as possible this should happen without losing any data. Depending on what was being allocated when memory ran out, it may be enough to back out of the action that required the extra memory (Figure 1.6). Alternatively, you might reduce the functionality provided by one or more components; or even shut down the component where the error occurred.

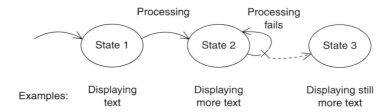

Figure 1.6   Failing the action that required the extra memory

What is vitally important is to ensure that from the user's point of view, an action succeeds completely or fails completely, leaving the system in a stable state in either case. User and component interfaces should make it clear when an important activity that affects the user has failed: if some data has been deleted, or a computation has not been performed.

Once a program has reached a stable state, it should continue as best it can. Ideally it should continue in a 'degraded mode', providing as much functionality as possible, but omitting less important memory-hungry features (Figure 1.7). You may be able to provide a series of increasingly degraded modes, to cater for increasing shortages of memory. Components can implement a degraded mode by hiding their memory exhaustion from their clients, perhaps accepting requests and queuing them for later processing, or otherwise offering a lower-quality service. For example, the Word-O-Matic's voice output module accepts but ignores commands from its clients in its 'out of memory' state, which makes programming its clients much simpler.

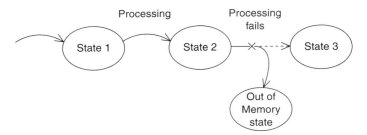

Figure 1.7   Failing to an out-of-memory state

Finally, a system should return to full operation when more memory becomes available. Memory is often in short supply while a system copes with high external loads, but once the load has passed its memory requirements will decrease. Users directly determine the load on multiprocessing environments like MS Windows and EPOC, so they can choose to free up memory by closing some system applications. A component running in a degraded mode should attempt to return to full operation periodically, to take advantage of any increase in available memory.

For example, when Word-O-Matic fails to allocate the memory required for voice output of a document, its display screen continues to operate as normal. If the text checker fails, Word-O-Matic stops highlighting spelling problems; if the floating window fails it doesn't appear yet the rest of the program carries on regardless. None of these fancier features are essential; and most users will be quite happy with just a text display and the means to enter more text.

Consequences

Supporting partial failure significantly improves a program's *usability*. With careful design, even the degraded modes can provide enough essential functionality that users can complete their work. By ensuring that the program can continue to operate within a given amount of memory, partial failure decreases the program's minimum *memory requirements* and increases the *predictability* of those requirements.

Supporting partial failure increases the program's *design quality* — if you support partial failure for memory exhaustion, it's easy to support partial failure (and other forms of failure handling) for other things, such as network faults and exhaustion of other resources. Systems that support partial failure properly can be almost totally *reliable*.

However: PARTIAL FAILURE is hard work to program, requiring *programmer discipline* to apply consistently and considerable *programmer effort* to implement.

Language mechanisms that support partial failure — exceptions and similar — considerably increase the implementation complexity of the system, since programmers must cater for alternative control paths, and for releasing resources on failure.

PARTIAL FAILURE tends to increase the *global* complexity of the systems, because *local* events — running out of memory — tend to have global consequences by affecting other modules in the system.

Supporting partial failure significantly increases the complexity of each module, increasing the *testing cost* because you must try to test all the failure modes.

❖   ❖   ❖

Implementation

Consider the following issues when implementing PARTIAL FAILURE:

1. Detecting memory exhaustion

How you detect exhaustion depends on the type of MEMORY ALLOCATION (219) you are using. For example, if you are allocating memory from a heap, the operation that creates objects will have some mechanism for detecting allocation failure. If you are managing memory allocation yourself, such as using FIXED ALLOCATION (226) or allocating objects dynamically from a POOL (251), then you need to ensure the program checks to determine when the fixed structure or the memory pool is full. The MEMORY ALLOCATION chapter discusses this in more detail.

How you communicate memory exhaustion within the program depends on the facilities offered by your programming language. In many languages, including early implementations of C and C++, the only way to signal such an error was to return an error code (rather than the allocated memory). Unfortunately, checking the value returned by every allocation requires a very high level of programmer discipline. More modern languages support variants of exceptions, explicitly allowing functions to return abnormally. In most environments an out-of-memory exception terminates the application by default, so components that implement PARTIAL FAILURE need to handle these exceptions.

2. Getting to a safe state

Once you have detected that you have run out of memory, you have to determine how to reach a safe state, that is, how much of the system cannot continue because it absolutely required the additional memory being available. Typically you will fail only the function that made the request; in other situations the component may need a degraded mode, or, if a separate executable, may terminate completely.

To determine how much of the system cannot be made safe, you need to examine each component in turn, and consider their invariants, that is, what conditions must be maintained for them to operate successfully (Hoare 1981; Meyer 1997). If a component's invariants are unaffected by running out of memory, then the component should be able to continue running as it is. If the invariants are affected by the memory failure, you may be able to restore a consistent state by deleting or changing other information within the component. If you cannot restore a component to a safe state, you have to shut it down.

If you have to fail entire applications, you may be able to use APPLICATION SWITCHING (84) to get to a safe state.

3. Releasing resources

A component that has failed to allocate memory must tidy up afterwards to ensure it has not left any side effects. Any resources it allocated but can no longer use (particularly memory) must be released, and its state (and that of any other affected components) must be restored to values that preserve its invariants.

In C++, exceptions 'unwind' the stack between a throw statement and a catch statement (Stroustrup 1997). By default, all stack-based pointers between them are lost, and any resources they own are orphaned. C++ exceptions guarantee to invoke the destructor on any stack-based object, however, so any object on the stack can clean up in its destructor so that it will be tidied up correctly during an exception. The standard template class auto_ptr wraps a pointer and deletes it when the stack is unwound.

```
auto_ptr<NetworkInterfaceClass> p(new NetworkInterfaceClass);
p->doSomethingWhichCallsAnException(); // the instance is deleted
```

Although Java has garbage collection, you still have to free objects (by removing all references to them) and release external resources as the stack unwinds. Rather than using destructors, the Java try.finally construct will execute the finally block whenever the try block exits, either normally or abnormally. This example registers an instance of a COMMAND (Gamma et al. 1995) subclass into a set, and then removes it from the set when an exception is thrown or the command's execute method returns normally.

```
Command cmd = new LongWindedCommand();
setOfActiveCommands.add(cmd);

try {
    cmd.execute();
}
finally {
    setOfActiveCommands.remove(cmd);
}
```

EPOC, as an operating system for limited-memory systems, has PARTIAL FAILURE as one of its most fundamental architectural principles (Symbian 1999a). Virtually every operation can fail due to memory exhaustion; but such failure is limited as much as possible and never permitted to cause a memory leak. EPOC's C++ environment does not use C++ exceptions, rather an operating system TRAP construct. Basically, a call to the leave method unwinds the stack (using the C longjmp function), until it reaches a TRAP harness call. Client code adds and removes items explicitly from a 'cleanup stack', and then the leave method automatically invokes a cleanup operation for any objects stored on the cleanup stack. The top-level EPOC system scheduler provides a TRAP harness for all normal user code. By default that puts up an error dialog box to warn the user the operation has failed, then continues processing.

Here's an example of safe object construction in EPOC (Tasker et al. 2000). A FACTORY METHOD (Gamma et al. 1995), NewL, allocates a zero-filled (i.e. safe) object using new(ELeave), then calls a second function, ConstructL, to do any operations that may fail. By pushing the uninitialized object onto the cleanup stack, if ConstructL fails then it will be deleted automatically. Once the new object is fully constructed it can be removed from the cleanup stack.

```
SafeObject* SafeObject::NewL(CEikonEnv* aEnv) {
    SafeObject* obj = new (ELeave) SafeObject(aEnv);
    CleanupStack::PushL(obj);
    obj->ConstructL();
    CleanupStack::Pop(); // obj is now OK, so remove it
    return obj;
}
```

The CAPTAIN OATES (57) pattern includes another example of the EPOC cleanup stack.

4. Degraded modes

Once you've cleaned up the mess after your memory allocation has failed, your program should carry on running in a stable state, even though its performance will be degraded. For example:

- Loading a font may fail; in this case you can use a standard system font.
- Displaying images may fail; you can leave them blank or display a message.
- Cached values may be unavailable; you can get the originals at some time cost.
- A detailed calculation may fail; you can use an approximation.
- Undo information may not be saved (usually after warning the user).

Wherever possible, components should conceal their partial failure from their clients. Such encapsulation makes the components easier to design and *localizes* the effect of the failure to the components that detect it. Component interfaces should not force clients to know about these failure modes, although they can provide additional methods to allow interested clients to learn about such failure.

You can often use MULTIPLE REPRESENTATIONS (209) to help implement partial failure.

5. Rainy day fund

Just as you have to spend money to make money, handling memory exhaustion can itself *require* memory. C++ and Java signal memory exhaustion by throwing an exception, which requires memory to store the exception object; displaying a dialog box to warn the user about memory problems requires memory to store the dialog box object. To avoid this problem, set aside some memory for a rainy day. The C++ runtime system, for example, is required to pre-allocate enough memory to store the `bad_alloc` exception thrown when it runs out of memory (Stroustrup 1997). Windows CE similarly sets aside enough memory to display an out-of-memory dialog box (Boling 1998). The Prograph visual programming language takes a more sophisticated approach — it supplies a rainy day fund class that manages a memory reserve that is automatically released immediately after the main memory is exhausted (MacNeil and Proudfoot 1985).

Example

The following Java code illustrates a simple technique for handling errors with partial failure. The method `StrapFont.font` attempts to find a font and ensure it is loaded into main memory. From the client's point of view, it must always succeed.

We implement a safe state by ensuring that there is always a font available to return. Here, the class creates a default font when it first initializes. If that failed, it would be a failure of process initialization — implemented by `new` throwing an uncaught `OutOfMemoryError` — preventing the user entering any data in the first place.

```
class StrapFont {
    static Font myDefaultFont = new Font("Dialog", Font.PLAIN, 12);

    public static Font defaultFont() {
        return myDefaultFont;
    }
```

The `StrapFont.font` method tries to create a new font object based on the description `privateGetFont` method, which can run out of memory and throw an `OutOfMemoryError`. If a new font object cannot be created then we return the default font. This mechanism also allows safe handling of a different problem, such as when the font does not exist:

```
    public static Font font(String name, int style, int size) {
        Font f;
        try {
            f = privateGetFont(name, style, size);
        }
        catch (BadFontException e) {
            return defaultFont();
        }
```

```
        catch (OutOfMemoryError e) {
          return defaultFont();
        }
        return f;
    }
  }
```

The client must reload the font using `StrapFont.font` every time it redraws the screen, rather than caching the returned value; this ensures that when memory becomes available the correct font will be loaded.

❖   ❖   ❖

Known uses

PARTIAL FAILURE is an important architectural principle. If a system is to support PARTIAL FAILURE, it must do so consistently. A recent project evaluated a third-party database library for porting to EPOC as an operating system service. Everything looked fine: the code was elegant; the port would be trivial. Unfortunately the library, designed for a memory-rich system, provided no support for partial failure; all memory allocations were assumed either to succeed or to terminate the process. In a service for simultaneous use by many EPOC applications that strategy was unacceptable; memory exhaustion is common in EPOC systems, and the designers couldn't allow a situation where it would cause many applications to fail simultaneously. The library was unsuitable because it did not support PARTIAL FAILURE.

Degraded modes are common in GUI applications. If Netscape fails to load a font due to insufficient memory, it continues with standard fonts. Microsoft PowerPoint will use standard fonts and omit images. PhotoShop warns the user and then stops saving undo information.

At a lower level, if the Microsoft Foundation Class framework detects an exception while painting a window, its default behaviour is to mark the window as fully painted. This allows the application to continue although the window display may be incorrect; the window will be repainted when it is subsequently changed by the application.

EPOC's word processor makes its largest use of memory when formatting part of a page for display. If this fails, it enters an out-of-memory mode where it displays as much of the text as has been formatted successfully. Whenever a user event occurs (scrolling, or a redisplay command), the word processor attempts to reformat the page, and leaves its degraded mode if it is successful. EPOC's architecture also has an interesting policy about safe states. The EPOC application framework is event-driven; every application runs by receiving repeated function calls from a central scheduler. Every application is in a safe state when it is not currently executing from the scheduler, so any EPOC application can fail independently of any other (Tasker et al. 2000).

See also

APPLICATION SWITCHING (84) can fail an entire application and begin running another application, rather than terminating an entire system of multiple applications. MULTIPLE REPRESENTATIONS (209) can also support partial failure, by replacing standard representations with more memory-efficient designs.

An alternative to failing the component that needed the memory is to use the CAPTAIN OATES (57) pattern and fail a different and less important component. The MEMORY ALLOCATION (219) chapter describes a number of strategies for dealing with allocation failures, such as deferring requests, discarding information, and signalling errors.

Ward Cunningham's CHECKS pattern language discusses several ways of communicating partial failure to the user (Cunningham 1995). *Professional Symbian Programming* (Tasker et al. 2000), *More Effective C++* (Meyers 1996) and *Exceptional C++* (Sutter 2000) describe in detail programming techniques and idioms for implementing PARTIAL FAILURE (48) with C++ exceptions.

Captain Oates

Also known as: Cache Release

How can you fulfil the most important demands for memory?

- Many systems have components that run in the background.

- Many applications cache data to improve performance.

- Users care more about what they are working on than about background activities the system is doing for its own sake.

To the operating system all memory requirements appear equal. To the user, however, some requirements are more equal than others (Orwell 1945).

For example, when someone is using the Strap-It-On PC's word processor to edit a document, they don't care what the fractal screen background looks like. You can increase a system's *usability* by spending scarce resources doing what users actually want.

Many systems include background components, such as screensavers, chat programs, cryptoanalysis engines (Hayes 1998), or Fourier analyses to search for extraterrestrial intelligence (Sullivan et al. 1997). Systems also use memory to make users' activities quicker or more enjoyable, by downloading music, caching web pages, or indexing file systems. Though important in the longer term, these activities do not help the user while they are happening, and take scarce resources from the urgent, vital demands of the user.

Therefore: **Sacrifice memory used by less vital components rather than fail more important tasks.**

Warn every component in the system when memory is running out, but while there is still some space left. When a component receives this warning it should release its inessential memory, or in more extreme situations, terminate activities.

If there is no support for signalling memory conditions, processes can keep track of the free memory situation by regular polling, and free inessential resources (or close down) when memory becomes short.

For example, when Word-O-Matic is about to run out of memory the IP networking stack empties its cache of IP address maps and the web browser empties its page cache. Background service processes such as the 'Fizzy' fractal generator automatically close down. Consequently, the word processor's *memory requirements* can be met. Figures 1.8 and 1.9 illustrate a system-wide implementation of the **CAPTAIN OATES** pattern.

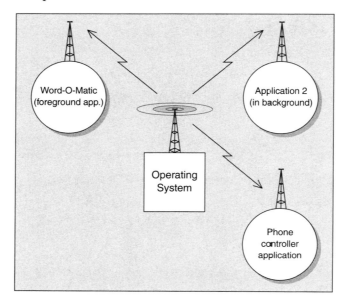

Figure 1.8   The memory-low event

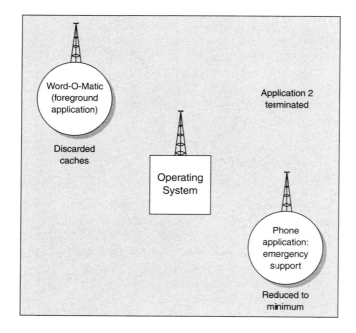

Figure 1.9   Result of the memory-low event

The name of this pattern celebrates a famous Victorian explorer, Captain Lawrence 'Titus' Oates. Oates was part of the British team led by Robert Falcon Scott, who reached the South Pole only to discover that Roald Amundsen's Norwegian team had got there first. Scott's team ran short of supplies on the way back, and a depressed and frostbitten Oates sacrificed himself to give the rest of his team a chance of survival, walking out into the blizzard leaving a famous diary entry: 'I may be some time'. Oates' sacrifice was not enough to save the rest of the team, whose remains were found in their frozen camp the next year. Thirty-five kilograms of rock samples, carried laboriously back from the Pole, were among their remains (Limb and Cordingley 1982; Scott 1913).

Consequences

By allocating memory where it is most needed this pattern increases the system's *usability*, and reduces its *memory requirements*. Programs releasing their temporary memory also increase the *predictability* of the system's memory use.

However: CAPTAIN OATES requires *programmer discipline* to consider voluntarily releasing resources. CAPTAIN OATES doesn't usually benefit the application that implements it directly, so the motivation for a development team to implement it isn't high — there needs to be strong cultural or architectural forces to make them do so. The pattern also requires *programmer effort* to implement and test.

CAPTAIN OATES introduces coupling between otherwise unrelated components, which decreases the *predictability* of the system. Releasing resources can reduce the program's *time performance*. Programs need to be *tested* to see that they do release resources, and that they continue to perform successfully afterwards. Because many programs must handle the memory-low signal, CAPTAIN OATES is easier with *operating system support*. This is another *global mechanism* that introduces *local complexity* to handle the signal.

❖   ❖   ❖

Implementation

The main point of the CAPTAIN OATES pattern is that it releases memory from low-priority activities so that high-priority activities can proceed. It is inappropriate for a component to release memory if it is supporting high-priority activities. Yet mechanisms that detect low-memory conditions are indiscriminate and notify all components equally. So how can you work out what components to sacrifice?

A user interface application can usually determine whether it is the current application, i.e. whether it has the input focus so users can interact with it (Figure 1.10). If so, it should not sacrifice itself when it receives low-memory warnings.

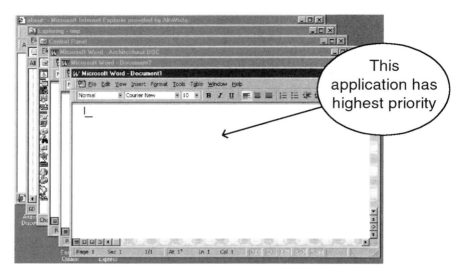

Figure 1.10 The current application

A background process, though, cannot usually ask the system how important it is. In MS Windows, for example, high-priority threads block waiting for some events — the Task Manager has a high priority when waiting for Ctrl+Alt+Del key strokes. When the Task Manager detects an event, however, it changes its priority down to normal. So, calling GetThreadPriority cannot give a true indication of how important the task is and whether it's being used.

Most processes, though, can determine how important they are from other information. A component managing network connections, for example, could check whether it had any active connections. Other background processes may not even have that information; a web page cache, for example, may have no direct information about the applications that it supports. Such processes, however, must not be directly interacting with the user (otherwise they would have more information about users' activities) and so can usually quite safely release inessential resources when required.

1. Detecting low-memory conditions

Many operating systems provide events that warn applications when memory is low. MS Windows and MS Windows CE send WM_COMPACTING and WM_HIBERNATE messages to all windows (though not, therefore, to background processes) to warn them that the system memory is getting low (Boling 1998; Microsoft 1997). Rather than send events, some operating systems or language runtimes call back to system components when memory is low — one example, C++'s new_handler, is discussed in the PARTIAL FAILURE (48) pattern.

As an alternative, if the system provides functions to show how much memory is in use, then each component can poll to see if memory is low, and release memory when it is. Polling can be unsatisfactory in battery-powered machines, however, since the processor activity uses battery power.

2. Handling low-memory events

When a low-memory event occurs, it's useful if each component can determine how short of memory the system is. In the Java JDK 1.2 environment, the runtime object's getMemoryAdvice() call answers one of four modes: 'green' meaning there's no shortage, 'yellow' then 'orange' meaning memory is getting low, and 'red' meaning memory is critically low. MS Windows' event, WM_COMPACTING, sends an indication of the proportion of time spent paging memory: ⅛ is equivalent to 'yellow', and is when the message is first sent; anything over ¼ is critically low (Microsoft 1997).

3. Good citizenship

Perhaps the simplest, and often the easiest, approach is for each process to voluntarily give up inessential resources they are not really using. By observing a simple timer, you can release latent resources after a specific time, regardless of the memory status of the rest of the system. For example, the EPOC web browser loads dynamic DLLs to handle specific types of web data. If a particular type of data occurs once, it may recur almost immediately, so the browser DLL loader caches each DLL. If the DLL isn't reused within a few seconds, however, the loader releases it.

Example

This C++ example implements a piece of operating system infrastructure to support a simple Captain Oates mechanism for the EPOC operating system. The Captain Oates application runs in the background and closes applications not currently in use when memory becomes low. Since closing an EPOC application automatically saves its state (a requirement of the PC-synchronization mechanisms), this does not lose any data. Transient editing states, such as the cursor position in a document or the current item displayed in a file browser, are not maintained, however.

The functionality is in class COatesTerminator, which is as follows (omitting function declarations):

```
class COatesTerminator : public CBase {
private:
   RNotifier iPopupDialogNotifier;      // Provides user screen output
   CPeriodic* iTimer;                   // Timer mechanism
   CEikonEnv* iApplicationEnvironment;  // User I/O Handler for this app.

   enum {
      EPollPeriodInSeconds = 10,        // How often to check memory
      EDangerPercentage = 5 };          // Close applications when less free
   };                                   // memory than this.
```

There are various construction and initialization functions (not included here) to set up the periodic timer and dialog notifier.

The core of the application is the `TimerTickL` function that polls the current memory status and closes applications when memory is low. The free memory reading can be deceptively low if other applications have allocated more memory than they are using. If free memory appears to be low on a first reading, we compress all the memory heaps; this claws back any free pages of memory at the end of each heap. Then a second reading will measure all free memory accurately. If the second reading is also low, we call `CloseAnApplicationL` to close an application.

```
void COatesTerminator::TimerTickL() {
    if ( GetMemoryPercentFree() <= EDangerPercentage ||
        (User::CompressAllHeaps(),
        GetMemoryPercentFree() <= EDangerPercentage )) {
      CloseAnApplicationL();
    }
}
```

`CloseAnApplicationL` must first select a suitable application to terminate — we do not want to close the current foreground application, the system shell, or this process. Of the other candidates, we'll just close the one lowest in the Z-order. Applications are identified to the system as 'window groups' (WG). To find the right window, we first get the identifiers of the window groups we don't want to close (focusWg, defaultWg, thisWg), next get the `WindowGroupList`, then work backwards through the list, and close the first suitable application we find.

Note also the use of the `CleanupStack`, as described in PARTIAL FAILURE (48). We push the array holding the `WindowGroupList` onto the stack when it is allocated, and then remove and destroy it as the function finishes. If the call to get the window group suffers an error, we immediately `leave` the `CloseAnApplicationL` function, automatically destroying the array as it is on the cleanup stack.

```
void COatesTerminator::CloseAnApplicationL() {
    RWsSession& windowServerSession =
        iApplicationEnvironment->WsSession();
  TInt foregroundApplicationWG =
        windowServerSession.GetFocusWindowGroup();
    TInt systemShellApplicationWG =
        windowServerSession.GetDefaultOwningWindow();
    TInt thisApplicationWG =
        iApplicationEnvironment->RootWin().Identifier();
    TInt nApplications=windowServerSession.NumWindowGroups(0);
    CArrayFixFlat<TInt>* applicationList =
        new (ELeave) CArrayFixFlat<TInt>(nApplications);
    CleanupStack::PushL(applicationList);
    User::LeaveIfError(
        windowServerSession.WindowGroupList(0,applicationList));
    TInt applicationWG = 0;
```

```
TInt i= applicationList->Count();
for (i -- ; i>=0; i -- ) {
    applicationWG = applicationList->At( i );
    if (applicationWG != thisApplicationWG &&
        applicationWG != systemShellApplicationWG &&
        applicationWG != foregroundApplicationWG)
      break;
    }
  }
```

If we find a suitable candidate, we use a standard mechanism to terminate it cleanly. Note that _LIT defines a string literal that can be stored in ROM — see the **READ-ONLY MEMORY** (65) pattern.

```
if (i >= 0) {
    TApaTask task(windowServerSession);
    task.SetWgId(applicationWG);
    task.EndTask();
    _LIT(KMessage, "Application terminated");
    iPopupDialogNotifier.InfoPrint( KMessage );
  }
  CleanupStack::PopAndDestroy(); // applicationList
}
```

This implementation has the disadvantage that it requires polling, consuming unnecessary CPU time and wasting battery power. A better implementation could poll only after writes to the RAM-based file system (straightforward), after user input (difficult), or could vary the polling frequency according to the available memory.

Known uses

The MS Windows application 'ObjectPLUS', a hypercard application by ObjectPLUS of Boston, responds to the WM_COMPACTING message. As the memory shortage becomes increasingly critical, it:

- stops playing sounds;
- compresses images;
- removes cached bitmaps taken from a database.

Though this behaviour benefits other applications in the system, it also benefits the HyperCard application itself by releasing memory for other more important activities. By implementing the behaviour in the Windows event handler, the designers have kept that behaviour architecturally separate from other processing in the application.

The Apple Macintosh memory manager (discussed in COMPACTION) supports 'purgeable memory blocks' that the memory manager reclaims when memory is low (Apple 1985). They are used for RESOURCE FILES, file system caches, and dynamically allocated program memory.

MS Windows CE Shell takes a two-phase approach to managing memory (Microsoft 1998; Boling 1998). When memory becomes low, it sends a `WM_HIBERNATE` message to every application. A CE application should respond to this message by releasing as many system resources as possible. When memory becomes even lower, it sends the message `WM_CLOSE` to the lowest-priority applications, asking those applications to close — like EPOC, Windows CE requires applications to save their state on `WM_CLOSE` without prompting the user. Alternatively, if more resources become available, applications can receive the `WM_ACTIVATE` message, requesting them to rebuild the internal state they discarded for `WM_HIBERNATE`.

A number of distributed internet projects take advantage of Captain Oates by running as screensavers. When a machine is in use, the screensavers do not run, but after a machine is idle for a few minutes the screensaver uses the idle processor to search for messages from aliens (Hayes 1998) or crack encrypted messages (Sullivan et al. 1997).

See also

Where CAPTAIN OATES (57) describes what a program should do when another process in the system runs out of memory, PARTIAL FAILURE (48) describes what a process should do when it runs out of memory itself. Many of the techniques for PARTIAL FAILURE (such as MULTIPLE REPRESENTATIONS (209) and APPLICATION SWITCHING (84)) are also appropriate for CAPTAIN OATES.

FIXED ALLOCATION (226) describes a simple way to implement a form of CAPTAIN OATES, where each activity is merely a data structure — simply make new activities overwrite the old ones.

Scott and his team are popular heroes of British and New Zealand culture. See *Captain Oates: Soldier and Explorer* (Limb and Cordingley 1982), and *Scott's Last Expedition: The Personal Journals of Captain R. F. Scott, R.N., C.V.O., on his Journey to the South Pole* (Scott 1913).

Read-Only Memory

Also known as: Use the ROM

What can you do with read-only code and data?

- Many systems provide read-only memory as well as writable memory.
- Read-only memory is cheaper than writable memory.
- Programs do not usually modify executable code.
- Programs do not modify resource files, lookup tables, and other pre-initialized data.

Programs often have lots of *read-only* code and data. For example, the Word-O-Matic word processor has a large amount of executable code, and large master dictionary files for its spelling checker, which it never changes. Storing this static information in main memory will take memory from data that does need to change, increasing the *memory requirements* of the program as a whole.

Many hardware devices — particularly small ones — support read-only memory as well as writable main memory. The read-only memory may be primary storage directly accessible from the processor, or indirectly accessible secondary storage. A wide range of technologies can provide read-only memory, from semiconductor ROMs and PROMS of various kinds, through flash ROMs, to read-only compact discs and even paper tape. Most forms of read-only memory are better in many ways than corresponding writable memory — simpler to build, less expensive to purchase, more reliable, more economical of power, dissipating less heat, and more resistant to stray cosmic radiation.

Therefore: **Store read-only code and data in read-only memory.**

Divide your system code and data into those portions that can change and those that never change. Store the immutable portions in read-only memory and arrange to re-associate them with the changeable portions at runtime.

Word-O-Matic's program code, for example, is contained in ROM memory in the Strap-It-On portable PC. Word-O-Matic's master dictionary and other resource files are stored in read-only secondary storage (flash ROM); only user documents and configuration files are stored in writable memory.

Consequences

This pattern trades off writable main storage for *read-only* storage, reducing the *memory requirements* for main storage and making it easier to test. Read-only storage is cheaper than writable storage, in terms of financial cost, power consumption and reliability. If the system can execute programs directly from read-only memory, then using read-only memory can decrease the system's *start-up time.*

Although you may need to copy code and data from *read-only secondary storage* to main memory, you can delete read-only information from main memory without having to save it back to secondary storage. Because they cannot be modified, read-only code and data can be shared easily between programs or components, further reducing the *memory requirements* of the system as a whole.

However: *Programmer effort* is needed to divide up the program into read-only and writable portions, and then *programmer discipline* to stick to the division. The distinction between read-only and writable information is fundamentally a *global* concern, although it must be made *locally* for every component in the program.

Code or data in read-only memory is more difficult to *maintain* than information in writable secondary storage. Often, the only way to replace code or data stored in read-only memory is to physically replace the hardware component storing the information. Updating flash memory, which can be erased and rewritten, usually requires a complicated procedure particuarly if the operating system is stored in the memory being updated.

❖   ❖   ❖

Implementation

Creating a 'ROM image' (a copy of the final code and data to be stored into read-only memory) is invariably a magical process, requiring major incantations and bizarre software ingredients that are specific to your environment. Across most environments, however, there are common issues to consider when using read-only memory.

1. Storing executable code

If you can run programs directly from read-only memory, then you can use it to store executable code. This generally poses two problems: how should the code be represented in read-only memory, and how can it get access to any data it needs?

Most environments store programs as object files — such as executables and dynamic linked libraries — that do not refer to any absolute addresses in memory, instead containing symbolic references to other files or libraries. Before object files can be executed, the operating system's runtime loader must bind the symbolic references to create completely executable machine code.

To store this executable code in read-only memory you need an extra tool, the 'ROM builder', which does the job of the runtime loader, reading in object files and producing a ROM Image. A ROM builder assigns each object file a base address in memory and copies it into the corresponding position in the ROM image, binding symbolic references and assigning writable memory for heap memory, static memory, and static data. For example, the EPOC system includes a Java ROM builder that takes the 'jar' or 'class' files and loads them into a ROM image, mimicking the actions of the Java runtime class loader.

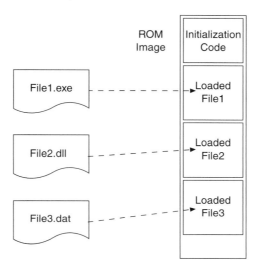

Figure 1.11   The ROM image

If the system starts up by executing code in read-only memory, then the ROM image will also need to contain initialization code to allocate main memory data structures and to bootstrap the whole system (Figure 1.11). The ROM builder can know about this bootstrap code and install it in the correct place in the image.

2. Including data within code

Most programs and programming languages include constant data as well as executable code — if the code is being stored in read-only memory, then this data should accompany it. To do this you need to persuade the compiler or assembler that the data is truly unchangeable.

The C++ standard (Ellis and Stroustrup 1990), for example, defines that instances of objects can be placed in the code segment — and thus in read-only memory — if:

- the instance is defined to be `const`, and
- it has no constructor or destructor.

Thus

```
const char myString[] = "Hello";   // In ROM
char* myString = "Hello";          // Not in ROM according to the
                                   Standard.
const String myString("Hello");    // Not in ROM, since it has a
                                   constructor
```

In particular, you can create C++ data tables that can be compiled into ROM:

```
const int myTable[] = { 1, 2, 3, 4, 5, 6, 7, 8, 9, 10 }; // In ROM
```

Note that non-const C++ strings are generally not placed in the code segment, since they can be modified, but some compilers support flags or #pragma declarations to change this behaviour.

The EPOC system uses a combination of C++ macros and template classes to create instances of strings in read-only memory, containing both a length and the text, as follows:

```
template <TInt S> class TLitC {
    // Various operators...
public:
    int iTypeLength; // This is the structure of a standard EPOC string
    char iBuf[S];
}

#define _LIT(name,s) const static TLitC<sizeof(s)> name={sizeof(s)-1,s}
```

This allows EPOC code to define strings in ROM using the _LIT macro:

```
_LIT(MyString, "Hello World");
User::InfoPrint(MyString); // Displays a message on the screen.
```

The linker filters out duplicate constant definitions, so you can even put _LIT definitions in header files.

2.1 Read-only objects in C++. C++ compilers enforce const as far as the bitwise state of the object is concerned: const member functions may not change any data member, nor may a client delete an object through a const pointer (Stroupstrup 1997). A well-designed class will provide logical const-ness by ensuring that any public function is const if it doesn't change the externally visible state of the object. For example, the simple String class below provides both a 'logically const' access operator, and a non-const one. A client given using a const String& variable can use only the former.

```
class String {
public:
    // Constructors etc. not shown...
    char operator[](int i) const { return rep[i]; }
    char& operator[](int i) { return rep[i]; }
private:
    char* rep;
}
```

C++ supports passing parameters by value, which creates a copy of the shared object on the stack. If the object is large and if the function does not modify it, it's common C++ style to **SHARE** the representation by passing the object as a `const` reference. Thus:

```
void function(const String& p);
```

is usually preferable to

```
void function(String p);
```

because it will use less stack space.

2.2 Read-only objects in Java. Java lacks `const`, and so is more restrictive on what data can be stored with the code in read-only memory — only strings and single primitive values are stored in Java constant tables. For example, the following code:

```
final int myTable[] = { 1, 2, 3, 4, 5, 6, 7, 8, 9, 10 }; // Don't do this!
```

compiles to a very large function that constructs `myTable`, assigning values to an array in main memory element by element. Storing data for Java programs in read-only memory is thus quite complex. You can encode the data as two-byte integers and store it in a string; use C++ to manage the data and access it via the Java Native Interface; or keep the data in a resource file and use file access calls (Lindholm and Yellin 1999).

3. Static data structures

Some programs require relatively large constant data structures, for example:

- encryption algorithms, such as the US Data Encryption Standard (DES);
- mathematical algorithms, such as log, sine and cosine functions;
- state transition tables, such as those generated by tools to support the Shlaer-Mellor object-oriented methodology (1991).

These tables can be quite large, so it's usually not a good idea to store them in main memory, but since they are constant, they can be moved to read-only memory. Managing the development of these data structures can be quite a large task, however.

If the table data changes often during the development process, the best approach is to use a tool to generate the table as a separate file that is incorporated by the ROM image builder. If the data changes very rarely, then it's usually easiest to copy the table manually into the code, and modify it or the surrounding code to ensure that the compiler will place it into read-only memory.

4. Read-only file systems

Some environments can treat read-only memory as if it were a file system. This has the advantage that file system structures can organize the read-only data, and that applications can read it through the normal file operations, although they cannot modify it. For example, EPOC supports a logical file system (Z:), normally invisible to users, which is stored in read-only memory and constructed by the EPOC ROM builder. All the resource files for ROM-based applications are stored in this file system.

File system access is usually slower than direct memory access. If read-only memory can be mapped into applications' address spaces, the data in a ROM filing system can be made available directly, as an optimization. For example, the EPOC Font and Bitmap Server uses the function `User::IsFileInROM` to access bitmap data directly from ROM.

5. Version control

Different versions of ROM images will place the same code or data at different addresses. You need to provide some kind of index so that other software in the system can operate with different ROM versions. For example, ROM images often begin with a table of pointers to the beginning of every routine and data structure: external software can find the correct address to call by indirection through this table (Smith 1985).

The **HOOKS** pattern describes how you can store the table in writable memory, so that routines can be extended or replaced with versions stored in writable memory.

Example

The following example uses a read-only lookup table to calculate the mathematical sine function for a number expressed in radians. Because the example is in Java, we must encode the table as a string (using hexadecimal values) because numeric arrays cannot be stored in Java constant tables. The following code runs on our development machine and calculates 256 values of the sine function as 16-bit integers.

```
final int nPoints = 256;
for (int i = 0; i<nPoints; i++) {
    double radians = i * Math.PI / nPoints;
    int tableValue = (int)(Math.sin(radians) * 65535);
    System.out.print("\\u"+Integer.toHexString(tableValue));
}
```

This code doesn't produce quite correct Java: a few of the escape codes at the start and end of the table lack leading zeros, but it's easier to correct this by hand than to spend more time on a program that's only ever run once.

The `sin` function itself does linear interpolation between the two points found in the table. For brevity, we've not shown the whole table:

```
static final String sinValues = "\u0000\u0324\u0648. . .\u0000";

public static float sin(float radians) {
    float point = (radians / (float)Math.PI) * sinValues.length();
    int lowVal = (int)point;
    int hiVal = lowVal + 1;
```

```
        float lowValSin = (float)sinValues.charAt(lowVal) / 65535;
        float hiValSin = (float)sinValues.charAt(hiVal) / 65535;
        float result = ((float)hiVal — point) * lowValSin
            + (point — (float)lowVal) * hiValSin;
        return result;
    }
```

On a fast machine with a maths co-processor this `sin` function runs orders of magnitude more slowly than the native `Math.sin()` function! Nevertheless, this program provides an accuracy of better than 1 in 20,000, and illustrates the lookup table technique. Lookup tables are widely used in environments that don't support mathematics libraries and in situations where you prefer to use integer rather than floating-point arithmetic, such as graphics compression and decompression on low-power processors.

❖   ❖   ❖

Known uses

Most embedded systems — from digital watches and washing machine controllers to mobile telephones and weapons systems — keep their code and some of their data in read-only memory, such as PROMs or EPROMs. Only runtime data is stored in writable main memory. Palmtops and Smartphones usually keep their operating system code in ROM, along with applications supplied with the phone. In contrast, third-party applications live in secondary storage (battery backed-up RAM) and must be loaded into main memory to execute. Similarly, many 1980s home computers, such as the BBC Micro, had complex ROM architectures (Smith 1985).

Even systems that load almost all their code from secondary storage still need some 'bootstrap' initialization code in ROM to load the first set of instructions from disk when the system starts up. PCs extend this bootstrap to the ROM-based Basic Input Output System (BIOS), which provides generic access to hardware, making it easy to support many different kinds of hardware with one (DOS or MS Windows) operating system (Chappel 1994).

See also

Data in read-only storage can be changed using COPY-ON-WRITE (91) and HOOKS (72). COPY-ON-WRITE and HOOKS also allow some kinds of infrequently changing (but not constant) data to be moved to read-only storage.

Anything in read-only storage is suitable for SHARING (182) between various programs and different components or for moving to SECONDARY STORAGE (79).

PAGING (119) systems often distinguish between read-only pages and writable pages, and ignore or prevent attempts to write to read-only pages. Several processes can safely share a read-only page, and the paging system can discard it without the cost of writing it back to disk.

Hooks

Also known as: Vector table, Jump table, Patch table, Interrupt table.

How can you change information in read-only storage?

- You are using read-only memory.

- It is difficult or impossible to change read-only memory once created.

- Code or data in read-only memory needs to be maintained and upgraded.

- You need to make additions and relatively small changes to the information stored in read-only memory.

The main disadvantage of read-only storage is that it is *read-only*. The contents of read-only memory are set at manufacturing time, or possibly upgrade time; whereupon they are fixed for eternity. Unfortunately, there are always bugs that need to be fixed, or functionality to be upgraded. For example, the released version of the Word-O-Matic code in the Strap-It-On's ROM is rather buggy, and fixes for these bugs need to be included into existing systems. In addition, Strap-It-On's marketing department has decreed that it needs an additional predictive input feature, to automatically complete users' input and so reduce the number of input keystrokes (Darragh et al. 1990).

If the information is stored in partly writable storage, such as EPROMs, you could issue a completely new ROM image and somehow persuade all the customers to invest the time and risk of upgrading it. Upgrading ROMs is painful for your customers, however, and often commercially impractical if you don't have control over the whole system. Moreover, a released ROM is unlikely to be so badly flawed as to demand a complete re-release. Often the amount of information that needs to be changed is small, even for significant changes to the system as a whole.

You could ignore the existing read-only memory, and store a new copy of the information in writable main memory. Even if there is enough writable memory in the system to hold a full copy of the contents of the read-only memory, you generally cannot afford to dedicate large amounts of main memory to storing copies of the ROM.

Therefore: **Access read-only information through hooks in writable storage and change the hooks to give the illusion of changing the information.**

The key to making read-only storage extensible is to link your system together through writable memory, rather than read-only memory. When designing a system that uses read-only storage, do not access that storage directly. Allocate a 'hook' in writable memory for each entry point (to a function, component, data structure, or resource) that is stored in read-only memory, and initialize each hook to refer to its corresponding entry point. Ensure that every access to the entry point is via the writable hook — all accesses, whether from read-only memory or writable memory, should use the hook.

To update the read-only memory you copy just that part of the memory you need to modify, and then make the required changes to the copy. Then, you can store the modified copy in writable store, and set the hooks to point to the modified portion. The modified portion can call other parts of the program, if necessary again by indirection through the hooks (Figure 1.12).

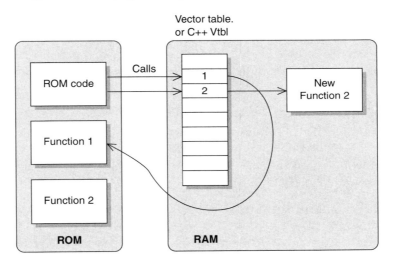

Figure 1.12 Code hooks

For example, the Strap-It-On was carefully designed so that every major function is called indirectly through a table of hooks that are stored in RAM and initialized when the system is booted. Bug fixes, extensions, and third-party code can be loaded into the system's main memory and the hooks changed to point to them. When an application uses a system function, the hooks ensure it finds the correct piece of code — either the original code in ROM, or the new code in RAM.

Consequences

Hooks let you extend read-only storage, and by making read-only storage easier to use, can reduce the program's writable *memory requirements*.

Providing good hooks increases the *quality* of the *program's design*, making it easier to *maintain* and extend in future. A ROM-based operating system that provides good hooks can enormously reduce the *programmer effort* required to implement any specific functionality.

However: Hooks require *programmer discipline* to design them into programs and then to ensure that they are used. They also increase the *testing* cost of the program, because the hooks have to be tested to see if they are called at the right times.

Indirect access via hooks is slower than direct access, reducing *time performance*; and the hook vectors take up valuable writable storage, slightly increasing *memory requirements*. Hook vectors are great places to attack system integrity, as any virus writer will tell you, so using hooks can make the system less *reliable*.

❖   ❖   ❖

Implementation

Consider the following issues when implementing the **Hooks** pattern.

1. Calling writable memory from read-only memory

You can't predict the addresses or entry points of code and data stored in main memory — indeed, because the memory is writable memory addresses can change between versions of programs (or even as a program is running). This makes it difficult for code in ROM to call code or rely on data that is stored in writable memory.

You can address this by using additional hooks that are stored at known addresses in main memory — hooks that point to code and data in main memory, rather than into read-only memory. Code in ROM can follow these hooks to find the addresses of main memory components that it needs to use.

2. Extending objects in read-only memory

Object-oriented environments associate operations with the objects they operate upon — called 'dynamic dispatch', 'message sending' or 'ad-hoc polymorphism'. You can use this to implement rather more flexible hooks. For example, both EPOC and Windows CE support C++ derived classes stored in RAM that inherit from base classes stored in ROM. When the system calls a C++ virtual function, the code executed may be in ROM or in RAM depending on the class of the object to which the function belongs. The compiler and runtime system ensure that the C++ virtual function tables (vtbls) have the correct entry for each function, so the vtbls behave like tables of hooks (Ellis and Stroustrup 1990). ROM programmers can use many object-oriented design patterns (such as **Factory Method** and **Abstract Factory**) to implement extensible code (Gamma et al. 1995) because the inheritance mechanism does not really distinguish between ROM and RAM classes.

This works equally well in a Java implementation. Java's dynamic binding permits ROM-based code to call methods that may be in ROM or RAM according to the target object's class.

3. Extending data in read-only memory

Replacing ROM-based data is simplest when the data exists as files in a ROM filing system. In this case, it is sufficient to ensure that application code looks for files in other file systems before the ROM one. EPOC, for example, scans for resource files in the same directory on each drive in turn, taking the drive letters in alphabetic order. Drive Z, the ROM drive, is therefore scanned last.

You can also use accessor functions to use data structures stored in read-only memory. Provided these functions are called through hooks, you can modify the data the rest of the system retrieves from read-only memory, by modifying these accessor functions.

If you access read-only memory directly, then you need *programmer discipline* to write code that can use both ROM and RAM simultaneously. When reading data, you should generally search the RAM first, then the ROM; when writing data, you can only write into the RAM. This ensures that if you replace the ROM data by writing to RAM, the updated version in RAM will be found before the original in ROM.

Example

The Strap-It-On's operating system is mostly stored in ROM, and accessed via a table of hooks. The operating system can be updated by changing the hooks. This example describes C code implementing the creation of the hook table and intercepting the operating system function memalloc, which allocates memory.

The basic data type in the Strap-It-On operating system is called a sysobj — it may be a pointer to a block of memory, a single 4-byte integer, two 2-byte short integers and so on. Every system call takes and returns a single sysobj, so the hook table is essentially a table of pointers to functions taking and returning sysobjs.

```
typedef void* sysobj;
const int SIO_HOOK_TABLE_SIZE = 100;
typedef sysobj (*sio_hook_function) (sysobj) ;


sio_hook_function sio_hook_table[SIO_HOOK_TABLE_SIZE];
```

As the system begins running, it stores a pointer to the function that implements memalloc in the appropriate place in the hook table.

```
extern sysobj sio_memalloc(sysobj);
const int SIO_MEMALLOC = 0;
sio_hook_table[SIO_MEMALLOC] = sio_memalloc;
```

Strap-It-On applications make system calls, such as the function memalloc, by calling 'trampoline functions' that indirect through the correct entry in the hook table.

```
void *memalloc(size_t bytesToAllocate) {
    return (void*)sio_hook_table[SIO_MEMALLOC]((sysobj)bytesToAllocate);
}
```

1. Changing a function using a hook

To change the behaviour of the system, say to implement a memory counter, we first allocate a variable to remember the address (in read-only memory) of the original implementation of the `memalloc` call. We need to preserve the original implementation because our memory counter will just count the number of bytes requested, but then needs to call the original function to actually allocate the memory.

```
static sio_hook_function original_memalloc = 0;
static size_t mem_counter = 0;
```

We can then write a replacement function that counts the memory requested and calls the original version:

```
sysobj mem_counter_memalloc(sysobj size) {
    mem_counter += (size_t)size;
    return original_memalloc(size);
}
```

Finally, we can install the memory counter by copying the address of the existing system `memalloc` from the hook table into our variable, and install our new routine into the hook table.

```
original_memalloc = sio_hook_table(SIO_MEMALLOC);
sio_hook_table(SIO_MEMALLOC) = mem_counter_memalloc;
```

Now, any calls to `memalloc` (in client code and in the operating system, as ROM also uses the hook table) will first be processed by the memory counter code.

Known uses

The Mac, BBC Micro, and IBM PC ROMs are all reached through hook vectors in RAM, and can be updated by changing the hooks. Emacs makes great use of hooks to extend its executable-only code — this way, many users can share a copy of the Emacs binary, but each one has his or her own, customized environment (Stallman 1984). NewtonScript allows objects to inherit from read-only objects, using both HOOKS (72) and COPY-ON-WRITE (191) so that they can be modified (Smith 1999).

The EPOC 'Time World' application has a large ROM-based database of world cities and associated time zones, dialling codes and locations. It also permits the user to add to the list; it stores new cities in a RAM database similar to the pre-defined ROM one, and searches both whenever the user looks for a city.

EPOC takes an alternative approach to updating its ROM. Patches to ROMs are supplied as device drivers that modify the virtual memory map of the system, to map one or more new pages of code in place of the existing ROM memory. This is awkward to manage as the new code must occupy exactly the same space as the code, and provide exactly the same entry points at exactly the same memory addresses.

See also

COPY-ON-WRITE (191) is a complementary technique for changing information in READ-ONLY MEMORY (65), and COPY-ON-WRITE and HOOKS (72) can often be used together.

Using HOOKS in conjunction with READ-ONLY storage is a special instance of the general use of hooks to extend systems one cannot change directly. Many of the patterns in *Object-Oriented Design Patterns* (Gamma et al. 1995) are also concerned with making systems extensible without direct changes.

HOOKS form an important part of the hot-spot approach to systems design (Pree 1995).

SECONDARY STORAGE

Application Switching

Data Files

Resource Files

Packages

Paging

2

SECONDARY STORAGE

What can you do when you have run out of primary storage?

- Your memory requirements are larger than the available primary storage.

- You cannot reduce the system's memory requirements sufficiently.

- You can attach secondary storage to the device executing the system.

Sometimes your system's primary memory is just not big enough to fulfil your program's memory requirements.

For example, the Word-O-Matic word processor for the Strap-It-On needs to be able to let users edit large amounts of text. Word-O-Matic also supports formatting text for display or printing, not to mention spelling checks, grammar checks, voice output, mail merging and the special StoryDone feature to write the endings for short stories. Unfortunately, the Strap-It-On has only 2 Mb of RAM. How can the programmers even consider implementing Word-O-Matic when its code alone will occupy most of the memory space?

There are a number of other techniques in this book which can reduce a program's memory requirements. COMPRESSION (135) can store the information in a smaller amount of memory. Testing applications using a MEMORY LIMIT (32) will ensure that programs fit well into a small memory space. You can reduce the system functionality by deleting features or reducing their quality. In many cases, however, these techniques will not reduce the program's memory requirements sufficiently: data that has to be accessed randomly is difficult to compress; programs have to provide the features and quality expected by the marketplace.

Yet for most applications there is usually some hope. Even in small systems, the amount of memory a program requires to make progress at any given time is usually a small fraction of the total amount of memory used. So the problem is not where to store the code and data needed by the program at any given moment; rather, the problem is where to store the rest of the code and data that may, or may not, be needed by the program in the future.

Therefore: **Use secondary storage as extra memory at runtime.**

Most systems have some form of reasonably fast *secondary storage*. Secondary storage is distinct from RAM, since the processor can't write to each individual memory address directly; but it's easy for applications to access secondary storage without user intervention. Most forms of secondary storage support *file systems* such that the data lives in files with text names and directory structures. Typically each file also supports *random access* to its data ('get me the byte at offset 301 from the start of the file').

If you can divide up your program and data into suitable pieces, you can load into main memory only those pieces of code and data that you need at any given time, keeping the rest of the program on secondary storage. When the pieces of the program currently in main memory are no longer required you can replace them with more relevant pieces from the secondary store.

There are many different kinds of secondary storage that can be modified and can be accessed randomly: floppy disks, hard disks, flash filing systems, bubble memory cards, CD-ROM drives, writable CD-ROM file systems, and gargantuan file servers accessed over a network. Palm Pilot systems use persistent 'memory records' stored in secondary RAM. Other forms of secondary storage provide only sequential or read-only access: tape, CD-ROM and web pages accessed over the internet.

For example, the Strap-It-On comes with a CyberStrap, which includes a 32 Mb bubble memory store built into its strap along with interfaces for wrist-mounted disk drives. So the Word-O-Matic developers can rely on plenty of 'disk' to store data. Thus Word-O-Matic consists of several separate executables for APPLICATION SWITCHING (84); it stores each unused document in a DATA FILE (92); dictionaries, grammar rules and skeleton story endings exist as RESOURCE FILES (101); optional features are generally shipped as PACKAGES (108); and the most complex operations use object PAGING (119) to make it seem that the RAM available is much larger than in reality.

Consequences

Being able to use SECONDARY STORAGE (79) can be like getting a lot of extra memory for free — it greatly reduces your program's *primary memory requirements*.

However: The secondary storage must be managed, and information transferred between primary and secondary storage. This management has a *time performance* cost, and may also cost *programmer effort* and *programmer discipline*, impose *local restrictions* to support *global* mechanisms, require *hardware or operating system support,* and reduce the program's *usability*. Most forms of secondary storage require additional devices, increasing the system's *power consumption*.

❖   ❖   ❖

Implementation

There are several issues you must address to use secondary storage effectively:

- What is divided up: code, data, configuration information or some combination?
- Who does the division: the programmer, the system or the user?
- Who invokes the loading and unloading: the programmer, the system or the user?
- When does loading or unloading happen?

Generally, the more the program is subdivided and the finer the subdivision, the less the program depends on main memory, and the more use the program makes of secondary storage. Coarser divisions, perhaps addressing only code or only data, may require more main memory but place less pressure on the secondary storage resources.

Making programmers subdivide the program manually requires more effort than somehow allowing the system, or the user, to subdivide the program; and a finer subdivision will require more effort than a coarser one. As a result, very fine subdivisions are generally only possible when the system provides them automatically; but creating an automatic system requires significant effort. Making the user divide up the program or data imposes little cost for programmers, but reduces the *usability* of the system.

There are similar trade-offs in deciding who controls the loading and unloading of the divisions. If the system does it automatically this saves work for everyone except the system-builders; otherwise the costs fall on the user and programmer. Sequential loading and unloading is the simplest to implement (and often the worst for the user). More complex schemes that load and unload code or data on demand can be much more seamless to the user, and can even make the reliance on secondary storage transparent to both users and programmers.

❖   ❖   ❖

Specialized patterns

The rest of this chapter contains five specialized patterns describing different ways to use SECONDARY STORAGE. Figure 2.1 shows the patterns and the relationships between them: arrows show close relationships; springs indicate a tension between the patterns.

The patterns also form a sequence starting with simple patterns which can be implemented locally, relying only upon programmer discipline for correct implementation, and finishing with more complex patterns which require hardware or operating system support but require much less, if any, programmer discipline. Each pattern occupies a different place in the design space defined by the questions above, as follows:

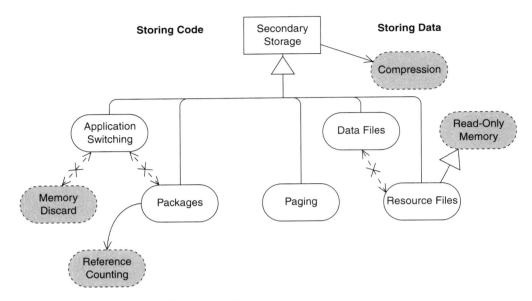

Figure 2.1   Secondary storage patterns

APPLICATION SWITCHING (84) requires the programmer to divide up the system into independent executables, only one of which runs at a time. The order in which the executables run can be determined by the executables themselves, by an external script, or by the user.

DATA FILES (92) use secondary storage as a location for inactive program data. These files may or may not be visible to the user.

RESOURCE FILES (101) store static read-only data. When the program needs a resource (such as a font, an error message, or a window description), it loads the resource from file into temporary memory; afterwards it releases this memory.

PACKAGES (108) store chunks of the program code. The programmer divides the code into packages, which are loaded and unloaded as required at runtime.

PAGING (119) arbitrarily breaks the program down into very fine units (pages) which are shuffled automatically between primary and secondary storage. Paging can handle code and data, support read-only information and information shared between different programs, and is transparent to most programmers and users.

All of these patterns in some sense trade facilities provided in the environment for work done by the programmer. The more complex the environment (compilation tools and runtime system), the less memory management work for the programmer; a complex runtime environment takes effort to develop, however, and has its own memory requirements at runtime. Figure 2.2 shows where each pattern fits in this scheme.

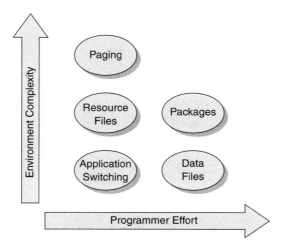

Figure 2.2 Implementation effort vs. environmental complexity

See also

READ-ONLY (65) pieces of program or data can be deleted from memory without having to be saved back to secondary storage.

You can use COMPRESSION (135) to reduce the amount of space taken on secondary storage.

Secondary Storage management is one of the primary functions of modern operating systems. More background information and detail on techniques for using Secondary Storage can be found in many operating systems textbooks (Tannenbaum 1992; Leffler et al. 1989; Goodheart and Cox 1994).

Application Switching

Also known as: Phases, Program Chaining, Command Scripts

How can you reduce the memory requirements of a system that provides many different functions?

- Systems are too big for all the code and data to fit into main memory.
- Users often need to do only one task at a time.
- A single task requires only its own code and data to execute; other code and data can live on secondary storage.
- It's easier to program only one set of related tasks — one application — at a time.

Some systems are big — too big for all of the executable code and data to fit into main memory at the same time.

For example, a Strap-It-On user may do word-processing, run a spreadsheet, read web pages, do accounts, manage a database, play a game, or use the 'StrapMan' remote control facilities to manage the daily strategy of a large telecommunications network. How can the programmers make all this functionality work in the 2 Mb of RAM they have available — particularly as each of the StrapMan's five different functions requires 1 Mb of code and 0.5 Mb of temporary RAM data?

Most systems need only a small subset of their functionality — enough to support one user task — at any given time. Much of the code and data in most systems is unused much of the time, but all the while it occupies valuable main memory space.

The more complex the system and the bigger the development team, the more difficult development becomes. Software developers have always preferred to split their systems architecture into separate components, and to reduce the interdependencies between these components. Components certainly make system development manageable, but they do not reduce main memory requirements.

Therefore: **Split your system into independent executables, and run only one at a time.**

Most operating systems support independent program components in the form of executable files on secondary storage. A running executable is called a process and its code and data occupy main memory. When a process terminates, all the main memory it uses is returned to the system.

Design the system so that behaviour the user will use together or in quick succession will be in the same executable. Provide facilities to start another executable when required, terminating the current one. The new process can reuse all the memory released by the terminated process.

In many operating systems this is the only approach supported; only one process may execute at a time. In MS-DOS the executable must provide functionality to terminate itself before another executable can run; in MacOS and PalmOs there is control functionality shared by all applications to support choosing another application and switching to it (Chappell 1994; Apple 1985; Palm 2000). In multi-tasking operating systems this pattern is still frequently used to reduce main memory requirements.

For example, no Strap-It-On user would want to do more than one of those tasks at any one time; it's just not physically possible given the small size of the screen. So each goes in a separate executable (word processor, spreadsheet, web browser, accounting, database, Doom), and the Strap-It-On provides a control dialog that allows the user to terminate the current application and start another. Each application saves its state on exit and restores it on restart, so that — apart from the speed of loading — the user has no way of telling that the application has terminated and restarted. The StrapMan application, however, wouldn't fit in RAM as a single executable. So the StrapMan's authors split it into six different executables (one for the main program and one for each function), and made the main one switch to each other executable as required.

Consequences

The *memory requirements* for each process are less than the *memory requirements* for the entire system. The operating system reclaims the memory when the process terminates, so this reduces *programmer effort* in managing memory and reduces the effects of 'memory leaks'.

Different executables may be in different implementation languages, and be interpreted or compiled as required. Some executables may also be existing 'legacy' applications, or utilities provided by the operating system. So APPLICATION SWITCHING may significantly reduce the *programmer effort* to produce the system, encouraging *reuse* and making *maintenance* easier. Script-based approaches can be very flexible, as scripts are typically very easy to modify. Also, applications tend to be geared to stopping and starting regularly, so errors that terminate applications may not be so problematic to the user, increasing the system's robustness.

In single-process environments, such as PalmOs, each process occupies the same memory space, so the amount of memory required is easy to *predict*, which improves *reliability*, makes *testing easier* and removes the effects of the *global* memory use on each *local* application. You only need to start the first process to get the system running, reducing *start-up times*. It's also easy to know what's happening in a single-process environment, simplifying *real-time* programming.

However: Dividing a large program into a good set of processes can be difficult, so a multi-process application can require significant *programmer effort* to design, and *local complexity* in the implementation.

If you have many executables, the cost of starting each and of transferring data can dominate the system's *runtime performance*; this is also a problem if the control flow between different processes is complex — if processes are started and terminated frequently.

In single-process environments the user can use only the functionality in the current executable, so switching tends to reduce the system's *usability*. If the user has to manage the processes explicitly, that also reduces *usability*.

This pattern does not support background activities, such as TCP/IP protocols, interfacing to a mobile phone, or background downloading of e-mail. Such activities must continue even when the user switches tasks. The code for background tasks must either be omitted (reducing *usability*), live in a separate process (increasing *programmer effort*), or be implemented using interrupt routing (requiring large amounts of specialized *programmer effort*).

❖   ❖   ❖

Implementation

To implement APPLICATION SWITCHING you have to divide up the system into separate components (see the SMALL ARCHITECTURE (25) pattern). Communication between running processes can be difficult, so in general the split must satisfy these rules:

- The control flow between processes is simple.
- There is little transient data passed between the processes.
- The division makes some kind of sense to the user.

Figure 2.3 shows the two main alternatives that you can use to implement application switching.

1. Program chaining

One process can pass control explicitly to the following process. This is called 'program chaining', after the CHAIN command in some versions of the BASIC programming language (Digital 1975; Steiner 1984). Program chaining requires each executable to know which executable to go to next. This can be programmed explicitly by each application, or as part of an application framework library. Given such an application framework, each executable can use the framework to determine which application to switch to next, and to switch to that application, without requiring much programmer effort. The MacOs (task switcher) and PalmOs application frameworks do this (Apple 1985; Palm 2000).

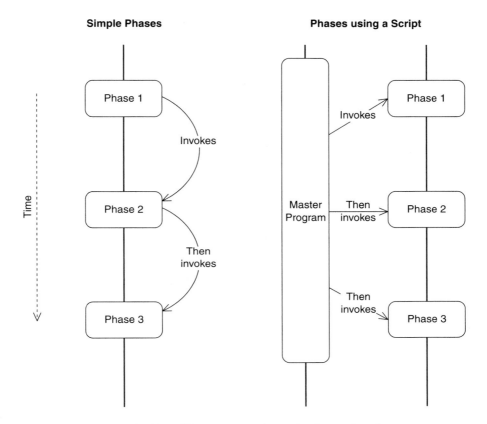

Figure 2.3   Two different approaches to implementing phases

2. Master program

Alternatively, a master script or top-level command program can invoke each application in turn. A master program encourages reuse because each executable doesn't need to know much about its context and can be used independently. The UNIX environment pioneered the idea of small interoperable tools designed to work together in this way (Kernighan and Pike 1984). Even with a master program, the terminating program can help determine which application to execute next by passing information back to the master program using exit codes, or by producing output or temporary files that are read by the master program.

3. Communicating between processes

How can separate components communicate when only one process is active at a time? You can't use main memory, because that is erased when each process terminates. Instead you need to use one or more of the following mechanisms:

- command line parameters and environment variables passed into the new process;
- secondary storage files, records or databases written by one process and read by another;
- environment-specific mechanisms. For example, many varieties of Basic complemented the CHAIN command with a COMMON keyword that specifies data preserved when a new process overwrites the current one (Steiner 1984).

4. Managing data

How do you make it seem to the user that an application never terminates, even when it is split up into separate processes? Many environments support only a small number of processes, maybe just one, but users don't want to have to re-create all their state each time they start up a new application. They want the illusion that the application is always running in the background.

The solution is for the application to save its state to **SECONDARY STORAGE** (79) on exit, and to restore this state when the application is restarted. Many OO libraries and environments support ways of 'streaming' all the important objects — data and state — as a single operation. The approach requires a binary 'file stream', which defines stream functions to read and write primitive types (e.g. int, char, float, string). Each class representing the application's state then defines its own streaming functions.

When you are streaming out an object-oriented application, you need to ensure that each object is streamed only once, no matter how many references there may be to it. A good way to deal with this is to have the 'file stream' maintain a table of object identifiers. Each time the stream receives a request to stream out an object it searches this table, and if it finds the object already there, it just saves a reference to the file location of the original instead of saving it again.

The Java libraries support persistence through the Serialization framework (Chan et al. 1998). Any persistent class implements the Serializable interface; it needs no other code — the runtime environment can serialize all its data members, following object references as required (and writing each object only once, as above). The classes ObjectOutputStream and ObjectInputStream provide methods to read and write a structure of objects: writeObject and readObject respectively. By convention the files created usually have the extension .ser; some applications ship initial .ser files with the Java code in the JAR archive.

Examples

Here's a very trivial example from an MS Windows 3.1 system. We cannot use the disk-checking program, scandisk, while MS Windows is running, so we run it first, then run Windows:

```
@REM AUTOEXEC.BAT Command file to start MS Windows 3.1 from DOS
@REM [Commands to set paths and load device drivers omitted]
```

```
C:\WINDOWS\COMMAND\scandisk /autofix /nosummary
win
```

The following Java routine chains to a different process, terminating the current process:

```
void ChainToCommand(String theCommand) throws IOException {
    Runtime.getRuntime().exec(theCommand);
    Runtime.getRuntime().exit( 0 );
}
```

Note that if this routine is used to execute another Java application, it will create a new Java virtual machine before terminating the current one, and the two VMs will coexist temporarily, requiring significant amounts of memory.

The UNIX exec family of functions is more suitable for single process chaining in low memory; each starts a new process in the space of the existing one (Kernighan and Pike 1984). The following C++ function uses Microsoft C++'s _execl variant (Microsoft 1997). It also uses the Windows environment variable 'COMSPEC' to locate a command interpreter, since only the command interpreter knows where to locate executables and how to parse the command line correctly.

```
void ChainToCommand( string command ) {
    const char *args[4];
    args[0] = getenv( "comspec" );
    args[1] = "/c";
    args[2] = command.c_str();
    args[3] = 0;
    _execv( args[0], args );
}
```

The function never returns. Note that although all the RAM memory is discarded, execl doesn't close file handles, which remain open in the chained process. See your C++ or library documentation for execl and the related functions.

The following is some EPOC C++ code implementing streaming for a simple class, to save data to files while the application is switched. The class, TSerialPortConfiguration, represents configuration settings for a printer port. Most of its data members are either C++ enums with a small range of values, or 1-byte integers (char in C++, TInt8 in EPOC C++); TOutputHandshake is a separate class:

```
class TSerialPortConfiguration {
    // Various function declarations omitted . . .
    TBps iDataRate;
    TDataBits iDataBits;
    TStopBits iStopBits;
    TParity iParity;
    TOutputHandshake iHandshake;
    };
```

The functions `InternalizeL` and `ExternalizeL` read and write the object from a stream. Although the values `iDataRate` are represented internally as 4-byte integers and enums, we know we'll not lose information by storing them as PACKED DATA, in a single byte. The class `TOutputHandshake` provides its own streaming functions, so we use them:

```
EXPORT_C void TSerialPortConfiguration::InternalizeL(
                RReadStream& aStream) {
    iDataRate = (TBps) aStream.ReadInt8L();
    iDataBits = (TDataBits) aStream.ReadInt8L();
    iStopBits = (TStopBits) aStream.ReadInt8L();
    iParity = (TParity) aStream.ReadInt8L();
    iHandshake.InternalizeL(aStream);
}

EXPORT_C void TSerialPortConfiguration::ExternalizeL(
            RWriteStream& aStream) const {
    aStream.WriteInt8L(iDataRate);
    aStream.WriteInt8L(iDataBits);
    aStream.WriteInt8L(iStopBits);
    aStream.WriteInt8L(iParity);
    iHandshake.ExternalizeL(aStream);
}
```

❖   ❖   ❖

Known uses

The PalmOs and early versions of the MacOS environments both support only a single user process at any one time; both provide framework functions to simulate multi-tasking for the user. MacOS uses persistence while PalmOs uses secondary storage 'memory records' to save application data (Apple 1985; Palm 2000).

The UNIX environment encourages programmers to use processes by supporting *scripts* and making them executable in the same way as binary executables, with any suitable scripting engine (Kernighan and Pike 1984). In MS Windows and the DOS environments the only fully supported script formats are the fairly simple BAT and CMD formats, although it's trivial to create a simple Windows BAT file to invoke more powerful scripting languages such as Tcl (Ousterhout 1994) and Perl (Wall et al. 1996).

The UNIX Make utility manages APPLICATION SWITCHING (and the DATA FILES (92) required) to compile a program, generally running any pre-processors and the appropriate compiler process for each input file in turn, then running one or more linker processes to produce a complete executable (Kernighan and Pike 1984).

See also

PACKAGES (108) provide similar functionality within a single process — by delaying code loading until it's required. However, whereas in APPLICATION SWITCHING the operating system will discard the memory, code and other resources owned by a task when the task completes, a PACKAGE must explicitly release these resources.

PAGING (119) provides much more flexible handling of both code and data.

The executables can be stored on SECONDARY STORAGE (79), using COMPRESSION (135).

The MEMORY DISCARD (244) pattern has a similar dynamic to this pattern but on a much smaller scale. Where APPLICATION SWITCHING recovers all the memory occupied by a process only when it terminates, MEMORY DISCARD allows an application to recover the memory occupied by a group of objects in the middle of its execution.

Data Files

Also known as: Batch Processing, Filter, Temporary File

What can you do when your data doesn't fit into main memory?

- Systems are too big for all the code and data to fit into RAM together.

- The code by itself fits into RAM (or can be fitted using other patterns).

- The data doesn't fit into RAM.

- Data is generally written sequentially.

Sometimes programs themselves are quite small, but need to process a large amount of data — the *memory requirements* mean that a program will fit into main memory, but the data requires too much memory.

For example, the input and output data for the Word-O-Matic Text Formatter can exceed the capacity of the Strap-It-On's main memory when formatting a large book. How should the Word-O-Matic designers implement the program to produce the output PostScript data, let alone to produce all the index files and update all the cross-references, when it's physically impossible to get them all into RAM memory?

Dividing the program up into smaller phases (as in APPLICATION SWITCHING (84)) can reduce the memory required by the program itself, but this doesn't help reduce the memory requirements for the input and output. Similarly, COMPRESSION (135) techniques may reduce the amount of secondary storage required to hold the data, but don't reduce the amount of main memory needed to process it.

Yet most systems don't need you to keep all data in RAM. Modern operating systems make it simple to read and write from files on secondary storage. And the majority of processing tasks do not require simultaneous access to all the data.

Therefore: **Process the data a little at a time and keep the rest on secondary storage.**

Use sequential or random file access to read each item to process; write the processed data sequentially back to one or more files. You can also write temporary items to secondary storage until you're ready to use them. If you are careful, the amount of main memory needed for processing each portion will be much less than the total memory that would be required to process all the data in main memory. You need to be able to store both input and output as files in SECONDARY STORAGE, so the input and output data must be partitioned cleanly.

For example, Word-O-Matic stores its chapters as separate text files. The Word-O-Matic Text Formatter (nicknamed the 'Wombat') makes several passes over these files; see Figure 2.4. The first pass scans all the chapter files in turn, locating the positions and targets of cross-references and index entries in the file data, and writes all the information it needs to create each cross-reference to a temporary 'cross-reference' file. Wombat's second pass then scans the cross-reference file to create an in-memory index to this file, then reads each chapter file, creating a transient version with the cross-references and indexes included. It reads the cross-reference data by random access to the index file using the in-memory index. Since the page numbering changes as a result of the updates, Wombat also keeps an in-memory table showing how each reference destination has moved during this update. Finally, Wombat's third pass reads each transient chapter file a bit at a time, and writes out the PostScript printout sequentially, making the corrections to the page numbers in the index and references using its in-memory table as it does so. Using these techniques Wombat can format an entire book using as little as 50 Kb of RAM memory.

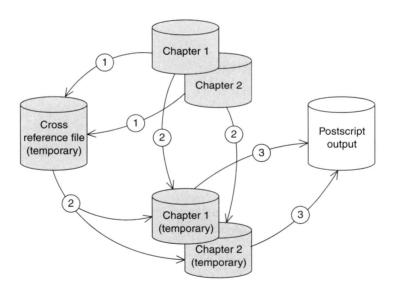

Figure 2.4   Wombat's data files and phases

Consequences

The *memory requirements* for processing data piecemeal are reduced, since most of the data lives on secondary storage. The system's main memory requirements are also much more *predictable*, because you can allocate a fixed amount of memory to support the processing, rather than a variable amount of memory to store a variable amount of data.

You can examine the input and output of functions in an application using utilities to look at the secondary storage files, which makes *testing* easier. DATA FILES also make it easy to split an application into different independent components linked only by their data files, reducing the *global* impact of *local* changes, and making *maintenance* easier. Indeed DATA FILES also make it much easier to implement phases, allowing APPLICATION SWITCHING (84); for example Wombat's phase 1 is in a different executable from phases 2 and 3.

However: *Programmer effort* is required to design the program so that the data can be processed independently. Processing data incrementally adds *local complexity* to the implementation, which you could have avoided by processing the data *globally* in one piece. If you need to keep extra context information to process the data, then managing this information can add *global complexity* to the program.

DATA FILES can provide slower *runtime performance* than processing all the input in one piece, since reading and writing many small data items is typically less efficient than reading or writing one large item. Repeated access to secondary storage devices can increase the system's *power consumption*, and can even reduce the lifetime of some secondary storage media, such as flash RAM and floppy disks. The limitations of data files — such as imposing ordering rules on the input, or needing the user or client software to manage files — can reduce the system's *usability*.

❖   ❖   ❖

Implementation

The Wombat example above illustrated the four main kinds of operation on data files:

1. simple sequential input (reading each chapter in turn);
2. simple sequential output (writing the final output file);
3. random access (reading the cross-reference file);
4. sequential output to several files (writing the temporary chapter files).

Here are some issues to consider when using data files.

1. Incremental processing

One simple and common way to manipulate data files is to read an entire file sequentially from input, and/or to write a second file sequentially to the output (see Figure 2.5). Incremental processing requires extra programmer effort to implement, because the program must be tailored specially to process its input file incrementally. Because the program processes one large file in small increments, the programmer is typically responsible for selecting the increments to process (although this can be left to the user by requiring him or her to indicate increment boundaries in the data file, or provide a collection of smaller data files).

Figure 2.5   Incremental processing

Because the whole input file is processed in a single operating system process, incremental processing makes it easier to maintain global contextual information between each processing stage, and easier to produce the final output — the final output is just written incrementally from the program. Unfortunately, precisely because it works in one single long-running process, it can be more difficult to keep the memory requirements down to a minimum.

2. Subfile processing

Rather than processing a single file sequentially, you can divide data up into a number of smaller subfiles. Write a program which processes one subfile, producing a separate output file. Run this program multiple times (typically sequentially) to process each subfile, and then combine the subfiles to produce the required output (see Figure 2.6).

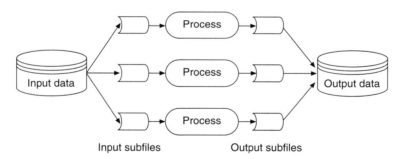

Figure 2.6   Subfile processing

Subfile processing has several advantages, provided it's easy to divide up the data. Subfile processing tends to require less memory, since only a subset of the data is processed at a time; and it is more robust to corruption and errors in the data files, since each such problem affects only one file. Unfortunately, splitting the files requires effort either on the part of the programmer or on the part of the user: co-ordinating the processing and combining the subfiles requires programmer effort. See APPLICATION SWITCHING (84) for a discussion of techniques for communication between such processes.

Many compilers use subfile processing: they compile each code file separately, and only combine the resulting temporary object files in a separate link phase. Because of its enormous potential for reducing memory use, subfile processing was ubiquitous in old-time batch tape processing (Knuth 1998).

3. Random access

Rather than reading and writing files sequentially (whether incrementally or using subfiles) you can access a single file randomly, selecting information and reading and writing it in any order (Figure 2.7). Random access generally requires more *programmer effort* than incremental or subfile processing, but is much more flexible: you don't have to determine the order in which items can be processed (and possibly divide them into subfiles) in advance.

To use random access, each process needs to be able to locate individual data items within the files on secondary storage. Generally, you will need an index, a list of offsets from the start of the file to each item of data required. Because the index will be used for most accesses to the file, it needs to be stored in main memory, or be easily accessible from main memory. Effective indexing of files is a major science in its own right, but for simple applications there are two straightforward options:

- The file may contain its own index, perhaps at the start of the file, which is read into RAM by the process. **RESOURCE FILES** (101) often use this approach.

- The application may scan the file on start-up, creating its own index. The Wombat text processor did this with its cross-reference file.

More complicated systems may use indexes in different files from the data, or even have indexes to the index files themselves. File processing is covered in texts such as Folk et al. (1988), Date (1999) and Elmasri and Navathe (2000).

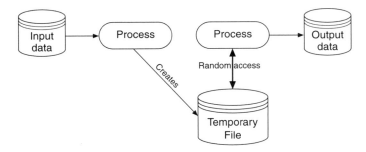

Figure 2.7 Random access

Examples

1. Simple subfile processing

File compilation provides a typical example of subfile processing. The user splits each large program into a number of files, and the compiler processes each file individually. Then the linker ld combines the various .o output files into an executable program, testprog.

```
cc main.c
cc datalib.c
cc transput.c
ld —o testprog main.o datalib.o transput.o
```

2. Incremental processing

The following Java code reverses the characters in each line in a file. It reads each line into a buffer, reverses the characters in the buffer, and then writes the buffer out into a second file. We call the reverse method with a BufferedReader and BufferedWriter to provide more efficient access to the standard input and output than direct access to the disk read and write functions, at a cost of some memory:

```
reverse(new BufferedReader(new InputStreamReader(System.in)),
        new BufferedWriter(new OutputStreamWriter(System.out)));
```

The reverse method does the work, using two buffers, a String and a StringBuffer, because Strings in Java cannot be modified.

```
public void reverse(BufferedReader reader, BufferedWriter writer)
    throws IOException {
    String line;
    StringBuffer lineBuffer;

    while ((line = reader.readLine()) != null) {
        lineBuffer = new StringBuffer(line);
        lineBuffer.reverse();
        writer.write(lineBuffer.toString());
        writer.newLine();
    }
    writer.close();
}
```

The important point about this example is that it requires only enough memory to hold the input and output buffers, and a single line of text to reverse, rather than the entire file, and so can handle files of any length without running out of memory.

3. Processing with multiple subfiles

Consider reversing all the bytes in a file rather than just the bytes in each line. The simple incremental technique above won't work, because it relies on the fact that processing one line does not affect any other lines. Reversing all the characters in a file involves the whole file, not just each individual line.

We can reverse a file without needing to store it all in memory by using subfiles on secondary storage. We first divide (scatter) the large file into a number of smaller subfiles, where each subfile is small enough to fit into memory, and then we can reverse each subfile separately. Finally, we can read (gather) each subfile in reverse order, and assemble a new completely reversed file.

```
public void run() throws IOException {
    scatter(new BufferedReader(new InputStreamReader(System.in)));
    gather(new BufferedWriter(new OutputStreamWriter(System.out)));
}
```

To scatter the file into subfiles, we read `SubfileSize` bytes from the input reader into a buffer, reverse the buffer, and then write it out into a new subfile.

```
protected void scatter(BufferedReader reader) throws IOException {
    int bytesRead;

    while ((bytesRead = reader.read(buffer, 0, SubfileSize)) > 0) {
        StringBuffer stringBuffer = new StringBuffer(bytesRead);
          stringBuffer.append(buffer, 0, bytesRead);
        stringBuffer.reverse();
        BufferedWriter writer =
          new BufferedWriter(new FileWriter(subfileName(nSubfiles)));
        writer.write(stringBuffer.toString());
        writer.close();
        nSubfiles++;
    }
}
```

We can reuse the buffer each time we reverse a file (an example of FIXED ALLOCATION (226)), but we have to generate a new name for each subfile. We also need to count the number of subfiles we have written, so that we can gather them all together again.

```
protected char buffer[] = new char[SubfileSize];

protected String subfileName(int n) {
    return "subxx" + n;
}

protected int nSubfiles = 0;
```

Finally, we need to gather all the subfiles together. Since the subfiles are already reversed, we just need to open each one starting with the last, read its contents, and write them to an output file.

```
protected void gather(BufferedWriter writer) throws IOException {
    for (nSubfiles -- ; nSubfiles >= 0; nSubfiles -- ) {
        File subFile = new File(subfileName(nSubfiles));
        BufferedReader reader =
            new BufferedReader(new FileReader(subFile));
        int bytesRead = reader.read(buffer, 0, SubfileSize);
        writer.write(buffer, 0, bytesRead);
        reader.close();
        subFile.delete();
    }
    writer.close();
}
```

❖   ❖   ❖

Known uses

Most programming languages compile using subfile processing. C, C++, FORTRAN and COBOL programs are all typically compiled one file at a time, and the output object files are then combined with a single link phase after all the compilation phases. C and C++ also force the programmer to manage the 'shared data' for the compilation process in the form of header files (Kernighan and Ritchie 1988). Java takes the same approach for compiling each separate class file; instead of a link phase Java class files are typically combined into a 'JAR' archive file using COMPRESSION (Chan et al. 1998).

The UNIX environment encourages programmers to use data files by providing many simple 'filter' executables: wc, tee, grep, sed, awk, troff, for example (Kernighan and Pike 1984). Programmers can combine these using 'pipes'; the operating system arranges that each filter need only handle a small amount of data at a time.

Most popular applications use data files, and make the names of the current files explicit to the user. Microsoft's MFC framework enshrines this application design in its Document-View architecture (Prosise 1999), supporting multiple documents, where each document normally corresponds to a single data file. EPOC's AppArc architecture (Symbian 1999) supports only one document at a time; depending on the look and feel of the particular environment this file's name may not be visible to the user.

Some word processors and formatters support subfiles — for example Microsoft Word, TeX, and FrameMaker (Microsoft Word 1997; Lamport 1986, Adobe 1997). The user can create a *master document* that refers to a series of subdocuments. These subdocuments are edited individually, but when the document is printed each subdocument is loaded into memory and printed in turn. The application need keep only a small amount of global state in memory across subdocuments.

EPOC supports a kind of subfile within each file, called a stream; each stream is identified using an integer ID and accessed using a simple persistence mechanism.

This makes it easy to create many output streams and to access each one separately, and many EPOC applications use this feature. Components that use persistence on large objects generally save each one in a separate stream; then they can defer loading each object in until it's actually required — the template class TSwizzle provides a **MULTIPLE REPRESENTATION** (209) to make this invisible to client code (Symbian 1999a). EPOC's relational database creates a new stream for every 12 or so database rows, and for every binary object stored. This makes it easy for the DBMS server to change entries in a database — by writing a new stream to replace an existing one and updating the database's internal index to all the streams (Thoelke 1999).

Printer drivers (especially those embedded in bitmap-based printers) often use 'banding', where the driver renders and prints only a part of the page at a time. Banding reduces the size of the output bitmap it must store, but also reduces the printing speed as each page must be rendered several times, once for each band.

See also

RESOURCE FILES (101) is an alternative for read-only data. PAGING (119) is much simpler for the programmer, though much more complex to implement. DATA FILES make it easier to implement APPLICATION SWITCHING (84). Each subfile can be stored on SECONDARY STORAGE, using COMPRESSION. (135)

You can use either FIXED ALLOCATION (226) and MEMORY DISCARD (244) or both to process each item read from a DATA FILE.

PIPES AND FILTERS (Shaw and Garlan 1996) describes a software architecture style based around filters.

Rather than a simple DATA FILE, you may need a full-scale database (Connolly and Begg 1999; Date 1999; Elmasri and Navathe 2000). Wolfgang Keller and Jens Coldewey (1998) provide a set of patterns to store objects from OO programs into relational databases.

Resource Files

How can you manage lots of configuration data?

- Much program data is *read-only* configuration information and is not modified by the program.

- The configuration data typically changes more frequently than program code.

- Data can be referenced from different phases of the program.

- You only need a few data items at any time.

- File systems support *random access*, which makes it easy to load a portion of a file individually.

Sometimes a program's *memory requirements* include space for a lot of read-only static data; typically the program uses only a small amount of this at any one time. For example Word-O-Matic needs static data such as window layouts, icon designs, font metrics, and spelling dictionaries. Much of this information may be requested at any arbitrary time within the program, but when requested it is typically needed for only a short time. If the information is stored in main memory — if, for example, you hard-coded it into your program — it will increase the program's overall *memory requirements*.

Furthermore, you may need to change the configuration information separately from the program itself. What may seem to be different variants of the program (for different languages, or with different user interface themes) may use the same code but require different configuration data. Within a given configuration, specific data items may be required at any time — window formats or fonts for example — so you cannot use APPLICATION SWITCHING (84) techniques to bring this data in. In general, however, much of the data will not be used at any given time.

Therefore: **Keep configuration data on secondary storage, and load and discard each item as necessary.**

Operating systems offer a simple way to store read-only static data: in a file on secondary storage. File systems provide random access, so it's easy to read just a single portion of a file, ignoring the remainder. You can load a portion of file into tempo-rary memory, use it for a while, then discard it; you can always retrieve it again if you need it. In fact, with only a little additional complexity, you can make a file into a read-only database, containing data items each associated with a unique identifier.

So rather than hard-code each item of data specifically in the program code, you can give each item a unique identifier. When the program requires the data, it invokes a special routine passing the identifier; this routine loads the data from a 'resource file' and returns it to the program. The program discards the loaded data item when it's no longer required. Typical resources are:

- strings
- screen layouts
- fonts
- bitmaps, icons, and cursors.

For example, all of Word-O-Matic's window layouts, icon designs and text strings are stored in resource files. When they are required, Word-O-Matic retrieves the data from the resource file, and stores it in a temporary memory buffer. The memory can be reused when the data is no longer required.

Consequences

The read-only static data doesn't clutter primary storage, reducing the program's *memory requirements*. Multiple programs can share the same resource file, reducing the *programmer effort* involved. Some operating systems share the loaded resources between multiple instances of the same program or library, further decreasing *memory requirements*. This also makes it easy to change the data without changing the program (e.g. to support multiple language strings), increasing the program's *design quality*.

However: This approach requires *programmer discipline* to place resources into the resource files, and to load and release the resources correctly. Loading and unloading resource files reduces the program's *time performance* somewhat. In particular, it can impact its *start-up time*. Resource files also need *programmer effort* to implement, because you need some mechanism to unload (and reload) the resources. It's best if the *operating system* environment provides this support.

❖   ❖   ❖

Implementation

Since resource files are accessed randomly, applications need an index to locate data items (see DATA FILES (92)). Most implementations of resource files hold this index in the resource file itself, typically at the start of the file. However, this means that the resource file cannot simply be human-readable text, but must be *compiled.* Resource compilers also typically convert the resource data into binary formats that can easily be managed by application code, reducing the memory occupied and improving application performance.

In practice you usually need a logical separation between different resources in a system: the resources for one component are distinct from those for another, and the responsibility of separate teams. Thus most resource file frameworks support more than one resource file at a time.

Here are some things to consider when implementing resource files.

1. Making it easy for the programmer

The task of loading and interpreting a resource is not a trivial one, so most systems provide library functions. You need basic functions to load and release the raw resources; typically you can also use more sophisticated functions:

- to manage the loading and release of resources, from multiple files;
- to build graphical dialogs and constructs from the information;
- to transfer bitmap and drawing resources (fonts, icons, cursors, drawing primitives) directly from the file to the screen without exposing their structure to the program;
- to insert parameters into the resource strings.

It's not enough just to be able to load and unload resources into systems at runtime; you also have to create the resources in the first place. Programming environments also provide facilities to help you produce resources:

- a resource compiler — which creates a resource file database from a text file representation;
- dialog editors. These allow programmers to 'screen paint' screens and dialogs with user controls; programmers can then create resource-file descriptions from the results. An example is Microsoft Developer Studio (see Figure 2.8), but there are many others.

2. Working with resource files to save memory

Some resource file systems support COMPRESSION (135). This has a small time overhead for each resource loaded, but reduces the file system space taken by the files. ADAPTIVE COMPRESSION (160) algorithms are inappropriate for compressing whole files, though, as it must be possible to decode any data item independently of the rest of the file. You can compress individual resources if they are large enough, such as images or sound files.

It's worthwhile to take some effort to understand how resource loading works on your specific system as this can often help save memory. For example, MS Windows supports two kinds of resource: PRELOAD and LOADONCALL. Preloaded resources are

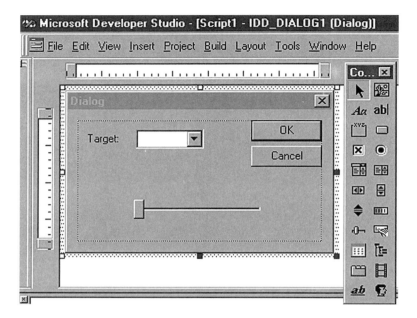

Figure 2.8 A dialog editor

loaded when the program is first executed; a LOADONCALL resource loads only when the user code requests the specific resource. Clearly, to save memory, you should prefer LOADONCALL. Similarly, Windows 3.1 doesn't load strings individually, but only in blocks of 16 strings with consecutive ID numbers. So you can minimize memory use by arranging strings in blocks, such that the strings in a single block are all used together. By way of contrast, the Windows LoadIcon function doesn't itself access the resource file; that happens later when a screen driver needs the icon — so calling LoadIcon doesn't in itself use much memory. Petzold (1998) discusses the memory use of Windows resource files in more detail.

3. Font files

You often want to treat font resources very differently from other kinds of resources. For a start, all applications will share the same set of fonts, and font descriptions tend to be much larger than other resources. A sophisticated font handling system will load only portions of each file as required by specific applications: perhaps only the implementation for a specific font size, or only the characters required by the application for a specific string. The last approach is particularly appropriate for fonts for the Unicode characters, which may contain many thousands of images (Pike and Thompson 1993).

4. Implementing a resource file system

Sometimes you need to implement your own resource file system. Here are some issues to consider.

4.1 Selecting variants. How will the system select which version of the resource files is loaded? There are various options. Some systems include only one resource file with each release. Others (e.g. most MS Windows applications) support variants for languages, but install only one; changing language means overwriting the files. Still other systems select the appropriate variant on program initialization; EPOC, for example, chooses the variant by file extension (if the current language is number 01, application Word loads resource file WORD.R01). Other systems may even permit the system to change its language 'on the fly', although this is bound to require complex interactions between applications.

4.2 Inserting parameters into strings. The most frequent use of resources is in strings. Now, displayed strings often contain variable parameters: "You have CC things to do, NN", where the number NN and the name CC vary according to the program needs. How do you insert these parameters?

A common way is to use C's printf format: "You have %d things to do, %s". This works reasonably, but has two significant limitations. First, the normal implementation of printf and its variants are liable to crash the program if the parameters required by the resource strings are not those passed to the strings. So a corrupt or carelessly constructed resource file can cause unexpected program defects. Second, the printf format isn't particularly flexible at supporting different language constructions — a German, for example, might want the two parameters in the other order: "%s: you have %d things to do".

A more flexible alternative is to use numbered strings in the resource strings: "You have %1 things to do, %2". The program code has responsibility to convert all parameters to strings (which is simple, and can be done in a locale-sensitive way), and a standard function inserts the strings into the resource string. It is a trivial task to implement this function to provide default behaviour or an error message if the number of strings passed doesn't match the resource string.

Examples

Here's an example of an MS Windows resource file for an about box:

```
// About Box Dialog
//

IDD_ABOUTBOX DIALOG DISCARDABLE 34, 22, 217, 55
STYLE DS_MODALFRAME | WS_POPUP | WS_CAPTION | WS_SYSMENU
CAPTION "About DEMOAPP"
FONT 8, "MS Sans Serif"
BEGIN
```

```
ICON                    2,IDC_STATIC,11,17,18,20
LTEXT                   "Demonstration Application by Charles Weir",
                        IDC_STATIC,40,10,79,8
LTEXT                   "Copyright \251 1999",IDC_STATIC,40,25,119,8
DEFPUSHBUTTON           "OK",IDOK,176,6,32,14,WS_GROUP
END
```

The C++ code to use this using the Microsoft Foundation Classes is remarkably trivial:

```
///////////////////////////////////////////////////////////////////////////
// CAboutDlg dialog

CAboutDlg::CAboutDlg(CWnd* pParent /*=NULL*/)
    : CDialog(CAboutDlg::IDD, pParent) {
//{{AFX_DATA_INIT(CAboutDlg)
        // NOTE: the ClassWizard will add member initialization here
//}}AFX_DATA_INIT
}
```

Note the explicit syntax of the comment, {{AFX_DATA_INIT(CAboutDlg); this allows other Microsoft tools and 'wizards' to identify the location; the Wizard can determine any variable fields in the dialog box, and insert code to initialize them and to retrieve their values after the dialog has completed. In this case there are no such variables, so no code is present.

❖   ❖   ❖

Known uses

Virtually all Apple Macintosh and MS Windows GUI programs use resource files to store GUI resources, especially fonts (Apple 1985; Petzold 1998). EPOC stores all language-dependent information (including compressed help texts) in resource files, and allows the system to select the appropriate language at runtime. EPOC's Unicode font handling minimizes the memory use of the font handler with a FIXED ALLOCATION (226) (Edwards 1997) buffer to store a cached set of character images. EPOC16 uses COMPRESSION to reduce the size of its resource files.

Many computer games use RESOURCE FILES — from hand-helds with extra static ROM, and early microcomputers backed with cassette tapes and floppies, to state-of-the-art game consoles based on CD-ROMs. The pattern allows them to provide many more screens, levels, or maps than could possibly fit into main memory. Each level is stored as a separate resource in secondary storage, and then loaded when the user reaches that level. Since the user only plays on one level at any time, memory requirements are reduced to the storage required for just one level. This works well for arcade-style games where users play one level, then proceed to the next (if they win) or die (if they lose), because the sequence of levels is always predictable. Similarly, many of the variations of multi-user adventure games keep the details of specific games: as resource files locations, local rules, monsters, weapons; as they tend to be large, they are often stored COMPRESSED (135).

See also

DATA FILES (92) provide writable data storage; APPLICATION SWITCHING (84) and PACKAGES (108) do for code what RESOURCE FILES does for unmodifiable data.

Each resource file can be stored in SECONDARY STORAGE (79) or READ-ONLY MEMORY (65), and may use COMPRESSION.

Petzold (1998) and Microsoft (1997) describe Microsoft Windows resource files. Tasker et al. (2000) describe using EPOC resource files.

Packages

Also known as: Components, Lazy Loading, Dynamic Loading, Code Segmentation

How can you manage a large program with lots of optional pieces?

- You don't have space in memory for all the code and its static data.

- The system has lots of functionality, but not all will be used simultaneously.

- You may require any arbitrary combination of different bits of functionality.

- Development works best when there's a clear separation between developed components.

Some big programs are really small programs much of the time — the *memory requirements* of all the code are much greater than the requirements for code actually used in any given run of the program. For example, Strap-It-On's Spin-the-Web web browser can view files of many different kinds at once, but it typically reads only the StrapTML local pages used by its help system. Yet the need to support other file types increases the program's code memory requirements even when they are not needed.

In these kinds of programs, there is no way of predicting in advance which features you'll need, nor of ordering them so that only one is in use at a time. So the APPLICATION SWITCHING (84) pattern cannot help, but you still want the benefits of that pattern — that the memory requirements of the system are reduced by not loading all of the program into main memory at the same time.

Therefore: Split the program into packages, and load each package only when it's needed.

Any runtime environment that stores code in disk files must have a mechanism to activate executables loaded from disk. With a relatively small amount of effort, you can extend this mechanism to load additional executable code into a running program. This will only be useful, though, if most program runs do not need to load most of this additional code.

You need to divide the program into a *main program* and a collection of independently loaded *packages*. The main program is loaded and starts running. When it needs to use a facility in a package, a code routine somewhere will load the appropriate package, and call the package directly.

For example, the core of Spin-the-Web is a main program that analyses each web page, and loads the appropriate viewer as a package.

Consequences

The program will *require less memory* because some of its code is stored on Sec-ondary Storage (79) until needed.

The program will *start up quicker*, as only the small main program needs to be loaded initially, and can begin running with *less memory* than would otherwise be required. Because each package is fairly small, subsequent packages can be loaded in quickly without pauses for changing phases (as would be caused by the Applica-tion Switching (84) pattern).

Because packages aren't statically linked into the application code, dynamic load-ing mechanisms allow third parties or later developers to add functionality without changing or even stopping the main program. This significantly increases the system's *usability* and *maintainability*.

However: *Programmer effort* is needed to divide up the program into packages.

Many environments never unload packages, so the program's *memory require-ments* can steadily increase, and the program can still run out of memory unless any given run uses only a small part of its total functionality. It takes *programmer effort* to implement the dynamic loading mechanism and to make the packages conform to it, and to define the strategy of when to load and unload the packages; or to optimize the package division and minimize the loading overhead. This mechanism can often be reused across programs, or it may be provided by the *oper-ating system;* on the other hand, many environments provide no support for dynamic loading.

Because a package isn't loaded until it's required, dynamic loading means that the system may not detect a missing package until well after the program has loaded; this slightly reduces the program's *usability*. Also, if access to the package is slow (for example, over the web), the time taken to load a package can reduce the program's responsiveness, which also reduces the program's *usability*. This arbitrary delay also makes Packages unsuitable for *real-time* operations.

Packages can be located remotely and changed independently from the main pro-gram. This produces *security* implications — a hostile agent may introduce viruses or security loopholes into the system by changing a package.

❖   ❖   ❖

Implementation

To support packages, you need three things:

1. a system that loads code into RAM to execute it;

2. a partition of the software into packages such that normally only a subset of the packages needs be active;

3. support for dynamically loadable packages — usually position independent or relocatable object code.

Here are some issues to consider when using or implementing packages as part of your system.

1. Processes as packages

Perhaps the simplest form of a package is just a separate process. With careful programming, two processes that run simultaneously can appear to users as a single process, although there can be a significant cost in performance and program complexity to achieve this. Implementing each package in a separate process has several key advantages:

- The package and main program will execute in separate address spaces, so a fatal error in the package will not necessarily terminate the main program.

- The memory allocated to the package can be discarded easily, simply by terminating the process when the package is no longer needed.

- In some cases, the desired package may already exist as an application in its own right. For example, we may want packages to do word-processing, drawing, or spreadsheet managing. Such applications exist already, and are implemented as separate processes.

There are two common approaches to using processes as packages:

1. The client can execute the process in the same way that, say, the operating system shell might do. It runs the process until it is complete, perhaps reading its standard output (see DATA FILES (92)).

2. The client can use operating system Inter-Process Communication (IPC) mechanisms to communicate with the process.

This second approach is taken by some forms of the Microsoft ActiveX ('COM') frameworks, by IBM's System Object Model (SOM) and by frameworks based on CORBA (Box 1998; Szyperski 1999; Henning and Vinoski 1999; Egremont 1998). Each uses some form of PROXY (Gamma et al. 1995; Buschmann et al. 1996) to give the client access to objects in the package object. See the *Essential Distributed Objects Survival Guide* (Orfali et al. 1996) for a discussion and comparison of these environments.

2. Using dynamically linked libraries as C++ packages

You can also consider using shared, or dynamically linked, libraries (DLLs) as packages. Normally an executable loads all its DLLs during initialization, so DLLs do not behave as packages by default. Most environments, however, provide additional mechanisms to load and unload DLLs 'on the fly'.

Some frameworks use delayed loading of DLLs: you can implement Microsoft COM objects, for example, as DLLs that load automatically when each object is first accessed. Although COM's design uses C++ virtual function tables, many other languages have provided bindings to access COM objects (Box 1998).

Other environments simply provide mechanisms to load the DLL file into RAM, and to invoke a function within the DLL. How can you use this to implement PACKAGES?

Typically you can identify their externally callable, *exported*, functions in DLLs either by function name or by function ordinal (the first exported function is ordinal 0, the second, 1, etc.). With either approach it would be quite a task to provide stubs for all the client functions and patch each to the correct location in the DLL.

Instead you can use object-orientation's dynamic binding to provide a simpler solution. This requires just a single call to one DLL entry point (typically at index 0 or 1). This function returns a pointer to a single instance of a class that supports an interface known to the client. From then on, the client may call methods on that instance; the language support for dynamic binding ensures that the correct code executes. Typically this class is an ABSTRACT FACTORY or provides FACTORY METHODS (Gamma et al. 1995). Figure 2.9 shows such a library and the classes it supports.

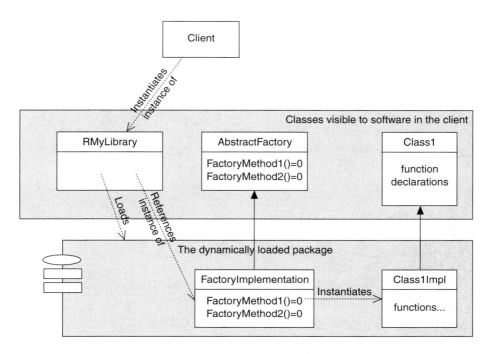

Figure 2.9 Dynamically loaded package with abstract factory

3. Implementing packages using code segmentation

Many processor architectures and operating systems provide *code segmentation*. This supports packages at the machine code or object code level. A segmented architecture considers a program and the data that it accesses to be made up of some number of independent segments, rather than one monolithic memory space (Tannenbaum 1992).

Typically each segment has its own memory protection attributes — a data segment may be readable and writable by a single process, where a code segment from a shared library could be readable by every process in the system. As with packages, individual segments can be swapped to and from secondary storage by the operating system, either automatically or under programmer control. Linkers for segmented systems produce programs divided up into segments, again either automatically or following directives in the code.

Many older CPUs supported segmentation explicitly, with several *segment registers* to speed up access to segments, and to ensure that the code and data in segments could be accessed irrespective of the segment's physical memory. Often processor restrictions limited the maximum size of each segment (64K in the 8086 architecture). More modern processor architectures tend to combine PACKAGES with PAGING (119).

4. Loading packages

If you're not using code segmentation or Java packages, you'll have to write some code somewhere in each application to load the packages. There are two standard approaches to where you put this code.

4.1. Manual loading.   The client loads the package explicitly. This is best when:

1. the client must identify which it requires of several packages with the same interface (e.g. loading a printer driver), or
2. the library provides relatively simple functionality, and it's clear when it needs to be unloaded.

4.2. Autoloading.   The client calls any function supported by the library. This function is actually a stub provided by the client; when called it loads the library and invokes the appropriate entry point. This is better when:

1. you want a simple interface for the client, or
2. there are many packages with complicated interdependencies, so there's no easy algorithm to decide when to load a package.

Both approaches are common. For example, Microsoft's COM framework and most EPOC applications do explicit loading; the Emacs text editor does autoloading (Box 1998; Tasker et al. 2000; Stallman 1984).

5. Unloading packages

You'll save most memory if there's a mechanism to unload packages that are no longer required. To do this you also need a way to detect when there is no longer a need for the loaded code. In OO-environments this is easy to decide: the loaded code is no longer needed when there are no instances of objects supported by the package. So you can use REFERENCE COUNTING (268) or GARBAGE COLLECTION (278) to decide when to unload the code.

Loading a package takes time, so some implementations choose to delay unloading packages even when clients notify them that they may do so. Ideally they must unload these cached packages when system memory becomes short — the CAPTAIN OATES (57) pattern.

6. Version control and binary compatibility

You need to make sure that each package loaded works correctly with the component that loaded it — even if the two pieces of code were developed and released at different times. This requirement is often called 'binary compatibility', and is distinct from 'source code compatibility'. The requirements of 'binary compatibility' depend both on the language and on the compilation system used, but typically include:

• New versions of the clients expect the same externally visible entry points, parameters and return values; new services provide them.

• New clients don't add extra parameter values; new services don't add extra returned values. This is related to the rules for subtyping — see Meyer (1997).

• New services support the same externally visible state as before.

• New services don't add new exceptions or error conditions unless existing clients have a way to handle them.

The problem of version control can become a major headache in development projects, when teams are developing several packages in parallel. Java, for example, provides no built-in mechanism to ensure that two packages are binary compatible; incompatible versions typically don't fail to load, but instead produce subtle program defects. To solve this problem, some environments provide version control in the libraries. Solaris, for example, supports major and minor version numbers for its DLLs. Minor version changes retain binary compatibility; major ones do not.

Drossopoulou et al. (1998) discuss the rules for Java in more detail. Symbian Knowledgebase (2000) discusses rules for C++ binary compatibility.

7. Optimizing packages

If you are using PACKAGES, you'll have only a fraction of the total code and data in memory at any given time — the *working set*. What techniques can you use to keep this working set to a minimum? You need to ensure that code that is used together is stored in the same package. Unfortunately, although organizing compiled code according to classes and modules is a good start, it doesn't provide an optimum solution. For example, each of the many visual objects in the Strap-it-On's Mind-Mapping application has functionality to create itself from vague text descriptions, to render animated pictures on the screen, to interact in weird and stimulating ways, to save itself to store and to restore itself again. Yet a typical operation on a mind-map will use only one of these types of functionality — but in every class (see Figure 2.10).

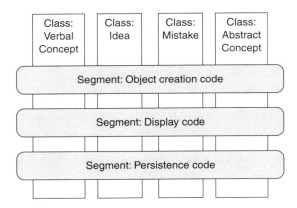

Figure 2.10 Example — class divisions don't give appropriate segments

You could reorganize the code so that the compilation units correspond to your desired segments — but the results would be difficult for programmers to manage and maintain. Using the terminology of Soni et al. (1995), the problem is that we must organize the compiled code according to the *execution architecture* of the system, while the source code is organized according to its *conceptual architecture*. Most development environments provide *profilers* that show this execution architecture, so it's possible for programmers to decide a segmentation structure — at the cost of some *programmer effort* — but how should they implement it?

Some compilation environments provide a solution. Microsoft's C++ Compiler and DEC's FORTRAN compiler, for example, allow the user to partition each compilation unit into separate units of a single function, called COMDATs. Programmers can then order these into appropriate segments using a Link option: /ORDER:@filename (Microsoft 1997). Sun's SparcWorks' analyzer tool automates the procedure still further, allowing 'experiments' with different segmentation options using profiling data, and providing a utility (er_mapgen) to generate the linker map file directly from these experiments.

For linkers without this option, an alternative is to pre-process the source files to produce a single file for each function, and then to order the resulting files explicitly in the linker command line. This requires additional *programmer discipline,* since it prevents you making code and data local to each source file.

Example

This EPOC C++ example implements the 'Dynamically loaded package with abstract factory' approach illustrated in Figure 2.11. This component uses animated objects in a virtual reality application. The animated objects are of many kinds (people, machinery, animals, rivers, etc.), only a few types are required at a time, and new implementations will be added later. Thus the implementations of the animated objects live in packages, and are loaded on demand.

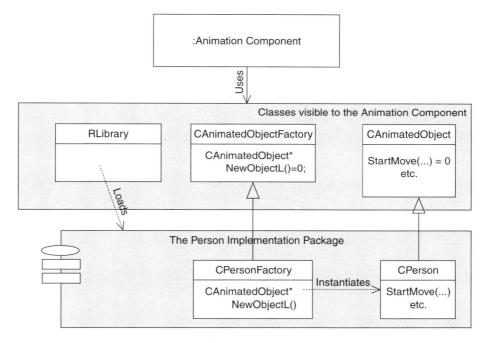

Figure 2.11 The example classes

1. Implementation of the animation component

EPOC implements packages as DLLs. The code in the animation component must load the DLL, and keep a handle to it for as long as it has DLL-based objects using its code. It might create a new CAnimatedObject using C++ something like the following (where the current object has a longer lifetime than any of the objects in the package, and iAnimatedObjectFactory is a variable of type CAnimatedObjectFactory*)

```
iAnimatedObjectFactory = CreateAnimatedObjectFactoryFromDLL(fileName);
CAnimatedObject* newAnimatedObject =
    iAnimatedObjectFactory->NewObjectL();
```

The implementation of CreateAnimatedObjectFactoryFromDLL is as follows. It uses the EPOC class RLibrary as a handle to the library; the function RLibrary::Load loads the library; RLibrary::Close unloads it again. As with all EPOC code, it must implement PARTIAL FAILURE (48) if loading fails. Also, libraryHandle is a stack variable, so we must ensure it is Closed if any later operations do a PARTIAL FAILURE themselves, using the cleanup stack function, CleanupClosePushL.

```
CAnimatedObjectFactory* CreateAnimatedObjectFactoryFromDLL(
                              const TDesC& aFileName) {
  RLibrary libraryHandle;
  TInt r = libraryHandle.Load(aFileName);
  if (r != KErrNone)
    User::Leave(r);
  CleanupClosePushL(libraryHandle);
```

We must ensure that the library is the correct one. In EPOC every library (and data file) is identified by three Unique Identifier (UID) integers at the start of the file. The second UID (index 1) specifies the type of file:

```
if(libraryHandle.Type()[1] != TUid::Uid(KUidAnimationLibraryModuleV01))
    User::Leave(KErrBadLibraryEntryPoint);
```

EPOC DLLs export functions by ordinal rather than by name (Tasker 1999b). By convention a call to the library entry point at ordinal one returns an instance of the FACTORY OBJECT, CAnimatedObjectFactory.

```
typedef CAnimatedObjectFactory* (*TAnimatedObjectFactoryNewL)();
TAnimatedObjectFactoryNewL libEntryL =
    reinterpret_cast<TAnimatedObjectFactoryNewL>(libraryHandle.Lookup(1));
if (libEntryL == NULL)
    User::Leave(KErrBadLibraryEntryPoint);
CAnimatedObjectFactory* factoryObject = (*libEntryL)();
CleanupStack::PushL(factoryObject);
```

We'll keep this factory object for the lifetime of the package, so we pass the RLibrary handle to its construction function:

```
    factoryObject->ConstructL(libraryHandle);
    CleanupStack::Pop(2); // libraryHandle, factoryObject
    return factoryObject;
}
```

The CAnimatedObjectFactory factory object is straightforward. It merely stores the library handle. Like almost all EPOC objects that own resources, it derives from the CBase base class, and provides a ConstructL function (Tasker et al. 2000). Some of its functions will be called across DLL boundaries; we tell the compiler to generate the extra linkup code using the EPOC IMPORT_C and EXPORT_C macros.

```
class CAnimatedObjectFactory : public CBase {
public:
    IMPORT_C ~CAnimatedObjectFactory();
    IMPORT_C void ConstructL(RLibrary& aLib);
```

```
      IMPORT_C virtual CAnimatedObject* NewAnimatedObjectL() = 0;
   private:
      RLibrary iLibraryHandle;
   };
```

The implementations of the construction function and destructor are simple:

```
   EXPORT_C void CAnimatedObjectFactory::ConstructL(RLibrary& aLib) {
      iLibraryHandle = aLib;
   }
   EXPORT_C CAnimatedObjectFactory::~CAnimatedObjectFactory() {
      iLibraryHandle.Close();
   }
```

2. Implementation of the package

The package itself must implement the entry point to return a new factory object , so it needs a class that derives from CAnimatedObjectFactory:

```
   class CPersonFactory : public CAnimatedObjectFactory {
   public:
      virtual CAnimatedObject* NewAnimatedObjectL();
   };
   CAnimatedObject* CPersonFactory::NewAnimatedObjectL() {
      return new(ELeave) CPerson;
   }
```

The package also needs the class to implement the CAnimatedObject object itself:

```
   class CPerson : public CAnimatedObject {
   public:
      CPerson();
      // etc.
   };
```

Finally, the library entry point simply returns a new instance of the concrete factory object (or null, if memory fails). EXPORT_C ensures that this function is a library entry point. In MS C++ we ensure that the function corresponds to ordinal one in the library by editing the 'DEF' file (Microsoft 1997).

```
   EXPORT_C CAnimatedObjectFactory* LibEntry() {
      return new CPersonFactory;
   }
```

Known uses

Most modern operating systems (UNIX, MS Windows, WinCE, EPOC, etc.) support dynamically linked libraries (Goodheart and Cox 1994; Petzold 1998, Symbian 1999b). Many applications delay the loading of certain DLLs, particularly for *add-ins* — added functionality provided by third parties. Lotus Notes loads viewer DLLs when needed; Netscape and Internet Explorer dynamically load viewers such as the Adobe PDF viewer; MS Word loads document converters and uses DLLs for add-in extensions such as support for web page editing. Some EPOC applications explicitly load packages: the Web application loads drivers for each transport mechanism (HTTP, FTP, etc.) and viewers for each data type.

Printer drivers are often implemented as PACKAGES. This allows you to add new printer drivers without restarting any applications. All EPOC applications dynamically load printer drivers where necessary. MS Windows 95 and NT do the same.

Many Lisp systems use dynamic loading. GNU Emacs, for example, consists of a core text editor package plus auto-loading facilities. Most of the interesting features of GNU Emacs exist as packages: intelligent language support, spelling checkers, e-mail packages, web browsers, terminal emulators, etc. (Stallman 1984).

Java makes great use of dynamic loading. Java loads each class only when it needs it, so each class is effectively a PACKAGES. Java implementations may discard classes once they don't need them any more, using garbage collection, although many environments currently do not. Java applets are also treated as dynamically loading PACKAGES by web browsers. A browser loads and run applets on pages it is displaying, and then stops and unloads applets when their containing pages are no longer displayed (Lindholm and Yellin 1999). The Palm Spotless JVM loads almost all classes dynamically, even those like String that are really part of the Java language (Taivalsaari et al. 1999).

Many earlier processors supported segmentation explicitly in their architecture. The 8086 and PDP-11 processors both implement segment registers. Programmers working in these environments often had to be acutely aware of the limitations imposed by fixed segment sizes; MS Windows 1, 2 and 3 all reflected the segmented architecture explicitly in the programming interfaces (Hamacher et al. 1984; Chappell 1994).

See also

APPLICATION SWITCHING (84) is a simpler alternative to this pattern, which is applicable when the task divides into independent phases. PAGING (119) is a more complex alternative. Unloaded packages can live on SECONDARY STORAGE (79), and maybe use COMPRESSION (135).

ABSTRACT FACTORY provides a good implementation mechanism to separate the client interfaces from the package implementations. VIRTUAL PROXIES can be used to autoload individual packages (Gamma et al. 1995). You may need REFERENCE COUNTING (268) or GARBAGE COLLECTION (278) to decide when to unload a package.

Coplien's *Advanced C++ Programming Styles and Idioms* (1994) describes dynamically loading C++ functions into a running program.

Paging

Also known as: Virtual Memory, Paging OO DBMS

How can you provide the illusion of infinite memory[1]?

- The memory requirements for the program's code and data are too big to fit into RAM.

- The program needs random access to all its code and data.

- You have a fast secondary storage device, which can store the code and data not currently in use.

- To decrease programmer effort and improve usability, programmers and users should not be aware that the program is using secondary storage.

Some systems' memory requirements are simply too large to fit into the available memory. Perhaps one program's data structures are larger than the system's RAM memory, or perhaps a whole system cannot fit into main memory, although each individual component is small enough on its own.

For example, the Strap-It-On's weather prediction system, Rain-Sight, loads a relatively small amount of weather information from its radio network link, and attempts to calculate whether the user is about to get rained on. To do that, it needs to work with some very large matrices indeed — larger than can fit in memory even if no other applications were present at all. So the Rain-Sight marketing team have already agreed to distribute a 5 Gb 'coin-disk' pack with every copy of the program, ample for the Rain-Sight data. The problem facing the Rain-Sight developers is how to use it.

You can manage data on secondary storage explicitly using a DATA FILE (92). This has two disadvantages.

- The resulting code needs to combine processing the data with shuffling it between primary and secondary storage. The result will be complex and difficult to maintain, costing programmer effort to implement and programmer discipline to use correctly, because programmers will have to understand both domain-specific requirements of the program and the finer points of data access.

---

[1] Sometimes the program is just too big, too complex, or you are too lazy to segment, subdivide, chain, phase, slice, dice, vitamize, or food process the code any more. Why **should** programmers have to worry about memory! Infinite memory for all is a **right**, not a privilege! Those small memory guys are just **no-life-losers**!

- In addition, this approach will tend to be *inefficient* for *random access* to data. If you read each item each time it's accessed, and write it back after manipulating it, this will require a lot of slow secondary storage access.

Other techniques, such as COMPRESSION (135) and PACKED DATA (174), will certainly reduce the RAM memory requirements, but can only achieve a finite reduction; ultimately any system can have more data than will fit into RAM.

Therefore: **Keep a system's code and data on secondary storage, and move them to and from main memory as required.**

No software is completely random in its access to memory; at any given time a typical system will be working with only a small subset of the code and data it has available. So you need to keep only a relatively small *working set* in memory; the rest of the system can stay on secondary storage. The software can access this working set very fast, since it's in main memory. If you need to access information on secondary storage, you must change the working set, reading the new data required, and writing or discarding any data that occupied that space beforehand.

You must ensure that the working set changes only slowly — that the software exhibits *locality of reference*, and tends to access the same objects or memory area in preference to completely random access. It helps that memory allocators will typically put items allocated together in the same area of memory. So objects allocated together will typically be physically near to each other in memory, particularly when you're using FIXED ALLOCATION (226).

There are three forms of this pattern in use today (Tannenbaum 1992; Goodheart and Cox 1994):

Demand paging is the most familiar form. The memory management hardware, or interpreter environment, implements *virtual memory* so that there is an additional *page table* that maps addresses used in software to *pages* of physical memory. When software attempts to access a memory location without an entry in the page table, the environment frees up a page by saving its data, and loads the new data from secondary storage into physical memory, before returning the address of the physical memory found.

Swapping is a simpler alternative to paging, where the environment stops a process, and writes out all its data to secondary storage. When the process needs to process an event, the environment reloads all the data from secondary storage and resumes. This approach is common on portable PCs, where the entire environment is saved to disk, though the intent there is to save power rather than memory.

Object-oriented databases are similar to demand paging, but the unit of paged memory is an object and its associated owned objects (or perhaps, for efficiency, a cluster of such objects). This approach requires more programmer effort than demand paging, but makes the data persistent, and allows multiple processes to share objects.

So, for example, the Rain-Sight team decided to use PAGING to make use of their disk. The Strap-OS operating system doesn't support hardware-based paging, so the team hacked a Java interpreter to implement paging for each Java object. The team then defined objects to implement each related part of the Rain-Sight matrices (which are always accessed together), giving them acceptable performance and an apparent memory space limited only by the size of the 'coin disk'.

Consequences

Paging is the ultimate escape of the memory-challenged programmer. The programmer is **much less** aware of paging than any other technique, since paging provides the illusion of essentially infinite memory — the program's *memory requirements* are no longer a problem. So paging tends to increase other aspects of a system's *design quality* and *maintainability* because memory requirements are no longer an overriding issue.

Paging needs little *programmer effort* and *programmer discipline* to use, because it doesn't need a logical decomposition of the program. Because paging does not require any artificial division of programs into phases or data into files it can make systems more *usable*. Programs using paging can easily accommodate more memory just by paging less, so paging improves *scalability* as well.

Paging can make good *local* use of the available memory where the program's memory use is distributed *globally* over many different components, since different components will typically use their data at different times.

However: Paging reduces a program's *time performance*, since some memory accesses require secondary storage reads and writes. It also reduces the predictability of response times, making it unsuitable for *real-time systems*. Paging performs badly if the memory accesses do not exhibit locality of reference, and this may require *programmer effort* to fix.

Paging needs fast secondary storage to perform well. Of course 'fast' is a relative term; lots of systems have used floppy disks for paging. Because paging tends to make lots of small data transfers rather than a few large ones, the latency of the secondary storage device is usually more important than its throughput. Furthermore, Paging's continuous use of secondary storage devices increases the system's *power consumption*, and reduces the lifetime of storage media such as flash RAM and floppy disks.

Since paging doesn't require *programmer discipline*, a program's *memory requirements* can tend to increase in paged systems, requiring more secondary storage and impacting the program's *time performance*. Paging requires no *local* support from within programs, but requires low-level *global* support, often provided by the *hardware and operating system*, or an interpreter or data manager. Because intermediate information can be paged out to secondary storage, paging can affect the *security* of a system unless the secondary storage is as well protected as the primary storage.

❖   ❖   ❖

Implementation

PAGING is typically supported by two main data structures; see Figure 2.12.

Page frames live in main memory, and contain the 'paged in' RAM data for the program. Each page frame also has control information: the secondary storage location corresponding to the current data and a *dirty bit*, set when the page memory has been changed since loading from secondary storage.

The *page table* also lives in main memory, and has an entry for each page on secondary storage. It stores whether that page is resident in memory, and if so, in which page frame it is stored. Figure 2.12 below shows a page table and page frames.

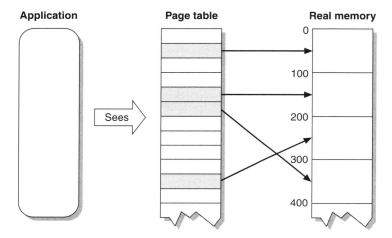

Figure 2.12   Page table and page frames

As you run a paging application, it accesses memory via the page table. Memory that is paged in can be read and written directly; writing to a page should set the page's dirty bit. When you try to access a page that is 'paged out' (not in main memory) the system must load the page from secondary storage, perhaps saving an existing page in memory back to secondary storage to make room for the new page. Trying to access a page in secondary storage is called a *page fault*. To handle a page fault, or to allocate a new page, the system must find a free page frame for the data. Normally, the frame chosen will already contain active data, which must be discarded, and if the dirty bit is set, the system must write the contents out to secondary storage. Once the new frame is allocated, or its contents are loaded from secondary storage, the page table can be updated and the program's execution continues.

Here are some issues to consider when implementing paging.

1. Intercepting memory accesses

Probably the single most difficult part of implementing paging is the need to intercept memory accesses. In addition, this intercept must distinguish access for writing, which must set the 'dirty bit', from access for reading, which doesn't.

There are several possible mechanisms:

1. *MMU*. Many modern systems have a memory management unit (MMU) in addition to the central processing unit (CPU). An MMU provides a set of *virtual memory maps (*typically one for each process), which map the memory locations requested by the code to different real memory addresses. If the program accesses an address that hasn't been loaded, this causes a page fault interrupt, and the interrupt driver will load the page from secondary storage.

   The MMU also distinguishes pages as read-only and read-write. An attempt to write to a read-only page also causes a page-fault interrupt, which makes it easy to set the dirty bit for that page.

2. *Interpreter*. It's fairly straightforward to implement paging for interpreted environments. The runtime interpreter must implement any accesses to the program or its data, so it is relatively easy to intercept accesses and to distinguish reads from writes.

3. *Process Swap*. When you swap entire processes, you don't need to detect memory access as processes are not running when they are swapped out.

4. *Data manager*. For programs in an environment with no built-in paging, we can use 'smart pointers' to classes to intercept each access to an object. Then a *data manager* can ensure that the object is in store and manage loading, caching, and swapping.

   In this case it's appropriate to page entire objects in and out, rather than arbitrarily sized pages.

2. Page replacement

How can you select which page frame to choose to free up to take a new or loaded page? The best algorithm is to remove the page that will be needed the furthest into the future — the least important page for the system's immediate needs (Tannenbaum 1992). Unfortunately this is usually impossible to implement, so instead you have to guess the future on the basis of the recent past. Removing the *least frequently used (LFU)* page provides the most accurate estimation, but is quite difficult to implement. Almost as effective but easier to implement is a *least recently used (LRU)* algorithm, which simply requires keeping a list of all page frames, and moving each page to the top of this list as it is used. Choosing a page to replace at random is easy to implement and provides sufficient performance for many situations.

   Most implementations of MMU paging incorporate segmentation techniques as well (see PACKAGES (108)). Since you already have the process's virtual data memory split into pages, it's an obvious extension to do the same for code. Code is READ-ONLY (65), and typically needs only very trivial changes when it's loaded from secondary storage to memory. So there's no point in wasting space in the swap file; you can take the code pages directly from the code file when you want them and discard them when they're no longer needed.

3. Working set size

A program's *working set size* is the minimum amount of memory it needs to run without excessive page faults. Generally, the larger the page size, the larger the working set size. A program's working set size determines whether it will run well under any given paging system. If the working set size is larger than the real memory allocated to page frames, then there will be an excessive number of page faults. The system will start *thrashing*, spending its time swapping pages from main memory to secondary storage and back but making little progress executing the software.

To avoid thrashing, do less with your program, add real memory to the system, or optimize the program's memory layout using the techniques discussed in the PACKAGES (108) pattern.

4. Program control of paging

Some programs do not have *locality of reference*. For example, a program might traverse all its data reading each page exactly once in order. In this case, each page will be paged in only once, and the best page to replace will be the **most** frequently or recently used. To help in such a case, some systems provide an interface so that the programmer can control the paging system. For example, the interface might support a request that a particular page be paged out. Alternatively it might allow a request that a particular page be *paged in* — for example, the program above will know which page will be needed *next* even before processing the current page.

Other program code may have real-time constraints. Device drivers, for example, must typically respond to interrupt events within microseconds. So device driver data must not be paged out. Most systems support this by 'tagging' certain areas of code with different attributes. For example, Microsoft's Portable Executable Format supports Pre-load and Memory-resident options for its 'virtual device driver' executable files (Microsoft 1997).

Example

The following code implements a simple framework to page individual C++ objects.

It's very difficult indeed to intercept all references to a C++ object without operating system support — in particular we can't intercept the 'this' pointer in a member function. So it's a bad idea to page instances of any C++ class that has member functions. Instead we make each object store its data in a separate data structure and access that structure through special member functions that control paging. The object itself acts as a PROXY (Gamma et al. 1995) for the data, storing a page number rather than a pointer to the data. Figure 2.13 below shows a typical scenario.

The page table optimizes access to the data in RAM: if its entry is non-null for a particular page, that page is loaded in RAM and the application object can access its data directly. If an application object tries to access a page with a null page table entry, it means that object's data isn't loaded. In that case the paging code will save or discard an existing page frame and load that object's data from disk.

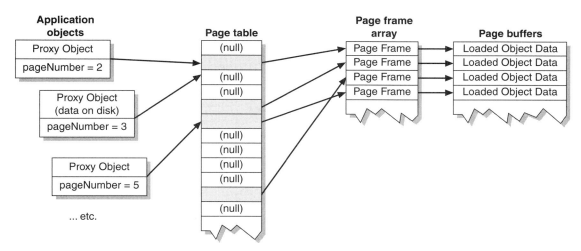

Figure 2.13   Objects in memory for the paging example

1. Example client implementation

Here's an example client implementation that uses the paging example. It's a simple bitmap image containing just pixels. Other paged data structures could contain any other C++ primitive data types or `structs`, including pointers to objects (though not pointers to the paged data structure instances, of course, as these will be paged out).

```
typedef char Pixel;

class BitmapImageData {
    friend class BitmapImage;
    Pixel pixels[SCREEN_HEIGHT * SCREEN_WIDTH];
};
```

The **PROXY** class, `BitmapImage`, derives its paging functionality from the generic `ObjectWithPagedData`. The main constraint on its implementation is that all accesses to the data object must be through the base class `GetPagedData` functions, which ensure that the data is paged into RAM. It accesses these through functions that cast these to the correct type:

```
class BitmapImage : public ObjectWithPagedData {
private:
    BitmapImageData* GetData()
        { return static_cast<BitmapImageData*>(GetPagedData()); }
    const BitmapImageData* GetData() const
        { return static_cast<const BitmapImageData*>(GetPagedData()); }
```

The constructor must specify the `PageFile` object and initialize the data structure. Note that all these functions can be inline:

```
public:
    BitmapImage(PageFile& thePageFile)
      : ObjectWithPagedData(thePageFile) {
        memset(GetData(), 0, sizeof(BitmapImageData));
    }
```

All other functions use the `GetData` functions to access the data. Note how the C++ const-correctness ensures that we get the correct version of the data function; non-const accesses to `GetData()` will set the 'dirty bit' for the page so it gets written back to file when paged out.

```
    Pixel GetPixel(int pixelNumber) const {
        return GetData()->pixels[pixelNumber];
    }
    void SetPixel(int pixelNumber, Pixel newValue) {
        GetData()->pixels[pixelNumber] = newValue;
    }
};
```

And that's the full client implementation. Simple, isn't it?

To use it we need to set up a page file — here's one with just four page buffers:

```
PageFile pageFile("testfile.dat", sizeof(BitmapImageData), 4);
```

And then we can use `BitmapImage` as any other C++ object:

```
BitmapImage* newImage = new BitmapImage(pageFile);
newImage->SetPixel(0, 0);
delete newImage;
```

2. Overview of the paging framework

Figure 2.14 below shows the logical structure of the paging framework using UML notation (Fowler and Scott 1999). The names in normal type are classes in the framework; the others are implemented as follows:

- *Page Table Entry* is a entry in the `pageTable` pointer array.
- *Page in RAM* is a simple (`void*`) buffer.
- *Page on Disk* is a fixed page in the disk file.
- *Client Implementation* is any client class, such as the `BitmapImage` class above.

The page frames and page table are a FIXED ALLOCATION, always occupying the same memory in RAM.

3. Implementation of `ObjectWithPagedData`

`ObjectWithPagedData` is the base class for the Client implementation classes. It contains only the page number for the data, plus a reference to the `PageFile` object. This allows us to have several different types of client object being paged independently.

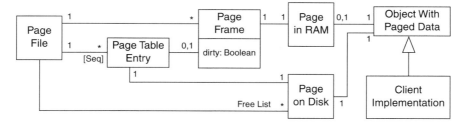

Figure 2.14 UML diagram: logical structure of the object paging system

```
class ObjectWithPagedData {
private:
    PageFile& pageFile;
    const int pageNumber;
```

All of its member operations are `protected`, since they're used only by the client implementations. The constructor and destructor use functions in `PageFile` to allocated and free a data page:

```
ObjectWithPagedData::ObjectWithPagedData(PageFile& thePageFile)
    : pageFile(thePageFile),
        pageNumber(thePageFile.NewPage())
{}

ObjectWithPagedData::~ObjectWithPagedData() {
    pageFile.DeletePage(pageNumber);
}
```

We need both `const` and non-`const` functions to access the paged data. Each ensures there's a page frame present, then accesses the buffer; the non-`const` version uses the function that sets the dirty flag for the page frame:

```
const void* ObjectWithPagedData::GetPagedData() const {
    PageFrame* frame = pageFile.FindPageFrameForPage( pageNumber );
    return frame->GetConstPage();
}

void* ObjectWithPagedData::GetPagedData() {
    PageFrame* frame = pageFile.FindPageFrameForPage( pageNumber );
    return frame->GetWritablePage();
}
```

4. Implementation of `PageFrame`

A `PageFrame` object represents a single buffer of 'real memory'. If the page frame is 'In Use', a client object has accessed the buffer and it hasn't been saved to disk or discarded. The member `currentPageNumber` is set to the appropriate page if the

frame is In Use, or else to INVALID_PAGE_NUMBER. PageFrame stores the 'dirty' flag for
the buffer, and sets it when any client accesses the GetWritablePage function.

```
class PageFrame {
    friend class PageFile;

private:
    enum { INVALID_PAGE_NUMBER = -1 };
    bool   dirtyFlag;
    int    currentPageNumber;
    void*  bufferContainingCurrentPage;
```

The constructor and destructor simply initialize the members appropriately:

```
PageFrame::PageFrame(int pageSize)
    : bufferContainingCurrentPage(new char[pageSize]),
      dirtyFlag(false),
      currentPageNumber(PageFrame::INVALID_PAGE_NUMBER)
{}

PageFrame::~PageFrame() {
    delete [] (char*)(bufferContainingCurrentPage);
}
```

GetConstPage and GetWritablePage provide access to the buffer:

```
const void* PageFrame::GetConstPage() {
    return bufferContainingCurrentPage;
}

void* PageFrame::GetWritablePage() {
    dirtyFlag = true;
    return bufferContainingCurrentPage;
}
```

And the other two member functions are trivial too:

```
int PageFrame::PageNumber() {
    return currentPageNumber;
}

bool PageFrame::InUse() {
    return currentPageNumber != INVALID_PAGE_NUMBER;
}
```

5. Implementation of PageFile

The PageFile object manages all of the important behaviour of the paging system.
It owns the temporary file, and implements the functions to swap data buffers to
and from it.

PageFile's main structures are as follows:

pageTable is a vector, with an entry for each page in the page file. These entries are null if the page is swapped to secondary storage, or point to a PageFrame object is the page is in RAM.

pageFrameArray contains all the PageFrame objects. It's an array to make it easy to select one at random to discard.

listOfFreePageNumbers contains a queue of pages that have been deleted. We cannot remove pages from the page file, so instead we remember the page numbers to reassign when required.

So the resulting private data is as follows:

```
class PageFile {
    friend class ObjectWithPagedData;
private:
    vector<PageFrame*> pageTable;
    vector<PageFrame*> pageFrameArray;
    list<int> listOfFreePageNumbers;
    const int pageSize;
    fstream fileStream;
```

PageFile's constructor must initialize the file and allocate all the FIXED ALLOCATION (226). It requires a way to abort if the file open fails; this example simply uses a variant of the ASSERT macro to check:

```
PageFile::PageFile(char* fileName, int pageSizeInBytes,
                   int nPagesInCache)
    : fileStream(fileName,
                 ios::in|ios::out|ios::binary|ios::trunc),
      pageSize(pageSizeInBytes) {
    ASSERT_ALWAYS( fileStream.good() );
    for (int i = 0; i<nPagesInCache; i++) {
        pageFrameArray.push_back(new PageFrame(pageSize));
    }
}
```

The destructor tidies up memory and closes the file. A complete implementation would delete the file as well:

```
PageFile::~PageFile() {
    for (vector<PageFrame*>::iterator i = pageFrameArray.begin();
         i != pageFrameArray.end(); i++)
      delete *i;
    fileStream.close();
}
```

The function NewPage allocates a page on disk for a new client object. It uses a free page on disk if there is one, or else allocates a new pageTable entry and expands the page file by writing a page of random data to the end.

```
int PageFile::NewPage() {
    int pageNumber;
    if (!listOfFreePageNumbers.empty()) {
        pageNumber = listOfFreePageNumbers.front();
        listOfFreePageNumbers.pop_front();
    } else {
        pageNumber = pageTable.size();
        pageTable.push_back(0);
        int newPos = fileStream.rdbuf()->pubseekoff(0, ios::end);
        fileStream.write(
            (char*)pageFrameArray[0]->bufferContainingCurrentPage,
            PageSize());
    }
    return pageNumber;
}
```

The corresponding DeletePage function is trivial:

```
void PageFile::DeletePage(int pageNumber) {
    listOfFreePageNumbers.push_front[pageNumber];
}
```

The function FindPageFrameForPage assigns a PageFrame for the given page number and ensures that the page is in RAM. If there's already a PageFrame for the page, it just returns the pointer; otherwise it finds a PageFrame and fills it with the requested page from disk.

```
PageFrame* PageFile::FindPageFrameForPage(int pageNumber) {
    PageFrame* frame = pageTable[pageNumber];
    if (frame == 0) {
        frame = MakeFrameAvailable();
        LoadFrame(frame, pageNumber);
        pageTable[pageNumber] = frame;
    }
    return frame;
}
```

The function MakeFrameAvailable assigns a frame by paging out or discarding an existing page, chosen at random.

```
PageFrame* PageFile::MakeFrameAvailable() {
    PageFrame* frame =
        pageFrameArray[(rand() * pageFrameArray.size()) / RAND_MAX];
    if (frame->InUse()) {
        SaveOrDiscardFrame( frame );
    }
    return frame;
}
```

The function that provides the meat of the paging algorithm is `SaveOrDiscardFrame`. This writes out the page to the corresponding location in file — if necessary — and resets the page table entry.

```
void PageFile::SaveOrDiscardFrame(PageFrame* frame) {
    if (frame->dirtyFlag) {
        int newPos = fileStream.rdbuf()->pubseekoff(
                         frame->PageNumber()*PageSize(), ios::beg);
        fileStream.write((char*)frame->bufferContainingCurrentPage,
                         PageSize());
        frame->dirtyFlag = false;
    }
    pageTable[frame->PageNumber()] = 0;
    frame->currentPageNumber = PageFrame::INVALID_PAGE_NUMBER;
}
```

And finally, the corresponding function to load a frame is as follows:

```
void PageFile::LoadFrame(PageFrame* frame, int pageNumber) {
    int newPos = fileStream.rdbuf()->pubseekoff(pageNumber * PageSize(),
                                                ios::beg);
    fileStream.read((char*)frame->bufferContainingCurrentPage, PageSize());
    frame->currentPageNumber = pageNumber;
}
```

❖   ❖   ❖

Known uses

Almost every modern disk operating system provides paged virtual memory, including most versions of UNIX, Linux, MacOS, and MS Windows (Goodheart and Cox 1994; Card et al. 1998; Microsoft 1997a).

OO Databases almost all use some form of object paging. ObjectStore uses the UNIX (or NT) paging support directly, but replaces the OS-supplied paging drivers with drivers that suit the needs of OO programs with persistent data (Chaudhri and Loomis 1997).

Infocom games implemented a paged interpreter on machines like Apple-IIs and early PCs, paging main memory to floppy disks (Blank and Galley 1980). This enabled games to run on machines with varying sizes of memory — although of course games would run more slowly if there was less main memory available. The LOOM system implemented paging in Smalltalk (Kaehler and Krasner 1983).

See also

The other patterns in this chapter — APPLICATION SWITCHING (226), DATA FILES (92), PACKAGES (108), and RESOURCE FILES (101) — provide alternatives to this pattern. PAGING can also use COPY-ON-WRITE (191) to optimize access to read-only storage, and can be extended to support SHARING (182). System memory is a global resource, so some operating systems implement CAPTAIN OATES (57), discarding segments from different processes rather than from the process that requests a new page.

An INTERPRETER (Gamma et al. 1995) can make PAGING transparent to user programs. VIRTUAL PROXIES and BRIDGES (Gamma et al. 1995) and ENVELOPE/LETTER or HANDLE/BODY (Coplien 1994) can provide PAGING for objects without affecting the objects' client interfaces.

COMPRESSION

Table Compression

Difference Coding

Adaptive Compression

3

COMPRESSION

How can you fit a quart of data into a pint pot of memory?

- The memory requirements of the code and data appear greater than the memory available, whether primary memory, secondary storage, read-only memory or some combination of these.

- You cannot reduce the functionality and omit some of the data or code.

- You need to transmit information across a communications link as quickly as possible.

- You cannot choose SMALL DATA STRUCTURES (169) to reduce the memory requirements further.

Sometimes you just don't have enough memory to go around. The most usual problem is that you need to store more data than the space available, but sometimes the executable code can be too large. You can often choose suitable SMALL DATA STRUCTURES to ensure that the right amount of memory is allocated to store the data; you can also use SECONDARY STORAGE (79) and READ-ONLY MEMORY (65) to move the data out of RAM. These techniques have one important limitation, however: they don't reduce the total amount of storage, of all kinds, needed to support the whole system.

For example, the Strap-It-On wrist-mounted PC needs to store the data for the documents the user is working on. It also needs sound files recorded by the internal microphone, data traces from optional body well-being monitors, and a large amount of executable code downloaded by the user to support 'optional applications' (typically Tetris, Doom, and Hunt-the-Wumpus, but sometimes work-related programs as well!). This information can certainly exceed the capacity of the Strap-It-On's primary memory and secondary storage combined. How can we improve the Strap-It-On's usability without forcing every user to carry around the optional 2 Gb disk backpack?

No matter how much memory such a system may have, you will always find users who need more. Extra storage is expensive, so you should use what you have as effectively as possible.

> *Therefore:* **Use a compressed representation to reduce the memory required.**

Store the information in a compressed form and decompress it when you need to access it. There are a wide variety of compression algorithms and approaches you can choose from, each with different space and time trade-offs.

So, for example, the Strap-It-On PC stores its voice sound files using GSM compression; its music uses MP3; its data traces use DIFFERENCE CODING (153); its databases use TABLE COMPRESSION (143); and its documents are stored using GZIP. The device drivers for Strap-It-On's secondary storage choose the appropriate ADAPTIVE COMPRESSION (160) technique based on the file type, ensuring all files are stored in a compressed form.

Consequences

The *memory requirements* of your system decrease because compressed code and data need less space than uncompressed code or data. Some forms of *time performance* may also improve — for example, reading from slow secondary storage devices or over a network.

However: Compressed information is often more difficult to process from within the program. Some compression techniques prevent random access to the compressed information. You may have to decompress an entire data stream to access any part of it — requiring enough *main memory* to store all the decompressed information, in addition to the *memory* needed for the decompression itself.

The program has to provide compression and decompression support, making it *more complex to maintain*, requiring a fair amount of *programmer effort* to implement, increasing the *testing cost* of the program and reducing the *real-time responsiveness*.

The compression process also takes *time* and *extra temporary memory*, increasing the possibilities for failure; compression can also increase a program's *power consumption*. In some cases — program code, resource file data, and information received via telecommunications — the compression cost may be paid once by large powerful machines better able to handle it. The amount of memory required to store a given amount of data becomes *less predictable*, because it depends upon how well the data can be compressed.

❖   ❖   ❖

Implementation

The key idea behind compression is that most data contains a large amount of *redundancy* — information that is not strictly required (Bell et al. 1990). The following sections explore several types of redundancy, and discuss compression techniques to exploit each type.

1. Mechanical redundancy

Consider the ASCII character set. ASCII defines around 100 printable characters, yet most text formats use 8, 16, or even 32 bits to store characters for processing on modern processors. You can store ASCII text using just 7 bits per character; this would reduce memory used at a cost of increased processing time, because most processors handle 8- or 32-bit quantities much more easily than 7-bit quantities. Thus, 1 bit in a single byte encoding, or 9 bits in a 16-bit Unicode encoding are redundant. This kind of redundancy is called mechanical redundancy.

For text compression, the amount of compression is usually expressed by the number of (compressed) bits required per character in a larger text. For example, storing ASCII characters in 7-bit bytes would give a compression of 7 bits per character. For other forms of data we talk about the *compression ratio* — the compressed size divided by the decompressed size. Using 7-bit ASCII to encode a normal 8-bit ASCII file would give a compression ratio of 7/8, or 87.5%.

TABLE COMPRESSION (143) and DIFFERENCE CODING (153) exploit other related forms of mechanical redundancy.

2. Semantic redundancy

Consider the traditional English song:

Verse 1:
Voice: Whear 'as tha been sin' I saw thee?
          Reply: I saw thee
Chorus: On Ilkley Moor bah t'at
Voice: Whear 'as tha been sin' I saw thee?
        Reply: I saw thee
Voice: Whear 'as tha been sin' I saw thee?
Chorus: On Ilkley Moor bah t'at
        Reply: Bah t'at
Chorus: On Ilkley Moor bah t'at
                  On Ilkley Moor bah t'at

Verse 2:
Voice: Tha's been a-coortin' Mary Jane
          Reply: Mary Jane
Chorus: On Ilkley Moor bah t'at

    . . . etc., for 7 more verses.

This song has plenty of redundancy because of all the repeats and choruses; you don't need to store every single word sung to reproduce the song. The songbook *Rise Up Singing* (Blood and Paterson 1992) uses bold type, parentheses and repetition marks to compress the complete song to 15 short lines, occupying a mere 6 square inches on the page without compromising readability:

1. Whear 'ast tha been sin' I saw thee (I saw thee)
On Ilkley Moor bah T'at
Whear 'ast tha been sin' I saw thee (2x)

On Ilkley Moor bah t'at (bah t'at) on Ilkley Moor bah t'at
On Ilkely Moor bah t'at.
2. Tha's been a-coortin' Mary Jane
3. Tha'll go an' get thee death o' cowld

. . . etc., for 6 more lines

LZ compression (see ADAPTIVE COMPRESSION (160)) and its variants use a similar but mechanical technique to remove redundancy in text or binary data.

3. Lossy compression

Compression techniques that ensure that the result of decompression is exactly the same data as before compression are known as *lossless*. Many of the more powerful forms of compression are *lossy*. With lossy compression, decompression will produce an approximation to the original information rather than an exact copy. Lossy compression needs knowledge of the specific kind of data being stored, and of the required uses for the data.

The key to understanding lossy compression is the difference between *data* and *information*. Suppose you wish to communicate the information represented by the word 'elephant' to an audience. Sent as a text string, 'elephant' occupies eight 7-bit ASCII characters, or 56 bits. Alternatively, as a spoken word encoded in 16-bit samples 8,000 times per second, 'elephant' requires 1 second of samples, i.e. 128 Kbits. A full-screen colour image of an elephant at 640×480 pixels might require 2.5 Mbits, and a video displayed for one second at 50 frames per second could take 50 times that, or 125 Mbits. None of the more expensive techniques convey much more information than just the text of 'elephant', however. If all you are interested in is the basic concept of an elephant, most of the data required by the other techniques is redundant. You can exploit this redundancy in various ways.

Simplest, you can omit irrelevant data. For example, you might be receiving uncompressed sound data represented as 16-bit samples. If your sound sampler isn't accurate enough to record 16-bit samples, the least significant 2 bits in each sample will be random, so you could achieve a simple compression by storing just 14 instead of 16 bits for each sample.

You can also exploit the nature of human perception to omit data that's less important. For example, we perceive sound on a 'log scale'; the ear is much less sensitive to differences in intensity when the intensity is high than when intensity is low. You can effectively compress sound samples by converting them to a log scale, and supporting only a small number of logarithmic intensities. This is the principle of some simple sound compression techniques, particularly μ-law and a-law, which compress 14-bit samples to 8 bits in this way (CCITT G.711, Brokish and Lewis 1997).

You can take this idea of omitting data further, and transform the data into a different form to remove data irrelevant to human perception. Many of the most effective techniques do this:

JPEG   The most commonly used variants of the JPEG standard represent each 8 × 8 pixel square as a composite of a standard set of 64 'standard pictures' — a fraction of each picture. The transformation is known as the 'cosine transform'. Then the fractions are represented in more or less detail according to the importance of each to human perception. This gives a format that compresses photographic data very effectively (ITU T.87; Gonzalez and Woods 1992).

GSM   GSM compression represents voice data in terms of a mathematical model of the human voice (Regular Pulse Excited Linear Predictive Coding)[1]. In this way it encodes separate 20 mS samples in just 260 bits, allowing voice telephony over a digital link of only 13 Kbps (Degener 1994).

GIF, PNG   The proprietary GIF and standard PNG formats both map all colours in an image to a fixed-size palette before encoding (CompuServe 1990, Boutell 1996).

MP3   MP3 represents sound data in terms of its composite frequencies — known as the 'Fourier transformation'. The MP3 standard specifies the granularity of representation of each frequency according to its importance to the human ear and the amount of compression required, allowing FM radio-quality sound in 56 Kb per second (MP3).

MPEG   The MPEG standard for video compression uses JPEG coding for initial frames. It then uses a variety of specific techniques — to spot motion in a variety of axes, changes of light, etc. — to encode the differences between successive frames in minimal data forms that fit in with the human perception of a video image (MPEG).

Some of these techniques exploit mechanical redundancy in the resulting data as well, using TABLE COMPRESSION (143), DIFFERENCE CODING (153) and ADAPTIVE COMPRESSION (160) techniques.

❖   ❖   ❖

Specialized patterns

The rest of this chapter contains specialized patterns describing compression and packing techniques (Figure 3.1). Each of these patterns removes different kinds of mechanical and semantic redundancy, with different consequences for accessing the compressed data.

---

[1] GSM was developed using Scandinavian voices; hence all voices tend to sound Scandinavian on a mobile phone.

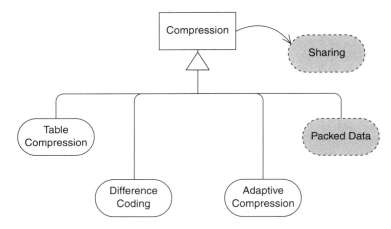

Figure 3.1   Compression patterns

The patterns are as follows:

TABLE COMPRESSION (143) reduces the average number of bits to store each character (or value) by mapping it to a variable number of bits, such that the most common characters require the fewest bits.

DIFFERENCE CODING (153) addresses data series or sequences, by storing only the differences between successive items. Alternatively or additionally, if several successive items are the same it stores simply a count of the number of identical items.

ADAPTIVE COMPRESSION (160) analyses the data before or while compressing it to produce a more efficient encoding, storing the resulting parameters along with the compressed data — or uses the data itself as a table to support the compression.

The PACKED DATA (174) pattern, which reduces the amount of memory allocated to store random-access data structures, can also been seen as a special kind of compression.

1. Evaluating compression techniques

There are many possible compression techniques. Here are some of the things to consider when choosing an appropriate technique.

1.1 Processing and memory required.   Different techniques vary significantly in the processing and memory costs they impose. In general, DIFFERENCE CODING has the lowest costs, followed by fixed TABLE COMPRESSION, and most forms of ADAPTIVE COMPRESSION have quite high costs on both counts — but there are many exceptions to this rule. *Managing Gigabytes* (Witten et al. 1999) examines the costs in some detail.

1.2 Encoding vs. decoding.   Some compression algorithms reduce the processing cost of decoding the data by increasing the cost of encoding. This is particularly advantageous if there is one large and powerful encoding system and many decoders with a lower specification. This is a situation common in broadcast systems.

MP3 and MPEG, for example, require much more processing, code and memory to encode than decode, which suits them for broadcast transmission (MP3; MPEG). Interestingly, LZ ADAPTIVE COMPRESSION has the same feature, so ZIP archives can be distributed with their relatively simple decoding software built-in (Ziv and Lempel 1977).

Some compressed representations can be used directly without any decompression. For example, Java and Smalltalk use byte coding to reduce the size of executable programs; intermediate codes can be smaller than full machine language (Goldberg and Robson 1983, Lindholm and Yellin 1999). These byte codes are designed so that they can be interpreted directly by a virtual machine, without a separate decompression step.

1.3. Programming cost.   Some techniques are simple to implement; others have efficient public domain or commercial implementations. Rolling your own complicated compression or decompression algorithm is unlikely to be a sensible option for many projects.

1.4. Random access and resynchronization.   Most compression algorithms produce a stream of bits. If this stream is stored in memory or in a file, can you access individual items within that file randomly, without reading the whole stream from the beginning? If you're receiving the stream over a serial line and some is corrupted or deleted, can you resynchronize that data stream, that is, can you identify the start of a meaningful piece of data and continue decompression? In general, most forms of TABLE COMPRESSION can provide both random access and resynchronization; DIFFERENCE CODING can also be tailored to handle both; ADAPTIVE COMPRESSION, however, is unlikely to work well for either.

Known uses

Compression is used very widely. Operating systems use compression to store more information on secondary storage, communications protocols use compression to transmit information more quickly, virtual machines use compression to reduce the memory requirements of programs, and general-purpose file compression tools are used ubiquitously for file archives.

See also

As well as compressing information, you may be able to store it in cheaper SECONDARY STORAGE (79) or READ-ONLY MEMORY (65). You can also remove redundant data using SHARING (182).

The excellent book *Managing Gigabytes* (Witten et al. 1999) explains all of this chapter's techniques for compressing text and images in much greater detail. *Text Compression* (Bell et al. 1990) focuses on text compression.

The online book *Information Engineering Across the Professions* (Cyganski et al. 1998) has explanations of many different kinds of text, audio, graphical, and video compression.

The FAQ of the newsgroup `comp.compression` describes many of the most common compression techniques. Steven Kinnear's web page (1999) provides an introduction to multimedia compression, with an excellent set of links to other sites with more detail.

Digital Video and Audio Compression (Solari 1997) has a good description of techniques for multimedia compression.

Table Compression

Also known as: Nibble Coding, Huffman Coding

How can you compress many short strings?

- You have lots of small-to-medium-sized strings in your program — all different.

- You need to reduce your program's memory requirements.

- You need random access to individual strings.

- You don't want to expend too much extra programmer effort, memory space, or processing time on managing the strings.

Many programs use a large number of strings — stored in databases, read from RESOURCE FILES (101), received via telecommunications links or hard-coded in the program. All these strings increase the program's memory requirements for main memory, read-only memory, and secondary storage.

Programs need to be able to perform common string operations such as determining their length and internal characters, concatenating strings, and substituting parameters into format strings, however strings are represented. Similarly, each string in a collection of strings needs to be individually accessible. If the strings are stored in a file on secondary storage, for example, we need random access to each string in the file.

Although storing strings is important, it is seldom the most significant memory use in the system. Typically you don't want to put too much programmer effort into the problem. Equally, you may not want to demand too much temporary memory to decompress each string.

For example, the Strap-It-On PC needs to store and display a large number of information and error messages to the user. The messages need to be stored in scarce main memory or read-only memory, and there isn't really enough space to store all the strings directly. The programs must be able to access each string individually, to display them to the user when appropriate. Given that many of the strings describe exceptional situations such a memory shortage, they need to be able to be retrieved and displayed quickly, efficiently, and without requiring extra memory.

Therefore: **Encode each element in a variable number of bits so that the more common elements require fewer bits.**

The key to TABLE COMPRESSION is that some characters are statistically much more likely to occur than others. You can easily map from a standard fixed-size representation to one where each character takes a different number of bits. If you analyse the kind of text you're compressing to find which characters are most probable, and map these characters to the most compact encoding, then on average you'll end up with smaller text.

For example, Figure 3.2 below shows the character frequencies for all the lowercase characters and spaces in a draft of this chapter.

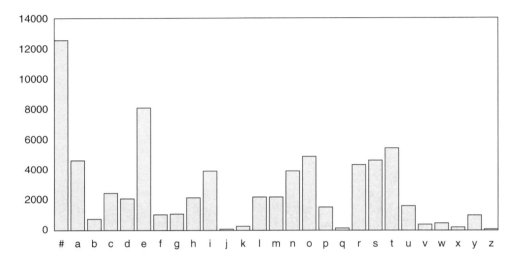

Figure 3.2   Distribution of characters in this chapter

Obviously some characters (space, 'e') appear much more often than others do ('z', 'j'). A surprisingly large proportion of the characters is hardly used at all. The most common character, space, occupies 15% of the memory required to hold the chapter. The 15 most common characters occupy 75% of the total memory.

Given that the Strap-It-On's information and error messages have a similar distribution of characters, its designers get a significant reduction in the storage space required by encoding the most common characters in fewer bits, and the less common characters in more bits. Using the Huffman encoding as described below, the designers of the Strap-It-On have achieved compression of 5 bits per character for its error messages, with negligible costs in runtime performance and temporary memory costs.

Consequences

Typically you get a reasonable compression for the strings themselves, reducing the program's *memory requirements*. Sequential operations on compressed strings execute almost as fast as operations on native strings, preserving *time performance*. TABLE

COMPRESSION is quite easy to implement, so it does not take much *programmer effort*. Each string in a collection of compressed strings can be accessed individually, without decompressing all proceeding strings.

However: The total compression of the program data — including non-string data — isn't high, so the program's *memory requirements* may not be greatly reduced.

String operations that rely on random access to the characters in the string may execute up to an order of magnitude slower than the same operations on decompressed strings, reducing the program's *time performance*. Because characters may have variable lengths, you can only access a specific character by scanning from the start of the string. If you want operations that change the characters in the string you have to uncompress the string, make the changes, and recompress it.

It requires *programmer discipline* to use compressed strings, especially for string literals within the program code. Compressed strings require either manual encoding or a string pre-processing pass, either of which increases complexity.

You have to *test* the compressed string operations, but these tests are quite straightforward.

❖   ❖   ❖

Implementation

There are many techniques used for table compression (Witten et al. 1999). The following sections explore a few common ones.

1. Simple coding

If the underlying character set has only 128 characters, such as ASCII, it certainly makes sense to store each character in 7 bits, rather than 8, 16, or 32 bits. But, as we discussed above, in fact a large proportion of normal text could be encoded in just 4 bits. Other non-European languages might be better with 5 or 6 bits.

If you encode most of the text into, say, small fixed-size characters, what do you do with the characters not within the most common set? The answer is to use *escape codes*. An escape code is a special character that changes the meaning of the following character (or sometimes of the characters up to the next escape code).

For example, a common simple coding technique is to use a *nibble code*, where each character is coded into 4 bits. A nibble code is easy to implement, because a nibble is always half a byte, making it easy to write the packed data. In a basic nibble code, we might have only one escape code, which is followed by the 8-bit ASCII code of the next character. So using the data in Figure 3.2 above to deduce the most common characters, we can construct an encoding and decoding table (Table 3.1).

Table 3.1   Encoding and decoding table

Plain text	Encoded nibbles	Encoded bits
—	0	0000
a	4	0100
b	F 6 1	1111 0110 0001
c	F 6 2	1111 0110 0010
d	D	1101
e	1	0001
f	F 6 5	1111 0110 0101
. . . etc		

Thus the phrase 'All the world's a stage' would encode as shown in Figure 3.3.

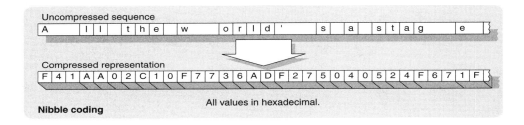

Figure 3.3   Encoding 'All the world's a stage'

Using this nibble code, 75% of characters in this chapter can be encoded in 4 bits; the remainder all require 12 bits. On this simple calculation the average number of bits required per character is 6 bits; when we implemented the nibble code and tested it on the file, we achieved 5.4 bits per character in practice.

2. Huffman coding

Why choose specifically 4 bits for the most common characters and 12 bits for the escaped characters? It would seem more sensible to have a more even spread, so that the most common characters (e.g. space) use fewer than 4 bits, fairly common characters ('u', 'w') require between 4 and 8 bits, and only the least common ones ('Q', '&') require more. Huffman coding takes this reasoning to its extreme. With Huffman coding, the 'Encoded bits' column in Table 3.1 will contain bit values of arbitrary lengths instead of either 4 or 12 (Huffman 1952).

Decoding Huffman data is a little trickier. Since you can't just look up an unknown length bit string in an array, Huffman tables are often represented as trees for decoding; each terminal node in the tree is a decoded character. To decode a bit string, you start at the root, then take the left node for each 1 and the right node for each 0. So, for example, if you had the following simple encoding table for a 4-character alphabet, where A is the most frequent character in your text, then D, then B and C:

Plain text	Encoded bits
A	1
B	010
C	011
D	00

this can be represented as a Huffman tree as shown in Figure 3.4.

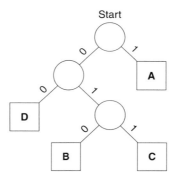

Figure 3.4   Huffman tree

For more about Huffman coding — more efficient decoding techniques and a discussion on generating the Huffman encoding tables — see *Managing Gigabytes* (Witten et al. 1999) or any other standard reference on text compression.

3. Encoding more than just characters

There's no need to limit TABLE COMPRESSION to strings; anything that contains data items of fixed numbers of bytes can be compressed in this way. Other compression techniques, for example, often apply Huffman coding to their intermediate representations to increase their compression ratios (see, for example, the ADAPTIVE COMPRESSION (160) technique GZIP).

TABLE COMPRESSION does not have to be restricted to compressing fixed-length items, as long as each item has a clearly defined end. For example, Huffman Word Compression achieves very high compression ratios (3 bits per character or so) by encoding each word separately (Witten et al. 1999). To achieve this ratio, Huffman Word Compression requires a very large compression table — the size of the dictionary used.

4. Compressing string literals

Compressed strings are more difficult to handle in program code. While programming languages provide string literals for normal strings, they do not generally support compressed strings. Most languages support escape codes (such as "\x34") that allow any numeric characters to be stored into the string. Escape codes can be used to store compressed strings in standard string literals. For example, here's a C++ string that stores the nibble codes for the 'All the world's a stage' encoding in Figure 3.3.

```
const char* AllTheWorldsAStage =
            "\xf4\x1a\xa0\x2c\x10\xf7\x73\x6a\xdf\x27\x50\x40\x52\x4f\x67\x1f";
```

You can also write a pre-processor to work through program texts, and replace standard encoded strings with compressed strings. This works particularly well when compressed strings can be written as standard string or array literals. Alternatively, in systems that store strings in RESOURCE FILES (101), the resource file compiler can compress the string, and the resource file reader can decompress it.

5. UTF8 encoding

To support internationalization, an increasing number of applications do all their internal string handling using 2-byte character sets — typically the Unicode standard (Unicode 1996). Given that the character sets for most European languages require fewer than 128 characters, the extra byte is clearly redundant. For storage and transmission, many environments encode Unicode strings using the UTF8 encoding.

In UTF8, each Unicode double byte is encoded into 1, 2 or 3 bytes (though the standard supports further extensions). The coding encodes the bits as follows:

Unicode value	1st byte	2nd byte	3rd byte
000000000xxxxxxx	0xxxxxxx		
00000yyyyyxxxxxx	110yyyyy	10xxxxxx	
Zzzzyyyyyyxxxxxx	1110zzzz	10yyyyyy	10xxxxxx

So in UTF8, the standard 7-bit ASCII characters are encoded in a single byte; in fact, the Unicode encoding is exactly the same as the 1-byte ASCII encoding for these characters. Common extended characters are encoded as 2 bytes, with only the least common characters requiring 3 bytes. Every UTF8 character starts and ends on a byte boundary, so you can identify a substring within a larger buffer of UTF8 characters using just a byte offset and a length.

UTF8 was designed to be especially suitable for transmission along serial connections. A terminal receiving UTF8 characters can always determine which byte represents the start of a Unicode character, because either their top bit is 0, or the top two bits are '11'. Any UTF8 bytes with the top bits equal to '10' are always second or third in sequence and should be ignored unless the terminal has received the initial byte.

Example

This example implements a nibble code to compress the text in this chapter. Figure 3.5 shows the distribution of characters in the text, sorted by frequency, with the 15 most common characters to the left of the vertical line.

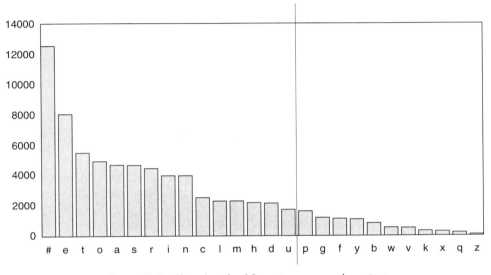

Figure 3.5 Choosing the 15 most common characters

Here is a Java example that implements this nibble code. The StringCompression class uses a byte array output stream to simplify creating the compressed string — the equivalent in C++ would use an ostrstream instance. The most common characters are represented in the string NibbleChars:

```
protected final String NibbleChars = "etoasrinclmhdu";
protected final int NibbleEscape = 0xf;
protected int lastNibble;
protected ByteArrayOutputStream outStream;
```

The encodeString method takes each fixed-size character and encodes it, character by character. This function has to deal with end effects, ensuring the last nibble gets written to the output file by padding it with an escape character.

```
protected byte[] encodeString(String string) {
        outStream = new ByteArrayOutputStream();
        lastNibble = -1;
        for (int i = 0; i < string.length(); i++) {
          encodeChar(string.charAt(i));
        }
```

```
    if (lastNibble != -1) {
            putNibble(NibbleEscape);
    }
    byte[] result = outStream.toByteArray();
    outStream = null;
    return result;
}
```

The most important routine encodes a specific character. The `encodeChar` method searches the `NibbleChars` string directly; if the character to be encoded is in the string it is output as a nibble, otherwise we output an escape code and a high and low nibble. A more efficient implementation could use a 256-entry lookup table.

```
protected void encodeChar(int charCode) {
    int possibleNibble = NibbleChars.indexOf(charCode);
    if (possibleNibble != -1) {
      putNibble(possibleNibble);
    } else {
      putNibble(NibbleEscape);
      putNibble(charCode >>> 4);
      putNibble(charCode & 0xf);
    }
}
```

The `putNibble` method simply adds one nibble to the output stream. We can only write whole bytes, rather than nibbles, so the `lastNibble` variable stores a nibble that has not been output. When another nibble is received, both `lastNibble` and the current nibble n can be written as a single byte:

```
protected void putNibble(int nibble) {
    if (lastNibble == -1) {
      lastNibble = nibble;
    } else {
      outStream.write((lastNibble << 4) + nibble);
      lastNibble = -1;
    }
}
```

Decoding is similar to encoding. For convenience, the decoding methods belong to the same class; they use a `ByteArrayInputStream` to retrieve data. The `decodeString` method reads a character at a time and appends it to the output:

```
protected ByteArrayInputStream inStream;

protected String decodeString(byte [] inBuffer) {
   inStream = new ByteArrayInputStream(inBuffer);
   StringBuffer outString = new StringBuffer();
   lastNibble = -1;
```

```
      int charRead;
      while ((charRead = decodeChar()) != -1) {
        outString.append((char)charRead);
      }
      return outString.toString();
  }
```

The decodeChar method reads as many input nibbles as are required to compose a single character.

```
  protected int decodeChar() {
      int s = getNibble();
      if (s == -1) return -1;
      if (s != NibbleEscape) {
        return NibbleChars.charAt(s);
      } else {
        s = getNibble();
        if (s == - -1) return -1;
        return (s << 4) + getNibble();
      }
  }
```

Method getNibble actually returns one nibble from the input stream, again keeping the extra nibble in the lastNibble field when a full byte is read but only one nibble returned.

```
  protected int decodeChar() {
      int nibble = getNibble();
      if (nibble == -1) {
        return -1;
      }
      if (nibble != NibbleEscape) {
        return NibbleChars.charAt(nibble);
      } else {
        nibble = getNibble();
        if (nibble == -1) {
            return -1;
        }
        return (nibble << 4) + getNibble();
      }
  }
```

Nibble encoding can be surprisingly effective. For example, a text-only version of this chapter compresses to just 5.4 bits per char (67%) using this technique. Similarly, the complete set of text resources for a release of the EPOC32 operating system would compress to 5.7 bits per character (though as the total space occupied by the strings is only 44 Kb, the effort and extra code required have so far not been worthwhile).

Known uses

Reuters' worldwide IDN network uses Huffman encoding to reduce the bandwidth required to transmit all the world's financial market prices worldwide. The IDN Huffman code table is reproduced and reimplemented in many different systems.

GZIP uses Huffman encoding as part of the compression process, though their main compression gains are from ADAPTIVE COMPRESSION (160) (Deutsch 1996).

The MNP5 and V42.bis modem compression protocols use Huffman encoding to get compression ratios of 75% to 50% on typical transmitted data (Held 1994).

Nibble codes were widely used in versions of text adventure games for small machines (Blank and Galley 1980). Philip Gage used a similar technique to compress an entire string table (Gage 97). Symbian's EPOC16 operating system for the Series 3 used table compression for its RESOURCE FILES (101) (Edwards 1997).

Variants of UTF8 encoding are used in Java, Plan 9, and Windows NT to store Unicode characters (Unicode 1996; Lindholm and Yellin 1999, Pike and Thompson 1993).

See also

Many variants of table compression also use ADAPTIVE COMPRESSION (160), calculating the optimal table for each large section of data and including the table with the compressed data.

Compressed strings can be stored in RESOURCE FILES (101) in SECONDARY STORAGE (79) or READ-ONLY MEMORY (65), as well as primary storage. Information stored in DATA FILES (92) can also be compressed.

Witten et al. (1999) and Cyganski et al. (1998) discuss Huffman encoding and other forms of TABLE COMPRESSION in much more detail than we can give here. Witten et al. also include discussions of memory and time costs for each technique.

Business Data Communications and Networking (Fitzgerald and Dennis 1995) provides a good overview of modem communications. Sharon Tabor's course materials for *Data Transmission* (2000) provide a good terse summary. The *Ultimate Modem Handbook* includes an outline of various modem compression standards (Lewart 1999).

Difference Coding

Also known as: Delta Coding, Run-Length Encoding

How can you reduce the memory used by sequences of data?

- You need to reduce your program's memory requirements.
- You have large streams of data in your program.
- The data streams will be accessed sequentially.
- There are significant time or financial costs of storing or transferring data.

Many programs use sequences or series of data — for example, sequential data such as audio files or animations, time series such as stock market prices, values read by a sensor, or simply the sequence of bytes making up program code. All these sequences increase the program's memory requirements, or worsen the transmission time using a telecommunications link.

This sort of streamed data is usually accessed sequentially, beginning at the first item and then processing each item in turn. Programs rarely or never require random access into the middle of the data. Although storing the data is important, it often isn't the largest problem you have to face — gathering the data is often much more work than simply storing it. Typically, you don't want to devote too much programmer effort, processing time, or temporary memory to the compression operations.

For example, the Strap-It-On PC needs to store results collected from the Snoop-Tronic series of body well-being monitors. These monitors are attached onto strategic points on the wearer's body, and regularly measure and record various physiological, psychological, psychiatric, and psychotronic metrics (heartbeats, blood-sugar levels, alpha-waves, influences from the planet Gorkon, etc.). This information needs to be stored in the background while the Strap-It-On is doing other work, so the recording process should not require much processor time or memory space. The recording is continuous, gathering data whenever the Strap-It-On PC and Snoop-Tronic sensors are worn and the wearer is alive, so large amounts of data are recorded. Somehow, we must reduce the memory requirements of this data.

Therefore: **Represent sequences according to the differences between each item.**

Continuous data sequences are rarely truly random — the recent past is often an excellent guide to the near future. So in many sequences:

- the values don't change very much between adjacent items, and
- there are runs, where there is no change for several elements.

These features result in two complementary techniques to reduce the number of bits stored per item:

- Delta Coding stores just differences between each successive item.
- Run-Length Encoding (RLE) replaces a run of identical elements with a repeat count.

For example, in the data stored by the Snoop-Tronic monitors, the values read are very close or the same for long periods of time. The Strap-It-On PC's driver for the Snoop-Tronic sensors uses sequence coding on the data streams as they arrive from each sensor, buffers the data, and stores it to secondary storage — without imposing a noticeable overhead on the performance of the system.

Consequences

Difference compression can achieve an excellent compression ratio for many kinds of data (particularly cartoon-style picture data and some forms of sound data), reducing the program's *memory requirements*. Sequential operations on the compressed data can execute almost as fast as operations on native values, preserving *time performance* and *real-time responsiveness,* and considerably improving *time performance* if there are slow disk or telecommunication links involved.

Difference compression is quite easy to implement, so it does not take much *programmer effort*, or extra *temporary memory*.

However: The compressed sequences are more difficult to manage than sequences of absolute data values. In particular, it is difficult to provide random access into the middle of compressed sequences without first uncompressing them, requiring *temporary memory* and *processing time*.

Some kinds of data — such as hi-fi sound or photographic images — don't reduce significantly with DIFFERENCE CODING.

You have to *test* the compressed sequence operations, but these tests are quite straightforward.

Implementation

Here are several difference coding techniques that you can consider.

1. Delta coding

Delta coding (or difference coding) stores differences between adjacent items, rather than the absolute values of the items themselves (Bell et al. 1990). Delta coding saves memory space because deltas can often be stored in smaller amounts of memory than absolute values. For example, you may be able to encode a slowly varying stream of 16-bit values using only 8-bit delta codes.

Of course, the range of values stored in the delta code is less than the range of the absolute item values (16-bit items range from 0 to 65536, while 8-bit deltas give you ± 127). If the difference to be stored is larger than the range of delta codes, typically the encoder uses an escape code (a special delta value, say –128 for an 8-bit code) followed by the full absolute value of the data item.

Figure 3.6 shows such a sequence represented using delta coding. All values are in decimal, and the escape code is represented as '■'.

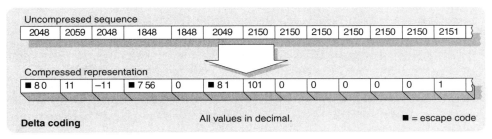

Figure 3.6   Delta coding

2. Run-length encoding

Run-length encoding (RLE) compresses a run of duplicated items by storing the value of the duplicated items once, followed by the length of the run (Bell et al. 1990). For example, we can extend the delta code above to compress runs by always following the escape code by a count byte as well as the absolute value. Runs of between 4 and 256 items can be compressed as the escape code, the absolute value of the repeated item, and the count. Runs of longer than 256 items can be stored as repeated runs of 256 characters, plus one more run of the remainder. Figure 3.7 shows RLE added to the previous example.

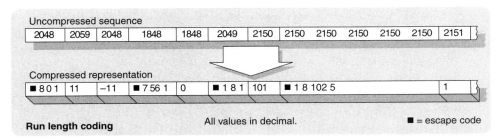

Figure 3.7   Run-length encoding and delta coding

3. Lossy difference compression

Here are some common techniques that increase the compression ratio of DIFFER-ENCE CODING by losing some of the information compressed:

1. You can treat a sequence with only negligible differences in values as if it was a run of items with identical values. For example, in the data series above, differences within a quarter of a percent of the absolute value of the data items may not be significant in the analysis. Quite possibly they could be due to noise in the recording sensor or the ambient temperature when the data item was recorded. A quarter of one percent of 2000 is 20 — so we can code the first three items as a run.

2. You can handle large jumps in delta values by allowing a lag in catching up. Thus, for example, the difference of 200 between 2048 and 1848 can be represented as two deltas, rather than an escape code.

Using these two techniques, we can code the example sequence as shown in Figure 3.8.

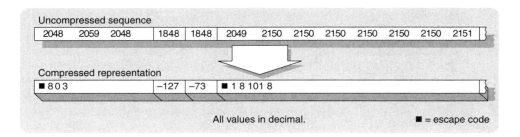

Figure 3.8 Lossy difference coding

3. You can increase the granularity of the delta values, so that each delta value is scaled by the magnitude of the items they are representing. So, for example, each delta step could be the nearest integer below 0.25% of the previous item's value, allowing much larger deltas.

4. Resynchronization

DIFFERENCE CODING algorithms are often used for broadcast communications and serial or network connections. In many cases, particularly with multimedia data streams, it doesn't matter very much if part of the sequence is lost or corrupted, so long as later data can be read correctly. Because difference codes assume the receiver knows the correct value for the last item (so that the next item can be computed by adding the difference), one wrong delta means that every subsequent delta will produce the wrong value. To avoid this problem, you can include resynchronization information; every now and again you can send a complete value as escape code, instead of a delta. The escape code resets the value of the current item, correcting any accumulated error due to corruption or lost data.

5. Non-numeric data

Difference coding can also be very effective at compressing non-numeric data structures. In delta coding, the deltas will be structures themselves; for RLE represents events where the structures haven't changed. For example, you can think some forms of the **OBSERVER** pattern (Gamma et al. 1995) as examples of delta compression: the observer is told only the changes that have happened.

Similarly, you can do run-length encoding using a count of a number of identical structures. For example, the X Window System can return a single compressed mouse movement event that represents a number of smaller movements — the compressed event contains a count of the number of uncompressed movements it represents (Scheifler and Gettys 1986).

Examples

The following Java example compresses a sequence of 2-byte values into a sequence of bytes using both difference compression and run-length encoding. The compression is lossless, and the only escape sequence contains both the complete value and the sequence length. As above, the bytes of the escape sequence are:

```
<escape> <high byte of repeated value> <low byte> <sequence count>
```

The encodeSequence method takes a sequence of shorts, and passes each one to the encodeShort method, which will actually encode them:

```
protected final int SequenceEscape = 0xff;
protected final int MaxSequenceLength = 0xfe;
protected short lastShort;
protected short runLength;

protected void encodeSequence(short[] inputSequence) {
    lastShort = 0;
    runLength = 0;

    for (int i = 0; i < inputSequence.length; i++) {
      encodeShort(inputSequence[i]);
    }
    flushSequence();
}
```

The encodeShort method does most of the work. It first checks if its argument is part of a sequence of identical values, and if so, simply increases the run-length count for the sequence — if the sequence is now the maximum length that can be represented, an escape code is written. If its argument is within the range of the delta coding (± 128 from the last value) an escape code is written if necessary, and a delta code is written. Finally, if the argument is outside the range, an escape code is written to terminate the current run-length encoded sequence if necessary. In any event, the current argument is remembered in the lastShort variable.

```
protected void encodeShort(short s) {
    if (s == lastShort) {
        runLength++;
        if (runLength >= MaxSequenceLength) {
            flushSequence();
        }
    } else if (Math.abs(s - lastShort) < 128 ) {
        flushSequence();
        writeEncodedByte(s - lastShort + 128);
    } else {
        flushSequence();
        runLength++;
    }
    lastShort = s;
}
```

The flushSequence method simply writes out the escape codes, if required, and resets the run length. It is called whenever a sequence may need to be written out — whenever encodeShort detects the end of the current sequence, or that the current sequence is the longest that can be represented by the run-length escape code.

```
protected void flushSequence() {
    if (runLength == 0) return;
    writeEncodedByte(SequenceEscape);
    writeEncodedByte(lastShort >>> 8);
    writeEncodedByte(lastShort & 0xff);
    writeEncodedByte(runLength);
    runLength = 0;
}
```

The corresponding decoding functions are straightforward. If an escape code is read, a run of output values is written, and if a delta code is read, a single output is written which differs from the last output value by the delta.

```
protected void decodeSequence(byte() inBuffer) {
    ByteArrayInputStream inStream =
        new ByteArrayInputStream(inBuffer);
    lastShort = 0;
    int byteRead;

    while ((byteRead = inStream.read()) != -1) {
        byteRead = byteRead & 0xff;

        if (byteRead == SequenceEscape) {
            lastShort = (short) (((inStream.read() &0xff ) << 8) +
                                 (inStream.read() & 0xff));
```

```
          for (int c = inStream.read(); c > 0; c --) {
            writeDecodedShort(lastShort);
          }
        } else {
          writeDecodedShort(lastShort += byteRead --128);
        }
      }
    }
```

❖   ❖   ❖

Known uses

Many image compression techniques use DIFFERENCE CODING. The TIFF image file format uses RLE to encode runs of identical pixels (Adobe 1992. The GIF and PNG formats do the same after (lossy) colour mapping (CompuServe 1990, Boutell 1996). The Group 3 and 4 Fax transmission protocols use RLE to encode the pixels on a line (Gonzalez and Woods 1992); the next line (in fine mode) or three lines (in standard mode) are encoded as differences from the first line.

MPEG video compression uses a variety of techniques to express each picture as a set of differences from the previous one (MPEG; Kinnear 1999). The V.42bis modem compression standard includes RLE and TABLE COMPRESSION (143) (Huffman coding), achieving a total compression ratio of up to 33% (Held 1994).

Many window systems in addition to X use run-length encoding to compress events. For example, MS Windows represents multiple mouse movements and key auto-repeats in this way, and EPOC's Window Server does the same (Petzold 1998, Symbian 1999).

Reuter's IDN system broadcasts the financial prices from virtually every financial exchange and bank in the world, aiming — and almost always succeeding — in transmitting every update to every interested subscriber in under a second. To make this possible, IDN represents each 'instrument' as a logical data structure identified by a unique name (Reuters Identification Code); when the contents of the instrument (prices, trading volume etc.) change, IDN transmits only the changes. To save expensive satellite bandwidth further, these changes are transmitted in binary form using Huffman coding (see TABLE COMPRESSION), and to ensure synchronization of all the Reuters' systems worldwide, the system also transmits a background 'refresh' stream of the complete state of every instrument.

See also

You may want to use TABLE COMPRESSION in addition to, or instead of, DIFFERENCE CODING. If you have a large amount of data, you may be able to tailor your compression parameters (ADAPTIVE COMPRESSION (160)), or use a more powerful ADAPTIVE algorithm.

The references discussed in the previous patterns are equally helpful on the subject of DIFFERENCE CODING. Witten et al. (1999) explain image compression techniques and trade-offs; Cyganski et al. (1998) and Solari (1997) explain audio, graphical and video compression techniques, and Held (1994) discusses modem compression.

Adaptive Compression

How can you reduce the memory needed to store a large amount of bulk data?

- You have a large amount of data to store, transmit, or receive.

- You don't have enough persistent memory space to store the information long term, or you need to communicate the data across a slow telecommunications link.

- You have transient memory space for processing the data.

- You don't need random access to the data.

A high proportion of the memory requirements of many programs is devoted to bulk data. For example, the latest application planned for the Strap-It-On PC is ThemePark:UK, a tourist guide being produced in conjunction with the Unfriendly Asteroid travel consultancy. ThemePark:UK is based on existing ThemePark products, which guide users around theme parks in Southern California. ThemePark:UK will treat the whole of the UK as a single theme park; the Strap-It-On will use its Global Positioning System together with an internal database to present interactive travel guides containing videos, music, voice-overs, and genuine people personalities for cute interactive cartoon characters. Unfortunately the UK is a little larger than most theme parks, and the designers have found that using TABLE COMPRESSION (143) and DIFFERENCE CODING (153) together cannot cram enough information into the Strap-It-On's memory.

This kind of problem is common in applications requiring very large amounts of data, whether collections of documents and e-mails or representations of books and multimedia. Even if systems have sufficient main memory to be able to process or display the parts of the data they need at any given time, they may not have enough memory to store all the information they will ever need, either in main memory or in secondary storage.

Therefore: **Use an adaptive compression algorithm.**

ADAPTIVE COMPRESSION algorithms can analyse the data they are compressing and modify their behaviour accordingly. These adaptive compression algorithms can provide high compression ratios, and work in several ways:

- Many compression mechanisms require parameters, such as the table required for TABLE COMPRESSION or the parameters to decide what data to discard with lossy forms of compression. An adaptive algorithm can analyse the data it's about to compress, choose parameters accordingly, and store the parameters at the start of the compressed data.

- Other adaptive techniques adjust their parameters 'on the fly', according to the data compressed so far. For example Move-To-Front (or MTF) transformations change the table used in, say, Nibble Compression, so that the table of codes translating to the minimum (4-bit) representation is always the set of most recently seen characters.

- Further techniques, predominantly the Lempel-Ziv family of algorithms, use the stream of data already encoded as a string table to provide a compact encoding for each string newly received.

Implementations of many ADAPTIVE COMPRESSION algorithms are available publicly, either as free or open source software, or from commercial providers.

For example, ThemePark:UK uses the *gzip* adaptive file compression algorithm for its text pages, which achieves typical compressions of 2.5 bits per character for English text, and requires fairly small amounts of RAM memory for decoding. ThemePark:UK also uses JPEG compression for its images, PNG compression for its maps and cartoons, and MP3 compression for sounds.

Consequences

Modern ADAPTIVE COMPRESSION algorithms provide excellent compression ratios, reducing your *memory requirements*. They are widely used and are incorporated into *popular industry standards* for bulk data.

Adaptive compression can also reduce *data transmission times* for telecommunication. File compression can also reduce the *secondary storage* requirements or *data transmission times* for program code.

However: ADAPTIVE COMPRESSION can require a significant *processing time* to compress and decompress large bulk data sets, and so is generally unsuitable for *real-time work*. Some *temporary memory* (primary and secondary storage) will be necessary to store the decompressed results and to hold intermediate structures.

The performance of compression algorithms can vary depending on the type of data being compressed, so you have to select your algorithm carefully, requiring *programmer effort*. If you cannot reuse an existing implementation you will need significant further *programmer effort* to code up one of these algorithms, because they can be quite complex. Some of the most important algorithms are *patented*, although you may able to use non-patented alternatives.

❖   ❖   ❖

Implementation

Designing efficient and effective ADAPTIVE COMPRESSION algorithms is a very specialized task, especially as the compression algorithms must be tailored to the type of data being compressed. For most practical uses, however, you do not need to design your own compression algorithms, as libraries of compression algorithms are available both commercially and under various open source licences. Sun's Java, for example, now officially includes a version of the *zlib* compression library, implementing the same compression algorithm as the *pkzip* and *gzip* compression utilities. In most programs, compressing and decompressing files or blocks of data is as simple as calling the appropriate routine from one of these libraries.

1. LZ compression

Many of the most effective compression schemes are variants of a technique devised by Ziv and Lempel (1977). Lempel-Ziv (LZ77) compression uses the data already encoded as a table to allow a compact representation of following data. LZ compression is easy to implement; and decoding is fast and requires little extra temporary memory.

LZ77 works by encoding sequences of tuples. In each tuple, the first two items reference a string previously coded — as an offset from the current position, and a length. The third item is a single character. If there's no suitable string previously coded, the first two items are zero. For example, Figure 3.9 shows the LZ77 encoding of the song chorus 'do do ron ron ron do do ron ron'.

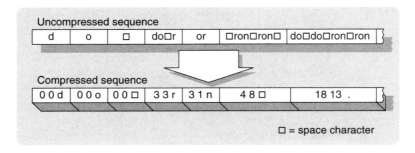

Figure 3.9 LZ77 compression

Note how the repeating sequence 'ron ron' is encoded as a single tuple; this works fine for decompression and requires only a small amount of extra effort in the compression code.

There are many variants of LZ compression, adding other forms of compression to the output, or tailored for fast or low-memory compression or decompression. For example, GZIP encodes blocks of 64 Kb at a time, and uses Huffman coding to compress the offset and length fields of each tuple still further.

Examples

We examine two examples of adaptive compression. The first, MTF compression, is a simple adaptive extension of TABLE COMPRESSION. The second, more typical of real-world applications, simply uses a library to do compression and decompression for us.

1. MTF compression

Move-To-Front (MTF) compression can adapt Nibble Compression to the data being encoded, by changing the compression table dynamically so that it always contains the 15 most recently used characters (Bell et al. 1990). The following code shows only the significant changes from the Nibble Coding example in TABLE COMPRESSION.

First, we need a modifiable version of the table. As with the fixed version, it can be a simple string.

```
protected String NibbleChars = " etoasrinclmhdu";
```

To start off, we set the table to be a best guess, so both the encodeString and decodeString methods start by resetting currentChars to the value NibbleChars (not shown here). Then we simply need to modify the table after encoding each character, by calling the new method updateCurrent in encodeChar:

```
protected void encodeChar(int charCode) {
    int possibleNibble = NibbleChars.indexOf(charCode);
    if (possibleNibble != -1) {
      putNibble(possibleNibble);
    } else {
      putNibble(NibbleEscape);
      putNibble(charCode >>> 4);
      putNibble(charCode & 0xf);
    }
    updateCurrent((char) charCode);
  }
```

The updateCurrent method updates the current table, by moving the current character to the front of the table. If that character is already in the table, it gets pushed to the front; if not, then the last (least recently used) character is discarded:

```
protected void updateCurrent(int c) {
    int position = NibbleChars.indexOf(c);
    if (position != -1) {
      NibbleChars = "" + c + NibbleChars.substring(0, position) +
          NibbleChars.substring(position+1);
    } else {
      position = NibbleChars.length() - 1;
      NibbleChars = "" + c + NibbleChars.substring(0, position);
    }
}
```

The decodeChar needs to do the same update for each character decoded:

```
protected int decodeChar() {
  int result;
  int nibble = getNibble();
  if (nibble == -1) {
    return -1;
  }
  if (nibble != NibbleEscape) {
    result = NibbleChars.charAt(nibble);
  } else {
    nibble = getNibble();
    if (nibble == -1) {
      return -1;
    }
    result = (nibble << 4) + getNibble();
  }
  updateCurrent(result);
  return result;
}
```

This example doesn't achieve as much compression as the fixed table for typical English text; for the text of this chapter it achieves only 6.2 bits per character. The MTF version does achieve some degree of compression on almost any non-random form of text, however, including executable binaries.

2. ZLIB compression

This example uses an existing compression library, and so is more typical of real-world applications of ADAPTIVE COMPRESSION. The Java Zlib libraries provide compressing streams that are DECORATORS of existing streams (Gamma et al. 1995; Chan et al. 1998). This makes it easy to compress any data that can be implemented as a stream. To compress some data, we open a stream on that data, and pass it through a compressing stream and then to an output stream.

```
protected static byte() encodeSequence(byte() inputSequence)
      throws IOException {
    InputStream inputStream = new ByteArrayInputStream(inputSequence);
    ByteArrayOutputStream outputStream = new ByteArrayOutputStream();
    GZIPOutputStream out = new GZIPOutputStream(outputStream);

    byte[] buf = new byte[1024];
    int len;
    while ((len = inputStream.read(buf)) > 0) {
      out.write(buf, 0, len);
    }
    out.close();
    return outputStream.toByteArray();
}
```

In this model, decompressing is much like compressing. This time, the compressing stream is on the reading side; but in all other respects the code is virtually the same.

```
protected static byte[] decodeSequence(byte[] s) throws IOException {
    GZIPInputStream inputStream =
      new GZIPInputStream(new ByteArrayInputStream(s));
    ByteArrayOutputStream outputStream =
      new ByteArrayOutputStream();

    byte[] buf = new byte[1024];
    int len;
    while ((len = inputStream.read(buf)) > 0) {
      outputStream.write(buf, 0, len);
    }
    outputStream.close();
    return outputStream.toByteArray();
}
```

Known uses

Lempel-Ziv and variant compression algorithms are an industry standard, evidenced by the many PKZip and gzip file compression utilities used to reduce the size of e-mail attachments, or to archive little-used or old versions of files and directories (Ziv and Lempel 1977, Deutsch 1996).

The PDF format for device-independent images uses LZ compression to reduce its file sizes (Adobe 1999). Each PDF file contains one or more streams, each of which may be compressed with LZ.

ADAPTIVE COMPRESSION is also used architecturally in many systems. Linux kernels can be stored compressed and are decompressed when the system boots, and MS Windows NT supports optional file compression for each disk volume (Ward 1999, Microsoft NT 1997a). Java's JAR format uses `gzip` compression (Chan et al. 1998), although designing alternative class file formats specially to be compressed can give two to five times better compression than `gzip` applied to the standard class file format (Horspool and Corless 1998; Pugh 1999). Some backup tape formats use compression, notably the Zip and Jaz drives, and the HTTP protocol allows any web server to compress data, though as far as we are aware this feature is little used (Fielding et al. 1999).

The current state-of-the-art library for adaptive file compression, Bzip2, achieves typical compressions of 2.3 bits per character on English text by transforming the text data before using LZ compression (Burrows and Wheeler 1994). BZip2 requires a couple of Mbytes of RAM to compress effectively. See Witten et al. (1999) and BZip2's home page (BZip2) for more detail.

See also

Table Compression (143) and Difference Coding (153) are often used with, or as part of, adaptive compression algorithms. You may also need to read a file a bit at a time (Data Files (92)) to compress it.

Text Compression (Bell et al. 1990) and *Managing Gigabytes* (Witten et al. 1999) describe and analyse many forms of adaptive compression, including LZ compression, arithmetic coding and many others.

SMALL DATA STRUCTURES

Packed Data

Sharing

Copy-on-Write

Embedded Pointers

Multiple Representations

4

SMALL DATA STRUCTURES

How can you reduce the memory needed for your data?

- The memory requirements of the data exceed the memory available to the system.

- You want to increase usability by allowing users to store as much of their data as possible.

- You need to be able to predict the program's use of memory.

- You cannot delete some of the data from the program.

The fundamental difference between code and data is that programmers care about code while users care about data. Programmers have some direct control over the size of their code (after all, they write it), but the data size is often completely out of the programmers' control. Indeed, given that a system is supposed to store users' data, any memory allocated to code, buffers, or other housekeeping is really overhead as far as the user is concerned. Often the amount of memory available to users can make or break a system's usability — a word processor that can store a hundred-thousand-word document is much more useful than one that can only store a hundred words.

Data structures that are appropriate where memory is unrestricted may be far too prodigal where memory is limited. For example, a typical implementation of an address database might store copies of information in indexes as well as the actual data, effectively storing everything in the database twice. Porting such an approach to the Strap-It-On wrist-top PC would halve the number of addresses that could be stored in the database.

Techniques like COMPRESSION (135) and using SECONDARY STORAGE (79) can reduce a program's main memory requirements, but both have significant liabilities when used to manage the data a program needs to work on. Many kinds of compressed data cannot be accessed randomly; if random access is required the data must be uncompressed first, costing time, and requiring a large amount of buffer memory for the uncompressed data. Data stored on SECONDARY STORAGE is similarly inaccessible, and needs to be copied into main memory buffers before it can be accessed.

Therefore: **Choose the smallest structure that supports the operations you need.**

For any given data set there are many different possible data structures that might support it. Suppose, for example, you need an unordered collection of object references with no duplicates — in mathematical terms, a set. You could implement it using a linear array of pointers, using a hash table, or using a variety of tree structures. Most class libraries will provide several different implementations of such collections; the best one to choose depends on your requirements. Where memory is limited, therefore, you must be particularly careful to choose a structure to minimize the program's memory requirements.

You can think of data structure design as a three-stage process. First, analyse the program's requirements to determine the information the program needs to store; unnecessary information requires no memory!

Second, analyse the characteristics of the data; what's its total volume; how does it vary over a single program run and across different runs; and what's its granularity — does it consist of a few large objects or many small objects? You can also analyse the way you'll access the data: whether it is read and written, or only ever read; whether it is accessed sequentially or randomly; whether elements are inserted into the middle of the data or only added at the end.

Third, choose the data structures. Consider as many different possibilities as you can — your standard class libraries will provide some basic building blocks, but consider also options such as embedding objects (**FIXED ALLOCATION** (226)), **EMBEDDED POINTERS** (198), or **PACKED DATA** (174). For each candidate of data structure design, work out the amount of memory it will require to store the data you need, and check that it can support all the operations you need to perform. Then consider the benefits and disadvantages of each design: for example, a smaller data structure may require more processing time to access, provide insufficient flexibility or give insufficient real-time performance. You'll need also to evaluate the resulting memory requirements for each possibility against the total amount of memory available — in some cases you may need to do simple trials using scratch code. If none of the solutions are satisfactory you may need to go back and reconsider your earlier analysis, or even the requirements of the system as a whole. On the other hand there's no need to optimize memory use beyond your given requirements (see the **THRESHOLD SWITCH** pattern (Auer and Beck 1996)).

For example, the Strap-It-On address program has enough memory to store the address records but not indexes. So its version of the address program uses a sorted data structure that does not need extra space for an index but that is slower to access than the indexed version.

Consequences

Choosing suitable data structures can reduce a program's *memory requirements*, and the time spent can increase the *quality of the program's design*.

By increasing the amount of users' information the program can store, careful data structure design can increase a program's *usability*.

However: Analysing a program's requirements and optimizing data structure design takes *programmer discipline* to do, and *programmer effort* and time to do well.

Optimizing data structure designs to suit limited memory situations can restrict a program's *scalability* should more memory become available.

The *predictability* of the program's memory use, the *testing costs*, and the program's *time performance* may or may not be affected, depending upon the chosen structures.

❖   ❖   ❖

Implementation

Every data structure design for any program must trade off several fundamental forces: memory requirements, time performance, and programmer effort being the most important. Designing data structures for a system with tight memory constraints is no different in theory from designing data structures in other environments, but the practical trade-offs can result in different solutions. Typically, you are prepared to sacrifice time performance and put in more programmer effort than in an unconstrained system, in order to reduce the memory requirements of the data structure.

There are several particular issues to consider when designing data structures to minimize memory use.

1. Predictability versus Exhaustion

The predictability of a data structure's memory use, and ultimately of the whole program, can be as important as the structure's overall memory requirements, because making memory use more predictable makes it easier to manage. Predictability is closely related to the need to deal with memory exhaustion: if you can predict the program's maximum memory use in advance then you can use FIXED ALLOCATION (226) to ensure the program will never run out of memory.

2. Space versus Flexibility

Simple, static, inflexible data structures usually require less memory than more complex, dynamic, and flexible data structures. For example, you can implement a one-to-one relationship with a single pointer or even an inline object (see FIXED ALLOCATION), while a one-to-many relationship will require collection classes, arrays, or EMBEDDED POINTERS (198). Similarly, flexible collection classes require more memory than simple fixed-sized arrays, and objects with methods or virtual functions require more memory than simple records (C++ structs) without them. If you don't need flexibility, don't pay for it; use simple data structures that need less memory.

3. Calculate versus Store

Often you can reduce the amount of main memory you need by calculating information rather than storing it. Calculating information reduces a program's time performance and can increase its power consumption, but can also reduce its memory requirements. For example, rather than keeping an index into a data structure, you can traverse the whole data structure using a linear search. Similarly, the PRESENTER pattern (Vlissides 1998) describes how graphical displays can be redrawn from scratch rather than being updated incrementally using a complex object structure.

❖   ❖   ❖

Specialized patterns

This chapter contains five specialized patterns that describe a range of techniques for designing data structures to minimize memory requirements. Figure 4.1 shows the relationships between the patterns.

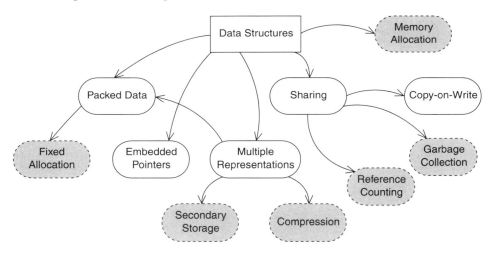

Figure 4.1   Data structure relationships

PACKED DATA (174) selects suitable internal representations of the data elements in an object, to reduce its memory footprint.

SHARING (182) removes redundant duplicated data. Rather than using multiple copies of functions, resources or data, the programmer can arrange to store only one copy, and use that copy wherever it is needed.

COPY-ON-WRITE (191) extends SHARING so that shared objects can be modified without affecting other client objects that use the shared objects.

EMBEDDED POINTERS (198) reduce the memory requirements for collection data structures, by eliminating auxiliary link objects and moving pointers into the data objects stored in the structures.

MULTIPLE REPRESENTATIONS (209) are effective when no single representation is simultaneously compact enough for storage yet efficient enough for actual use.

Known uses

Like Elvis, data structures are everywhere.

The classic example of designing data structures to save memory is the technique of allocating only two BCD digits to record the year when storing dates. This had unfortunate consequences, although not the disasters predicted in the lead-up to the millennium (Berry, Buck, Mills, Stipe 1987). Of course these data structure designs were often made with the best of motives: in the 1960s disk and memory were much more expensive than they are today; and allocating two extra characters per record could cost millions.

An object-oriented database built using Smalltalk needed to be scaled up to cope with millions of objects, rather than several thousand. Unfortunately, a back-of-the-envelope calculation showed that the existing design would require a ridiculous amount of disk space and thus buffer memory. Examination of the database design showed that Smalltalk Dictionary (hash table) objects occupied a large proportion of its memory; further investigation showed that these Dictionaries contained only two elements: a date and a time. Redesigning the database to use Smalltalk Timestamp objects that stored a date and time directly, rather than the dictionary, reduced the number of objects needed to store each timestamp from at least eight to three, and made the scaled-up database project feasible.

See also

Once you have designed your data structures, you then have to allocate the memory to store them. The MEMORY ALLOCATION (219) chapter presents a series of patterns describing how you can allocate memory in your programs.

In many cases, good data structure design alone is insufficient to manage your program's memory. The COMPRESSION (135) chapter describes how memory requirements can be reduced by explicitly spending processor time to build very compact representations of data that generally cannot be used directly in computations. Moving less important data into SECONDARY STORAGE and constant data into READ-ONLY MEMORY (65) can further reduce the demand for writable primary storage.

There are many good books describing data structure design in depth. Knuth (1997) remains a classic, though its examples are effectively in assembly language. Hoare (1972) is another seminal work, though nowadays difficult to find. Aho et al. (1983) is a standard text for university courses, with examples in a Pascal-style pseudo-code. Cormen et al. (1990) is a more in-depth Computer Science text, emphasizing the mathematical analysis of algorithms. Finally Segewick's series, beginning with *Algorithms* (1988), provides a more approachable treatment, with editions quoting source code in different languages — for example *Algorithms in C++* (Segewick 1999).

Packed Data

Also known as: Bit Packing

How can you reduce the memory needed to store a data structure?

- You have a data structure (a collection of objects) that has significant memory requirements.

- You need fast random access to every part of every object in the structure.

- You need to store the data in these objects in main memory.

No matter what else you do in your system, sooner or later you end up having to design the low-level data structures to hold the information your program needs. In an object-oriented language, you have to design some key classes whose objects store the basic data and provide the fundamental operations on that data. In a program of any size, although there may be only a few key data storage classes, there can be a large number of instances of these classes. Storing all these objects can require large amounts of memory, certainly much more than storing the code to implement the classes.

For example, the Strap-It-On's Insanity-Phone application needs to store all of the names and numbers in an entire local telephone directory (200,000 personal subscribers). All these names and numbers should just about fit into the Strap-It-On's memory, but would leave no room for the program that displayed the directory, let alone any other program in the wrist-top PC.

Because these objects (or data structures) are the core of your program, they need to be easily accessible as your program runs. In a program of any complexity, the objects will need to be accessed randomly (rather than in any particular order) and then updated. Taken together, random access with updating requires that the objects are stored in main memory.

You might consider using COMPRESSION (135) on each object or on a set of objects, but this would make processing slow and difficult, and makes random access to the objects using references almost impossible. Similarly, moving objects into SECONDARY STORAGE (79) is not feasible if the objects need to be accessed rapidly and frequently. Considering the Insanity-Phone example again, the data cannot be placed in the Strap-It-On's secondary memory because that would be too slow to access; and the data cannot be compressed effectively while maintaining random access because each record is too small to be compressed individually using standard adaptive compression algorithms.

Therefore: **Pack data items within the structure so that they occupy the minimum space.**

There are two ways to reduce the amount of memory occupied by an object:

1. Reduce the amount of memory required by each field in the object.

2. Reduce the amount of unused memory allocated between fields.

Consider each individual field in turn, and consider how much information that field really needs to store. Then, choose the smallest possible representation for that information. This may be the smallest suitable language-level data type, or even smaller, using different bits within, say, a machine word, to encode different data items.

Once you have analysed each field, analyse the class as a whole to ensure that extra memory is not allocated between fields. Compilers or assemblers often ensure that fields are aligned to take advantage of CPU instructions that make it easier to access aligned data, so, for example, all 2-byte fields may be stored at even addresses, and all 4-byte fields at addresses that are multiples of four. Aligning fields wastes the memory space between the end of one field and the start of the next (Figure 4.2).

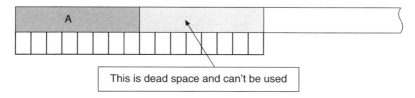

Figure 4.2   Wasted space caused by aligning fields

Figure 4.3 shows how packing an object can almost halve the amount of memory that it requires. The normal representation on the left allocates 4 bytes for each Boolean variable (presumably to use faster CPU instructions) and aligns 2- and 4-byte variables to 2- or 4-byte boundaries; the packed representation allocates only 1 byte for each Boolean variable and dispenses with alignment for longer variables.

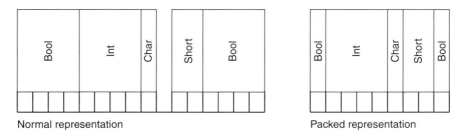

Figure 4.3   Saving memory by packing

Considering the Insanity-Phone again, the designers realized that local phone books never cover more than 32 area codes — so each entry requires only 5 bits to store the area code. A seven-digit decimal number requires 24 bits. Surnames are duplicated many times, so the Insanity-Phone stores each surname just once — an example of SHARING (182) — and therefore gets fewer than 30,000 unique names in each book; this requires 18 bits. Storing up to three initials (5 bits each — see TABLE COMPRESSION (143) costs a further 15 bits. The total is 62 bits, and this can be stored in one 64-bit long integer for each entry.

Consequences

Each instance occupies less memory, reducing the total *memory requirements* of the system, even though the same amount of data can be stored, updated, and accessed randomly. Choosing to pack one data structure is usually a *local* decision, with little *global* effect on the program as a whole.

However: The *time performance* of a system suffers, because CPUs are slower at accessing unaligned data. If accessing unaligned data requires many more instructions than aligned data, it can impact the program's *power consumption*. More complicated packing schemes such as bit packing can have even higher overheads.

Packing data requires *programmer effort* to implement, and produces less intuitive code which is harder to *maintain*, especially if you use non-standard data representations. More complicated techniques can increase *testing costs*.

Packing schemes that rely on particular aspects of a machine's architecture, such as word sizes or pointer formats, will reduce *portability*. If you're using non-standard internal representations, it is harder to exchange objects with other programs that expect standard representations.

Finally, packing can reduce *scalability*, because it can be difficult to unpack data structures throughout a system if more memory becomes available.

Implementation

The default implementation of a basic type is usually chosen for time performance rather than speed. For example, Boolean variables are often allocated as much space as integer variables, even though they need only a single bit for their representation. You can pack data by choosing smaller data types for variables; for example, you can represent Booleans using single byte integers or bit flags, and you may be able to replace full-size integers (32 or 64 bits) with 16- or even 8-bit integers (C++'s short and char types).

Compilers tend to align data members on machine-word boundaries, which wastes space (see Figure 4.2). Rearranging the order of the fields can minimize this padding, and can reduce the overhead when accessing non-aligned fields. A simple approach is to allocate fields within words in decreasing order of size.

Because packing has significant overheads in speed and maintainability, it is not worthwhile unless it will materially reduce the program's memory requirements. So, pack only the data structures that consume significant amounts of memory, rather than packing every class indiscriminately.

Here are some other issues to consider when applying the PACKED DATA pattern.

1. Compiler and language support

Compilers, assemblers and some programming language definitions support packing directly. Many compilers provide a compilation flag or directive that ensures all data structures use the tightest alignment for each item, to avoid wasted memory at the cost of slower runtime performance. In Microsoft C++, the directive:

```
#pragma pack(n)
```

sets the packing alignment to be based on n-byte boundaries, so pack(1) gives the tightest packing; the default packing is 8 (Microsoft 1996). G++ provides a pack attribute for individual fields to ensure they are allocated directly after the preceding field (Stallman 1999).

2. Packing objects into basic types

Objects can impose a large memory overhead, especially when they contain only a small amount of data. Java objects impose an allocation overhead of at least one additional pointer, and C++ objects with virtual functions require a pointer to a virtual function table. You can save memory by replacing objects by more primitive types (such as integers or pointers), an example of MULTIPLE REPRESENTATIONS (209).

When you need to process the data, wrap each primitive type in a first-class object, and use the object to process the data; when you've completed processing, discard the object, recover the basic type, and store it once again. To avoid allocating lots of wrapper objects, you can reuse the same wrapper for each primitive data item. The following Java code sketches how a BigObject can be repeatedly initialized from an array of integers for processing. The become method reinitializes a BigObject from its argument, and the process method does the work.

```
BigObject obj = new BigObject(0);

for (int i=1; i<10; i++) {
  obj.become(bigarray[i]);
  obj.process();
}
```

In C++, we can define operators to convert between objects and basic types, so that the two can be used interchangeably:

```
class BigIntegerObject {
public:
    BigIntegerObject(int anInt=0) : i(anInt) {}
    operator int() { return i; }
private:
    int i;
};

int main() {
    BigIntegerObject i(2), j(3);
    BigIntegerObject k = i*j; // Uses conversion operators
}
```

3. Packing pointers using tables

Packing pointers is more difficult, because they don't obviously contain redundant data. To pack pointers you need to look at what they reference.

If a given pointer may point to only one of a given set of items then it may be possible to replace the pointer with an index into an array; often, an array of pointers to the original item (Figure 4.4). Since the size of the array is usually much less than the size of all the memory in the system, the number of bits needed for an array index can be much less than the number of bits needed for a general pointer.

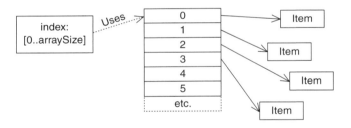

Figure 4.4   Index into an array

Take, for example, the Insanity-Phone application. Each entry apparently needs a pointer to the corresponding surname string: 32 bits, say. But if we implement an additional array of pointers into the string table, then each entry need only store an index into this array (16 bits). The additional index costs memory: 120 Kb using 4-byte pointers.

If you know that each item is guaranteed to be within a specific area of memory, then you can just store offsets within this memory. This might happen if you've built a string table, or if you're using POOLED ALLOCATION (251), or VARIABLE ALLOCATION (236) within a heap of known size. For example, if all the Insanity-Phone surname strings are stored in a contiguous table (requiring less than 200K with TABLE COMPRESSION (143)), the packed pointer need only hold the offset from the start of the table: 18 bits rather than 32.

4. Packing pointers using bitwise operations

If you are prepared to sacrifice portability, and have an environment such as C++ that allows you to manipulate pointers as integers, then you have several possible ways to pack pointers. In some architectures, pointers contain redundant bits that you do not need to store. Long pointers in the 8086 architecture had at least 8 redundant bits, for example, so could be stored in 3 bytes rather than 4.

You can further reduce the size of a pointer if you can use knowledge about the heap allocation mechanism, especially about alignment. Most memory managers allocate memory blocks aligned on word boundaries; if this is an 8-byte boundary, for example, then you can know that any pointer to a heap object will be a multiple of eight. In this case, the lowest 3 bits of each pointer are redundant, and can be reused or not stored. Many garbage collectors, for example, pack tag information into the low bits of their pointers (Jones and Lins 1996).

Example

Consider the following simple C++ class:

```
class MessageHeader {
    bool          inUse;
    int           messageLength;
    char          priority;
    unsigned      short channelNumber;
    bool          waitingToSend;
};
```

With 8-byte alignment, this occupies 16 bytes, using Microsoft C++ on MS Windows NT. With the compiler packing option turned on it occupies just 9 bytes. Note that the packed structure does not align the integer i1 to a 4-byte boundary, so on some processors it will take longer to load and store.

Even without compiler packing, we can still improve the memory use just by reordering the data items within the structure to minimize the gaps. If we sort the fields in decreasing order of size:

```
class ReorderedMessageHeader {
    int           messageLength;
    unsigned      short channelNumber;
    char          priority;
    bool          inUse;
    bool          waitingToSend;
};
```

the class occupies just 12 bytes, a saving of four bytes. If you're using compiler field packing, both MessageHeader and ReorderedMessageHeader occupy 9 bytes, but there's still a benefit to the latter since it puts all the member items on the correct machine boundaries where they can be manipulated fast.

We can optimize the structure even more using bitfields. The following version contains the same data as before:

```
class BitfieldMessageHeader {
    int       messageLength;
    unsigned  channelNumber:   16;
    unsigned  priority:         8;
    unsigned  inUse:            1;
    unsigned  waitingToSend:    1;

public:
    bool IsInUse() { return inUse; }
    void SetInUseFlag(bool isInUse) { inUse = isInUse; }
    char Priority() { return priority; }
    void SetPriority( char newPriority ) { priority = newPriority; }
    // etc.
};
```

but occupies just 8 bytes, a further saving of 4 bytes — or 1 byte if you're using compiler packing.

Unfortunately compiler support for Booleans in bitfields tends to be inefficient. This problem isn't actually a sad reflection on the quality of C++ compiler writers today; the real reason is that it requires a surprising amount of code to implement the semantics of, say, the SetInUseFlag function above. We can improve performance significantly by using bitwise operations instead of bitfields, and implement the member functions directly to expose these operations:

```
class BitwiseMessageHeader {
    int             messageLength;
    unsigned        short channelNumber;
    char            priority;
    unsigned        char flags;
public:
    enum FlagName { InUse = 0x01,  WaitingToSend = 0x02 };
    bool GetFlag(FlagName f)        { return (flags & f) != 0; }
    void SetFlag(FlagName f)        { flags |= f; }
    void ResetFlag(FlagName f)      { flags &= ~f; }
};
```

This optimizes performance, at the cost of exposing some of the implementation.

Known uses

Packed data is ubiquitous in memory-limited systems. For example, virtually all Booleans in the EPOC system are stored as bit flags packed into integers. The Pascal language standard includes a special PACKED data type qualifier, used to implement the original Pascal compiler.

To support dynamic binding, a C++ object normally requires a vtbl pointer to support virtual functions (Stroustrup 1995, 1997). EPOC requires dynamic binding to support MULTIPLE REPRESENTATIONS (209) for its string classes, but a vtbl pointer would impose a 4-byte overhead on every string. The EPOC string base class (TDesC) uses the top 4 bits of its 'string length' data member to identify the class of each object:

```
class TDesC8 {
private:
   unsigned int iLength:28;
   unsigned int iType:4;
   /* etc... */
```

Dynamically bound functions that depend on the actual string type are called from TDesC using a switch statement on the value of the iType bitfield.

Bit array classes are available in both the C++ Standard Template Library and the Java Standard Library. Both implement arrays of bits using arrays of machine words. Good implementations of the C++ STL also provide a template specialization to optimize the special case of an array of Booleans by using a bitset (Stroustrup 1997; Chan et al. 1998).

Java supports object wrapper versions for many primitive types (Integer, Float). Programmers typically use the basic types for storage and the object versions for complicated operations. Unfortunately Java collections store objects, not basic types, so every basic type must be wrapped before it is stored into a collection (Gosling et al. 1996).

See also

EMBEDDED POINTERS (198) provide a way to limit the space overhead of collections and similar data structures. FIXED ALLOCATION (226) and POOLED ALLOCATION (251) provide ways to reduce any additional memory management overhead.

Packing string data often requires TABLE COMPRESSION (135).

The VISITOR and PRESENTER (Vlissides 1998) patterns can provide behaviour for collections of primitive types (bit arrays etc.) without having to make each basic data item into an object. The FLYWEIGHT pattern (Gamma et al. 1995) allows you to process each item of a collection of packed data within the context of its neighbours.

Sharing

Also known as: Normalization

How can you avoid multiple copies of the same information?

- The same information is repeated multiple times.

- Very similar objects are used in different components.

- The same functions can be included in multiple libraries.

- The same literal strings are repeated throughout a program.

- Every copy of the same information uses memory.

Sometimes the same information occurs many times throughout a program, increasing the program's memory requirements. For example, the Strap-It-On user interface design includes many icons showing the company's bespectacled founder. Every component displaying the icon needs to have it available, but every copy of that particular gargoyle wastes memory.

Duplication can also enter the program from outside. Data loaded from RESOURCE FILES (161) or from an external database must be re-created inside a program, so loading the same resource or data twice (possibly in different parts of the program) will also result in two copies of the same information.

Copying objects has several benefits. Architecturally, it is important that components take responsibility for the objects they use, so copying objects between components can simplify ownership relationships. Some language constructs (such as C++ value semantics and Smalltalk cloning) assume object copying; and sometimes copying objects to where they are required can avoid indirection, making systems run faster.

Unwanted duplication doesn't just affect data objects. Unless care is taken, every time a separately compiled or built component of the program uses a library routine, a copy of that routine will be incorporated into the program. Similarly, every time a component uses a string or a constant a copy of that string may be made and stored somewhere.

Unfortunately, for whatever reason information is duplicated, every copy takes up memory that could otherwise be put to better use.

Therefore: **Store information once, and share it everywhere it is needed.**

Analyse your program to determine which information is duplicated, and which information can be safely shared. Any kind of information can be duplicated — images, sounds, multimedia resources, fonts, character tables, objects, and functions, as well as application data.

Once you have found common information, check that it can be shared. In particular, ensure that it never needs to be changed, or that all its clients can cope whenever it is changed. Modify the information's clients so that they all refer to a single shared copy of the information, typically by accessing the information through a pointer rather than directly.

If the shared information can be discarded by its clients, you may need to use REFERENCE COUNTING (268) or GARBAGE COLLECTION (278) so that it is only released once it is no longer needed anywhere in the program. If individual clients may want to change the data, you may need to use COPY-ON-WRITE (191).

For example, the Strap-It-On PC really only needs one copy of Our Founder's bitmap. This bitmap is never modified, so a single in-memory copy of the bitmap is shared everywhere it is needed in the system.

Consequences

Judicious SHARING can reduce a program's *memory requirements,* because only one copy is required of a shared object. SHARING also increases the *quality* of the design, since there's less chance of code duplication. SHARING generally does not affect a program's *scalability* when more memory is made available to the system, nor its *portability*. Since there's no need to allocate space for extra duplicate copies, SHARING can reduce *start-up times*, and to a lesser extent *runtime performance*.

However: *Programmer effort* and *discipline,* and *team co-ordination* are required to design programs to take advantage of SHARING. Designing sharing also increases the complexity of the resulting system, adding to *maintenance* and *testing* costs since shared objects create interactions between otherwise independent components.

Although it does not affect the *scalability* of centralized systems, SHARING can reduce the *scalability* of distributed systems, since it can be more efficient to make one copy of each shared object for each processor.

SHARING can introduce many kinds of aliasing problems, especially when read-only data is changed accidentally (Hogg 1991; Noble et al. 1998), and so can increase *testing costs*. In general, SHARING imposes a *global* cost on programs to achieve *local* goals, as many components may have to be modified to share a duplicated data structure.

❖   ❖   ❖

Implementation

SHARING effectively changes one-to-one (or one-to-many) relationships into many-to-one (or many-to-many) relationships. Consider the example shown in Figure 4.5, part of a simple word processor, in UML notation (Fowler 1997). A `Document` is made up of many `Paragraphs`, and each `Paragraph` has a `ParagraphFormat`.

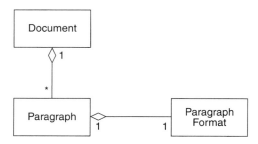

Figure 4.5 Part of a simple word processor

Considering each class in turn, it is unlikely that `Documents` or `Paragraphs` will be duplicated, unless, for example, many documents have many identical paragraphs. Yet many paragraphs within a document will have the same format. This design, however, gives each `Paragraph` object its own `ParagraphFormat` object. This means that the program will contain many `ParagraphFormat` objects (one for each `Paragraph`), while many of these objects will have exactly the same contents. `ParagraphFormats` are obvious candidates for sharing between different `Paragraphs`.

We can show this sharing as a many-to-one relationship (Figure 4.6).

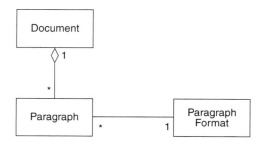

Figure 4.6 A many-to-one relationship

In the revised design, there will only be a few `ParagraphFormat` objects, each one different, and many `Paragraphs` will share the same `ParagraphFormat` object.

The design activity of detecting repeated data and splitting it into a separate object is called *normalization*. Normalization is an essential part of relational database design theory, and boasts an extensive literature (Connolly and Begg 1999; Date 1999; Elmasri and Navathe 2000).

You should consider the following issues when applying the **SHARING** pattern.

1. Making objects sharable

Aliasing problems make it difficult to share objects in object-oriented programs (Hogg 1991; Noble et al. 1998). Aliasing problems are the side effects caused by changing a shared object: if a shared object is changed by one of its clients the change will affect any other client of the shared object, and such changes can cause errors in clients that do not expect them. For example, changing the font in a shared `ParagraphFormat` object will change the fonts for all `Paragraphs` that share that format. If the new font is, say, a printer-only font, and is changed to suit one particular paragraph that will never be displayed on screen, it will break other paragraphs using that format which do need to be displayed on screen, because a printer-only font will not work for them.

The only kinds of objects that can be shared safely without side effects are *immutable* objects, objects that can never be changed. The immutability applies to the object itself — it's not enough just to make some clients read-only, since other clients may still change the shared object 'behind their back'. To share objects safely you typically have to change clients so that they make new objects rather than changing existing ones (see COPY-ON-WRITE (191)). You should consider removing any public methods or fields that can be used to change shared objects' state: in general, every field should only be initialized in the object's constructor (in Java, all fields should be `final`). The FLYWEIGHT pattern (Gamma et al. 1995) can be used to move dynamic state out of shared objects and into their clients.

2. Establishing sharing

For two or more components to be able to share information, each component must be able to find the information that is shared.

In small systems, where only a few distinguished objects are being shared, you can often use a global variable to store each shared object, or store shared instances within the objects' classes using the SINGLETON pattern (Gamma et al. 1995). The shared global variables can be initialized statically when the program starts, or the first time a shared object is accessed using LAZY INITIALIZATION (Beck 1997).

To provide a more general mechanism you can implement a *shared cache*, an in-memory database mapping from keys to shared objects. To find a shared object, a component checks the cache. If the shared object is already in the cache you use it directly; if not you create the object and store it back into the cache. For this to work you need a unique key for each shared object to identify it in the cache. A shared cache works particularly well when several components are loading the same objects from resource files databases, or networks such as the world wide web. Typical keys could be the fully qualified file names, web page URLs, or a combination of database table and database key within that table — the same keys that identify the data being loaded in the first place.

3. Deleting shared objects

Once you've created shared objects, you may need to be able to delete them when no longer required. There are three standard approaches to deleting shared objects: REFERENCE COUNTING (268), GARBAGE COLLECTION (278) and object owner-ship. REFERENCE COUNTING keeps a count of the number of objects interested in a shared object; when this becomes zero the object can be released (by removing the reference from the cache and, in C++, deleting the object). A GARBAGE COLLECTOR can detect and remove shared objects without requiring reference counts. Note that if a shared object is accessed via a cache, the cache will always have a reference to the shared object, preventing the garbage collector from deleting it, unless you can use some form of weak reference (Jones and Lins 1996).

With object ownership, you can identify one other single object or component that has the responsibility of managing the shared object (see the SMALL ARCHITECTURE (25) pattern). The object's owner accepts the responsibility of delet-ing the shared object at the appropriate time; generally it needs to be an object with an overview of all the objects that use the shared object (Weir 1996; Cargill 1996).

4. Sharing literals and strings

In many programs literals occupy more space than variables, so you can assign often used literals to variables and then replace the literals by the variables, effec-tively SHARING one literal in many places. For example, LaTeX uses this technique, coding common literals such as 1, 2, and –1 as the macros '\@ne', '\tw@', and '\m@on'. Smalltalk shares literals as part of the language environment, by representing strings as *symbols*. A symbol represents a single unique string, but can be stored internally as if it were an integer. The Smalltalk system maintains a *symbol table* that maps all known symbols to the strings they represent, and the compilation and runtime system must search this table to encode each string as a symbol, potentially adding a new entry if the string has not been presented before. The Smalltalk environment uses symbols for all method names, which both compresses code and increases the speed of method lookup.

5. Sharing across components and processes

It's more difficult to implement sharing between several components in different address spaces. Most operating systems provide some kind of shared memory, but this is often difficult to use. In concurrent systems, you need to prevent one thread from modifying shared data while another thread is accessing it. Typically this requires at least one semaphore, and increases code complexity and testing cost.

Alternatively, especially when data is shared between many components, you can consider encapsulating the shared data in a component of its own and use client–server techniques to access it. For example, EPOC accesses its relational databases through a single database server process. This server keeps a cache of indexes for its open data-bases; if two applications use the same database they share the same index.

Example

This Java example outlines part of the simple word processor described above. Documents contain Paragraphs, each of which has a ParagraphFormat. ParagraphFormats are complex objects, so to save memory several Paragraphs share a single ParagraphFormat. The code shows two mechanisms to ensure this:

- When we duplicate a Paragraph, both the original and the new Paragraph share a single ParagraphFormat instance.

- ParagraphFormats are referenced by name, such as 'bold', 'normal' or 'heading 2'. A Singleton ParagraphFormatCatalog contains a map of all the names to ParagraphFormat objects, so when we request a ParagraphFormat by name, the result is the single, shared, instance with that name.

The most important class in the word processor is Document: basically a sequence of Paragraphs, each of which has a (shared) ParagraphFormat.

```
class Document {
    Vector paragraphs = new Vector();
    int currentParagraph = -1;
```

The Paragraph class uses a StringBuffer to store the text of the paragraph, and also stores a reference to a ParagraphFormat object.

```
class Paragraph implements Cloneable {
    ParagraphFormat format;
    StringBuffer text = new StringBuffer();
```

A new Paragraph can be constructed either by giving a reference to a format object (which is then stored, without being copied, as the new Paragraph's format) or by giving a format name, which is then looked up in the ParagraphFormatCatalog. Note that neither initializing nor accessing a paragraph's format copies the ParagraphFormat object, rather it is passed by reference.

```
Paragraph(ParagraphFormat format) {
    this.format = format;
}

Paragraph(String formatName) {
    this(ParagraphFormatCatalog.catalog().findFormat(formatName));
}

ParagraphFormat format() {return format;}
```

Paragraphs are copied using the clone method (used by the word processor to implement its cut-and-paste feature). The clone method only copies one object, so the new clone's fields automatically point to exactly the same objects as the old object's fields. We don't want a Paragraph and its clone to share the StringBuffer, so we must clone that explicitly and install the cloned StringBuffer into the cloned Paragraph; however, we don't want to clone the ParagraphFormat reference, because

ParagraphFormats can be shared.

```
public Object clone() {
   try {
      Paragraph myClone = (Paragraph) super.clone();
      myClone.text = new StringBuffer(text.toString());
      return myClone;
   } catch (CloneNotSupportedException ex) {
      return null;
   }
}
```

Paragraphs find their formats using the `ParagraphFormatCatalog`. The catalog is a **SINGLETON** (Gamma et al. 1995):

```
class ParagraphFormatCatalog {
   private static ParagraphFormatCatalog systemWideCatalog
      = new ParagraphFormatCatalog();
   public static ParagraphFormatCatalog catalog() {
      return systemWideCatalog;
   }
```

that implements a map from format names to shared `ParagraphFormat` objects:

```
   Hashtable theCatalog = new Hashtable();
   public void addNewNamedFormat(String name, ParagraphFormat format) {
      theCatalog.put(name,format);
   }
   public ParagraphFormat findFormat(String name) {
      return (ParagraphFormat) theCatalog.get(name);
   }
}
```

Since the `ParagraphFormat` objects are shared, we want to restrict what clients can do with them. So `ParagraphFormat` itself is just an interface that does not permit clients to change the underlying object.

```
interface ParagraphFormat {
   ParagraphFormat nextParagraphFormat();
   String defaultFont();
   int fontSize();
   int spacing();
}
```

The class `ParagraphFormatImplementation` actually implements the `ParagraphFormat` objects, and includes a variety of accessor methods and constructors for these variables:

```
class ParagraphFormatImplementation implements ParagraphFormat {
   String defaultFont;
   int fontSize;
```

```
int spacing;
String nextParagraphFormat;
```

Each ParagraphFormat object stores the name of the ParagraphFormat to be used for the next paragraph. This makes it easier to initialize the ParagraphFormat objects, and will give the correct behaviour if we replace a specific ParagraphFormat in the catalog with another.

To find the corresponding ParagraphFormat object, it must also refer to the catalog:

```
public ParagraphFormat nextParagraphFormat() {
    return ParagraphFormatCatalog.catalog().
      findFormat(nextParagraphFormat);
}
```

When the Document class creates a new Paragraph, it uses the shared ParagraphFormat returned by the format of the current Paragraph: Note that ParagraphFormat objects are never copied, so they will be shared between all paragraphs that have the same format.

```
public Paragraph newParagraph() {
    ParagraphFormat nextParagraphFormat =
      currentParagraph().format().nextParagraphFormat();
    Paragraph newParagraph = new Paragraph(nextParagraphFormat);
    insertParagraph(newParagraph);
    return newParagraph;
}
```

❖   ❖   ❖

Known uses

Java's String instances are immutable, so implementations share a single underlying buffer between any number of copies of the same String object (Gosling et al. 1996). All implementations of Smalltalk use symbols for pre-compiled strings, as discussed above.

C++'s template feature often generates many copies of very similar code, leading to 'code bloat'. Some C++ linkers detect and share such instances of duplicated object code — Microsoft, for example, call this 'COMDAT folding' (Microsoft 1997a). Most modern operating systems provide dynamic link libraries (DLLs) or shared libraries that allow different processes to use the same code without needing to duplicate it in every executable (Kenah and Bate 1984; Card et al. 1998).

The EPOC Font and Bitmap server stores font and image data loaded from RESOURCE FILES (101) in shared memory (Symbian 1999b). These are used both by applications and by the Window Server that handles screen output for all applications. Each client requests and releases the font and bitmap data using remote procedure calls to the server process; the server loads the data into shared memory or locates an already-loaded item, and thereafter the application can access it directly (read-only). The server uses REFERENCE COUNTING (268) to decide when to delete each item; an application will normally release each item explicitly but the EPOC operating system will also notify the server if the application terminates abnormally, preventing memory leaks.

To avoid storing multiple copies of the same information the Palm Spotless JVM carefully shares whatever objects it can, such as constant strings defined in different class files (Taivalsaari et al. 1999).

See also

SHARING was first described as a pattern in the *Design Patterns Smalltalk Companion* (Alpert et al. 1998).

COPY-ON-WRITE (191) provides a mechanism to change a shared object as seen by one object, without impacting any other objects that rely on it. The READ-ONLY MEMORY (65) pattern describes how you can ensure that objects supposed to be read-only cannot be modified. Shared things are often READ-ONLY, and so often end up stored on SECONDARY STORAGE (79).

The FLYWEIGHT pattern (Gamma et al. 1995) describes how to make objects read-only so that they can be shared safely. Ken Auer and Kent Beck (1996) describe techniques to avoid SHARING Smalltalk objects by accident.

Copy-on-Write

How can you change a shared object without affecting its other clients?

- You need the system to behave as if each client has its own mutable copy of some shared data.

- To save memory you want to share data.

- You need to modify data in read-only memory.

Often you want the system to behave as though there are lots of copies of a piece of shared data, each individually modifiable, even though there is only one shared instance of the data. For example, in the Word-O-Matic word processor, each paragraph has its own format, which users can change independently of any other paragraph. Giving every paragraph its own ParagraphFormat object ensures this flexibility, but duplicates data unnecessarily because there are only a few different paragraph formats used in most documents.

We can use the SHARING (182) pattern instead, so that each paragraph format object describes several paragraphs. Unfortunately, a change to one shared paragraph format will change all the other paragraphs that share that format, not just the single paragraph the user is trying to change.

There's a similar problem if you're using READ-ONLY MEMORY (65). Many operating systems load program code and read-only data into memory marked as read-only, allowing it to be shared between processes; in palmtops and embedded systems the code may be loaded into ROM or flash RAM. Clients may want changeable copies of such data; but making an automatic copy by default for every client will waste memory.

Therefore: **Share the object until you need to change it, then copy it and use the copy in future.**

Maintain a flag or reference count in each sharable object, and ensure it's set as soon as there's more than one client to the object. When a client calls any method that modifies a shared object's externally visible state, create a duplicate of some or all of the object's state in a new object, delegate the operation to that new object, and ensure that the client uses the new object from then on. The new object will initially not be shared (with flag unset or reference count of one), so further modifications won't cause a copy until the new object in turn then gets multiple clients.

You can implement COPY-ON-WRITE for specific objects in the system, or implement it as part of the operating system infrastructure using PAGING (119) techniques. The latter approach is particularly used with code, which is normally read-only but allows a program to modify its own code on occasion, in which case a paging system can make a copy of part of the code for that specific program instance.

Thus Word-O-Matic keeps a reference count of the number of clients sharing each ParagraphFormat object. In normal use many Document objects will share the same ParagraphFormat, but on the few occasions that a user modifies the format of a paragraph, Word-O-Matic makes a copy of its ParagraphFormat and keeps that separate to the modified Paragraph and to any other Paragraphs with the new format.

Consequences

COPY-ON-WRITE gives programmers the illusion of many copies of a piece of data, without the waste of memory that would imply. So, it reduces the *memory requirements* of the system. In some cases it increases a program's *execution speed*, and particularly its *start-up time*, since copying can be a slow operation.

COPY-ON-WRITE also allows you to make it appear that data stored in read-only storage can be changed. So you can move infrequently changed data into read-only storage, reducing the program's *memory requirements*.

Once COPY-ON-WRITE has been implemented it requires little *programmer discipline* to use, since clients don't need to be directly aware of it.

However: COPY-ON-WRITE requires *programmer effort* or *hardware or operating system* support to implement, because the system must intercept writes to the data, make the copy and then continue the write as if nothing had happened.

If there are many write accesses to the data, then COPY-ON-WRITE can decrease *time performance*, since each write access must ensure the data's not shared. COPY-ON-WRITE can also lead to lots of copies of the same thing cluttering up the system, decreasing the *predictability* of the system's performance, making it *harder to test*, and ultimately increasing the system's *memory requirements*.

COPY-ON-WRITE can cause problems for object identity if the identity of the copy and the original storage is supposed to be the same.

Implementation

Here are some issues to consider when implementing the COPY-ON-WRITE pattern.

1. Copy-On-Write proxies

The most common approach to implementing **COPY-ON-WRITE** is to use a variant of the **PROXY** Pattern (Gamma et al. 1995; Buschmann et al. 1996; Coplien 1994). Using the terminology of Buschmann et al. (1996), a **PROXY** references an underlying *original* object and forwards all the messages it receives to that object.

To use **PROXY** to implement **COPY-ON-WRITE**, every client uses a different **PROXY** object, which distinguishes *accessors*, methods that merely read data, from *mutators* that modify it. The Original object contains a flag that records whether it has more than one proxy sharing it (Figure 4.7). Any updator method checks this flag and if the flag is set, makes a (new, unshared) copy of the representation, installs it in the proxy, and forwards the mutator to that copy instead.

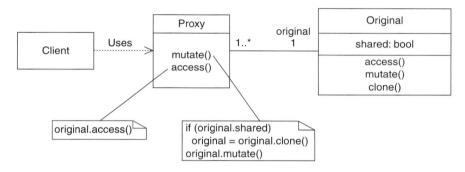

Figure 4.7 Using a proxy

In this design, the `shared` flag is stored in the original object, and it's the responsibility of the representation's `clone` method to create an object with the flag unset. A valid alternative implementation is to place the flag into the proxy object; in this case the proxy must reset the flag after creating and installing a new original object. As a third option, you can combine the client and proxy object, if the client knows about the use of **COPY-ON-WRITE**, and if no other objects need to use the original (other than via the combined client/proxy, of course).

You can also combine the function of **COPY-ON-WRITE** with managing the lifetime of the underlying representation object by replacing the `shared` flag in the representation object with a reference count. A reference count of exactly one implies the object is not shared and can be modified. See the **REFERENCE COUNTING** (268) pattern for a discussion of reference counting in detail.

2. Copying changes to objects

You do not have to copy all of any object when it is changed. Instead you can create a *delta* object that stores only the changes to the object, and delegates requests for unchanged data back to the main object. For example, when a user changes the font in a paragraph format, you can create a `FontChange` delta object that returns the new font when it is asked, but forwards all other requests to the underlying, and

unchanged, `ParagraphFormat` object. A delta object can be implemented as a
DECORATOR on the original object (Gamma et al. 1995). Figure 4.8 shows a possible implementation as a UML collaboration diagram (Fowler 1997).

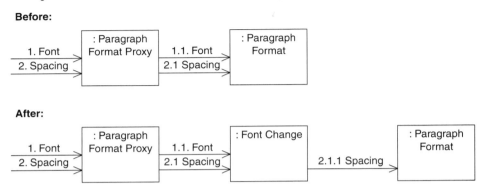

Figure 4.8   Creating a delta object

3. Writing to objects in read-only memory

You can use COPY-ON-WRITE so that shared representations in ROM can be
updated. Clearly the `shared` flag must be set in the ROM instance and cleared in the
copy, but otherwise this is no different from a RAM version of the pattern.

In C++ the rule is that only instances of classes without a constructor may be
placed in ROM. So a typical implementation must use static initialization for the
flag, and must therefore have public data members. The restriction on constructors
means that you can't implement a copy constructor and assignment operator;
instead you'll need to write a function that uses the default copy constructor to copy
the data.

Example

This example extends the word processor implementation from the SHARING (182)
pattern, to allow the user to change the format of an individual paragraph. In this
example the `Paragraph` object combines the role of proxy and client, since we've
restricted all access to the `ParagraphFormat` object to via the `Paragraph` object. We
don't need to separate out the read-only aspects to a separate interface as no clients
will ever see `ParagraphFormat`s directly.

The `Document` class remains unchanged, being essentially a list of paragraphs. The
`ParagraphFormat` class is also straightforward, but now it supports mutator methods
and needs to implement the `clone` method. For simplicity we only show one mutator — to set the font.

```
class ParagraphFormat implements Cloneable {
   String defaultFont;
   int fontSize;
   int spacing;
   String nextParagraphFormat;

   public Object clone() throws CloneNotSupportedException {
      return super.clone();
   }

   void privateSetFont(String aFont) {defaultFont = aFont;}
}
```

As in the previous example, the Paragraph class must also implement cloning. This implementation keeps the shared flag in the Paragraph class (i.e. in the proxy), as the member paragraphFormatIsUnique.

```
class Paragraph implements Cloneable {
   ParagraphFormat format;
   boolean paragraphFormatIsUnique = false;
   StringBuffer text = new StringBuffer();

   Paragraph(ParagraphFormat format) {
      this.format = format;
   }
   Paragraph(String formatName) {
      this(ParagraphFormatCatalog.catalog().findFormat(formatName));
   }
```

The Paragraph implementation provides two private utility functions: aboutToShareParagraphFormat and aboutToChangeParagraphFormat. The method aboutToShareParagraphFormat should be invoked whenever we believe it's possible that we may be referencing a ParagraphFormat object known to any other object.

```
protected void aboutToShareParagraphFormat() {
   paragraphFormatIsUnique = false;
}
```

If any external client obtains a reference to our ParagraphFormat object, or passes in one externally, then we must assume that it's shared:

```
ParagraphFormat format() {
   aboutToShareParagraphFormat();
   return format;
}

public void setFormat(ParagraphFormat aParagraphFormat) {
   aboutToShareParagraphFormat();
   format = aParagraphFormat;
}
```

And similarly, if a client clones this `Paragraph` object, we don't want to clone the format, but instead simply note that we're sharing it:

```
public Object clone() {
   try {
      aboutToShareParagraphFormat();
      Paragraph myClone = (Paragraph) super.clone();
      myClone.text = new StringBuffer(text.toString());
      return myClone;
   } catch (CloneNotSupportedException ex) {
      return null;
   }
}
```

Meanwhile, any method that modifies the `ParagraphFormat` object must first call `aboutToChangeParagraphFormat`. This method makes sure the `ParagraphFormat` object is unique to this `Paragraph`, cloning it if necessary.

```
protected void aboutToChangeParagraphFormat() {
   if (!paragraphFormatIsUnique) {
      try {
         format = (ParagraphFormat) format().clone();
      } catch (CloneNotSupportedException e) {}
      paragraphFormatIsUnique = true;
   }
}
```

Here's a simple example of a method that modifies a `ParagraphFormat`:

```
void setFont(String fontName) {
   aboutToChangeParagraphFormat();
   format.privateSetFont(fontName);
}
```

Known uses

Many operating systems use COPY-ON-WRITE in their paging systems. Executable code is very rarely modified, so it's usually SHARED (182) between all processes using it, but this pattern allows modification when processes need it. By default each page out of an executable file is flagged as read-only and shared between all processes that use it. If a client writes to a shared page, the hardware generates an exception, and the operating system exception handler then creates a writable copy for that process alone (Kenah and Bate 1984; Goodheart and Cox 1994).

Rogue Wave's Tools.h++ library uses COPY-ON-WRITE for its `CString` class (Rogue Wave Software 1994). A `CString` object represents a dynamically allocated string.

C++'s pass-by-value semantics mean that the CString objects are copied frequently, but very seldom modified. So each CString object is simply a wrapper referring to a shared implementation. CString's copy constructor and related operators manipulate a reference count in the shared implementation. If any client does an operation to change the content of the string, the CString object simply makes a copy and does the operation on the copy. One interesting detail is that there is only one instance of the null string, which is always shared. All attempts to create a null string, for example by initializing a zero-length string, simply access that shared object.

Because modifiable strings are relatively rare in programs, Sun Java implements them using a separate class, StringBuffer. However, StringBuffer permits its clients to retrieve String objects with the method toString. To save memory and speed up performance the resulting String uses the underlying buffer already created by StringBuffer. However, the StringBuffer object has a flag to indicate that the buffer is now shared; if a client attempts to make further changes to the buffer, StringBuffer creates a copy and uses that (Chan et al. 1998).

Objects in NewtonScript are defined using inheritance, so that common features can be declared in a parent object and then shared by all child objects that needed them. Default values for objects' fields are defined using COPY-ON-WRITE slots. If a child object doesn't define a field it will inherit that field's value from its parent object, but when a child object writes to a shared field a local copy of the field is automatically created in the child object (Smith 1999).

See also

HOOKS (72) provide an alternative technique for changing the contents of read-only storage.

Embedded Pointers

How can you reduce the space used by a collection of objects?

- Linked data structures are built out of pointers to objects.

- Collection objects (and their internal link objects) need large amounts of memory to store large collections.

- Traversing through a linked data structure can require temporary memory, especially if the traversal is recursive.

Object-oriented programs implement relationships between objects by using collection objects that store pointers to other objects. Unfortunately, collection objects and the objects they use internally can require a large amount of memory. For example, the Strap-It-On's 'Mind Reader' brainwave analysis program must receive brainwave data in real time from an interrupt routine, and store it in a list for later analysis. Because brainwaves have to be sampled many times every second, a large amount of data can accumulate before it can be analysed, even though each brainwave sample is relatively small (just a couple of integers). Simple collection implementations based on linked lists can impose an overhead of at least three pointers for every object they store, so storing a sequence of two-word samples in such a list more than doubles the sequence's intrinsic memory requirements — see Figure 4.9.

As well as this memory overhead, linked data structures have other disadvantages. They can use large numbers of small internal objects, increasing the possibility of fragmentation (see Chapter 5). Allocating all these objects takes an unpredictable amount of time, making it unsuitable for real-time work. Traversing the structure requires following large numbers of pointer links; this also takes time, but more importantly, traversals of recursive structures like graphs and trees can also require an unbounded amount of temporary memory; in some cases, similar amounts of memory to that required to store the structure itself. Finally, any function that adds an object to such a collection may fail if there is insufficient memory, and so must carry all the costs of PARTIAL FAILURE (48).

Of course, linked structures have many compensating advantages. They can describe many different kinds of structures, including linked lists, trees, queues, all of a wide variety of different subtypes (Knuth 1997). These structures can support a

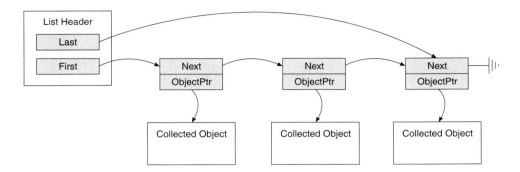

Figure 4.9   Linked list using external pointers

wide variety of operations quite efficiently (especially insertions and deletions in the middle of the data). Linked structures support VARIABLE ALLOCATION (236), so they never need to allocate memory that is subsequently unused. The only real alternative to building linked structures is to use some kind of FIXED ALLOCATION (226), such as a fixed-size array. But fixed structures place arbitrary limits on the number of objects in the collection, waste memory if they are not fully occupied, and insertion and deletion operations can be very expensive. So, how can you keep the benefits of linked data structures while minimizing the disadvantages?

Therefore: **Embed the pointers maintaining the collection into each object.**

Design the collection data structure to store its pointers within the objects that are contained in the structure, rather than in internal link objects. You will need to change the definitions of the objects that are to be stored in the collection to include these pointers, and possibly to include other collection-related information as well.

You will also need to change the implementation of the collection object to use the pointers stored directly in objects. For a collection that is used by only one external client object, you can even dispense completely with the object that represents the collection, and incorporate its data and operations directly into the client. To traverse the data structure, use iteration rather than recursion to avoid allocating stack frames for every recursive call, and use extra (or reuse existing) pointer fields in the objects to store any state related to the traversal.

So, for example, rather than store the Brainwave sample objects in a collection, Strap-it-On's Brainwave Driver uses an embedded linked list (Figure 4.10). Each Brainwave sample object has an extra pointer field, called `Next`, that is used to link brainwave samples into a linked list. As each sample is received, the interrupt routine adjusts its `Next` field to link it into the list. The main analysis routine adjusts the sample object's pointers to remove each from the list in its own time for processing.

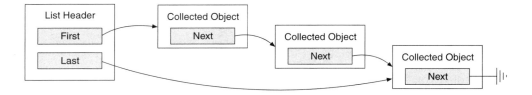

Figure 4.10   Linked list using embedded pointers

Consequences

EMBEDDED POINTERS remove the need for internal link objects in collections, reducing the number of objects in the system and thus the system's *memory requirements,* while increasing the *predictability* of the system's memory use (especially if traversals are iterative rather than recursive). The routines to add and remove items from the linked structure cannot suffer memory allocation failure.

Using EMBEDDED POINTERS reduces or removes the need for dynamic memory allocation, improving the *real-time performance* of the system. Some operations may have better *runtime performance*; for example with an embedded doubly-linked list you can remove an element in the collection simply by using a pointer to that element directly. With an implementation using external pointers (such as STL's Deque (Austern 1998)) you'd need first to set an iterator to refer to the right element, which requires a linear search.

However: EMBEDDED POINTERS don't really belong to the objects they are embedded inside. This pattern reduces those objects' encapsulation, gaining a *local* benefit but reducing the *localization* of the design. The pattern tightly couples objects to the container class that holds them, making it more difficult to reuse either class independently, increasing the *programmer effort* required because specialized collections often have to be written from scratch, reducing the *design quality* of the system and making the program harder to *maintain.*

In many cases a given collected object will often need to be in several different collections at different times during its lifetime. It requires *programmer discipline* to ensure that the same pointer field is never used by two collections simultaneously.

❖   ❖   ❖

Implementation

Applying the EMBEDDED POINTER pattern is straightforward: place pointer members into objects and build up linked data structures using those pointers, instead of using external collection objects. You can find the details in any decent textbook on data structures, from Knuth (1997) onwards, which will describe the details, advantages, and disadvantages of the classical linked data structure designs, from simple singly and doubly linked lists to subtle complex balanced trees. See the SMALL DATA STRUCTURES (169) pattern for a list of such textbooks.

1. Reuse

The main practical issue when using EMBEDDED POINTERS is how to incorporate the pointers into objects in a way that provides some measure of reuse, to avoid reimplementing all the collection operations for every single list. The key idea is for objects to somehow present a consistent interface for accessing the embedded pointers to the collection class (or the functions that implement the collection operations). In this way, the collection can be used with any object that provides a compatible interface. There are three common techniques for establishing interfaces to embedded pointers: inheritance, inline objects, and pre-processor constructs.

1.1. Inheritance.   You can put the pointers and accessing functionality into a super-class, and make the objects to be stored in a collection inherit from this class (Figure 4.11). This is straightforward, and provides a measure of reuse. However, you can't have more than one instance of such a pointer for a given object. In single-inheritance languages such as Smalltalk this prevents any other use of inheritance for the same object, and so limits any object to being in only one collection at a time. In languages with multiple inheritance, objects could be in multiple collections provided each collection accesses the embedded pointers through a unique interface, supplied by a unique base class (C++).

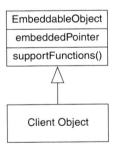

Figure 4.11   Inheritance

1.2. Inline objects.   In languages with inline objects, such as C and C++, you can embed a separate link object that contains the pointers directly into the client object (Figure 4.12). This doesn't suffer from the disadvantages of using inheritance, but you need to be able to find the client object from a given link object and vice versa. In C++ this can be implemented using pointers to members, or (more commonly) as an offset in bytes.

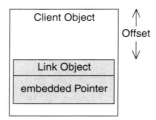

Figure 4.12   Inline object

For example, EPOC's collection libraries find embedded pointers using byte offsets. Whenever a new collection is created, it must be initialized with the offset inside its client objects where its pointers are embedded.

1.3. Pre-processors.   C++ provides two kinds of pre-processing: the standard pre-processor cpp, and the C++ template mechanisms. So in C++ a good approach is to include the embedded pointers as normal (possibly public) data members, and to reuse the management code via pre-processing. You can also pre-process code in almost any other language given a suitable pre-processor, which could be either a special-purpose program such as m4, or a general-purpose program such as perl.

2. Pointer differences

Sometimes an object needs to store two or more pointers; for example, a circular doubly-linked list node needs pointers to the previous and next item in the list. You can reduce the amount of memory needed by storing the difference (or the bitwise exclusive or) of the two pointers, rather than the pointer itself. When you are traversing the structure forwards, for example, you take the address of the previous node and add the stored difference to find the address of the next node; reverse traversals work similarly.

   For example, in Figure 4.13, rather than node c storing the dotted forward and back pointers (i.e. the addresses of nodes b and d) node c stores only the difference between these two addresses. Given a pointer to node b and the difference stored within c, you can calculate the address of node d as (b — (d–c)). Similarly, traversing the list the other way, given the address of node d and (b–c) you can calculate the address of node b as (d + (b–d)). For this to work, you need to store two initial pointers, typically a head and tail pointer for a circular doubly-linked list (Knuth 1997).

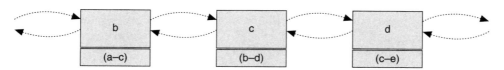

Figure 4.13   Pointer differences

3. Traversals

A related, but different, problem occurs when you need to traverse an arbitrarily deep structure, especially if the traversal has to be recursive. Suppose, for example, you have an unbalanced binary tree, and you need to traverse through all the elements in order (Figure 4.14). A traversal beginning at E will recursively visit C, then F; the traversal at C will visit B and D, and so on. Every recursive call requires extra memory to store activation records on the stack, so traversing larger structures can easily exhaust a process's stack space.

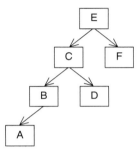

Figure 4.14   A binary tree

3.1. Iterative traversals using extra embedded pointers.   Consider the traversal more closely: at each object it needs to store one thing on the stack: the identity of the object it's coming from (and possibly any working data or parameters passed through the iteration). So, for example, when C invokes the operation on D, it must store that it needs to return to E on completion. You can use EMBEDDED POINTERS in each object to store this data (the parent pointer, and the traversal state — two Boolean flags that remember whether the left and right leaves have been processed). This allows you to iterate over the structure using a loop rather than recursion, but imposes the overhead of an extra pointer or two in each object (Figure 4.15).

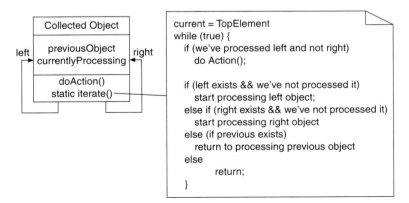

Figure 4.15   Iterative traversal using extra embedded pointers

3.2. Iterative traversals using pointer reversal.   Consider the iteration process further. At any time one of the three pointers in each element, left leaf, right leaf or parent, is redundant. If there is no iteration, the parent pointer is redundant; if a left or right leaf is currently being processed that leaf pointer is redundant (because the traversal has already reached that leaf). Pointer reversal allows iterative traversals of linked structures by temporarily using pointers to leaf nodes as parent pointers: as the traversal proceeds around the object, the pointers currently being followed are *reversed*, that is, used to point to parent objects.

In Figure 4.16, for example, when a traversal is at node A, node B's left leaf pointer would be reversed to point to its parent, node C; because B is C's left child, C's left child pointer would also be reversed to point to node E.

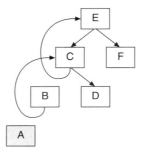

Figure 4.16   Iterative traversal using pointer reversal

Example

Here's an example using EMBEDDED POINTERS to store a data structure and traverse it using pointer reversal. The example program implements a sorting algorithm using a simple binary tree. To start with we'll give the objects that are stored in the tree (the BinaryTreeObjects) a single character of local data. We also need a greaterThan operation and an operation called to do the action we need (doIt).

```
class BinaryTreeObject {
   char data;

   BinaryTreeObject(char data) {
      this.data = data;
   }
   Object doIt(Object param) {
      return ((String) param + data);
   }
   boolean greaterThan(BinaryTreeObject other) {
      return data > other.data;
   }
}
```

A binary tree needs a left pointer and a right pointer corresponding to each node. Using the EMBEDDED POINTER pattern, we implement each within the structure itself:

```
BinaryTreeObject left;
BinaryTreeObject right;
```

Adding an element to the binary tree is fairly easy. We can traverse the tree starting at the top, going left when our new element is less than the current item, right when it's greater, until we get to a vacant position in the tree.

```
static void insert(BinaryTreeObject top, BinaryTreeObject newItem) {
    BinaryTreeObject current = top;

    for (;;) {
      if (current.greaterThan(newItem)) {
        if (current.left == null) {
          current.left = newItem;
          return;
        } else {
          current = current.left;
        }
      } else {
        if (current.right == null) {
          current.right = newItem;
          return;
        } else {
          current = current.right;
        }
      }
    }
}
```

Note that this method is not recursive and so should allocate no memory other than one stack frame with one local variable (`current`).

Traversing the tree is more difficult, because the traversal has to visit all the elements in the tree, and this means backtracking up the tree when it reaches a bottom-level node. To traverse the tree without using recursion, we can add two embedded pointers to every tree node: a pointer to the previous (parent) item in the tree, and a marker noting which action, left node or right node, the algorithm is currently processing.

```
BinaryTreeObject previous;
static final int Inactive = 0, GoingLeft = 1, GoingRight = 2;
int action = Inactive;
```

The `traversal` method, then, must move through each node in infix order. Each iteration visits one node; however, this may mean up to three visits to any given node (from parent going left, from left going right, and from right back to parent); we use the stored action data for the node to see which visit this one is. The `traversal` method must also call the `doIt` method at the correct point — after processing the left node, if any.

```
static Object traversal(BinaryTreeObject start, Object param) {
  BinaryTreeObject current = start;
  for (;;) {
    if (current.action == GoingLeft ||
        (current.action == Inactive && current.left == null)) {
      param = current.doIt(param);
    }
    if (current.action == Inactive && current.left != null) {
      current.action = GoingLeft;
      current.left.previous = current;
      current = current.left;
    } else if (current.action != GoingRight && current.right != null) {
      current.action = GoingRight;
      current.right.previous = current;
      current = current.right;
    } else {
      current.action = Inactive;
      if (current.previous == null) {
        break;
      }
      current = current.previous;
    }
  }
  return param;
}
```

Of course, a practical implementation would improve this example in two ways. First, we can put the `left`, `right`, `action`, `previous` pointers and the `greaterThan` stub into a base class (`SortableObject`, perhaps) or into a separate object. Second, we can make the `traversal` method into a separate **ITERATOR** object (Gamma et al. 1995), avoiding the need to hard-code the `doIt` method.

We can extend this example further, to remove the parent pointer from the data structure using pointer reversal. First, we'll need two additional methods, to save the parent pointer in either the left or the right pointer:

```
BinaryTreeObject saveParentReturningLeaf(BinaryTreeObject parent) {
  BinaryTreeObject leaf;

  if (action == GoingLeft) {
    leaf = left;
    left = parent;
  } else {
    leaf = right;
    right = parent;
  }
  return leaf;
}
```

and then to restore it as required:

```
BinaryTreeObject
restoreLeafReturningParent(BinaryTreeObject leafJustDone) {
   BinaryTreeObject parent;
   if (action == GoingLeft) {
     parent = left;
     left = leafJustDone;
   } else {
     parent = right;
     right = leafJustDone;
   }
   return parent;
}
```

Now we can rewrite the `traversal` method to remember the previous item processed, whether it's the parent of the current item or a leaf node, and to reverse the left and right pointers using the methods above:

```
static Object reversingTraversal(BinaryTreeObject top, Object param) {

   BinaryTreeObject current = top;
   BinaryTreeObject leafJustDone = null;
   BinaryTreeObject parentOfCurrent = null;

   for (;;) {

     if (current.action == GoingLeft ||
         (current.action == Inactive && current.left == null)) {
       param = current.doIt(param);
     }

     if (current.action != Inactive)
       parentOfCurrent = current.restoreLeafReturningParent(leafJustDone);

     if (current.action == Inactive && current.left != null) {
       current.action = GoingLeft;
       BinaryTreeObject p = current;
       current = current.saveParentReturningLeaf(parentOfCurrent);
       parentOfCurrent = p;
     } else if (current.action != GoingRight && current.right != null) {
       current.action = GoingRight;
       BinaryTreeObject p = current;
       current = current.saveParentReturningLeaf(parentOfCurrent);
       parentOfCurrent = p;
     } else {
       current.action = Inactive;
       if (parentOfCurrent == null) {
         break;
       }
```

```
            leafJustDone = current;
            current = parentOfCurrent;
        }
    }
    return param;
}
```

We're still wasting a word in each object for the action parameter. In Java we could perhaps reduce this to a byte but no further. In a C++ implementation we could use the low bits of, say, the left pointer to store it (see PACKED DATA (174) — packing pointers), thereby reducing the overhead of the traversing algorithm to nothing at all.

❖   ❖   ❖

Known uses

EPOC provides at least three different linked list collection classes using EMBEDDED POINTERS (Symbian 1999b). The EMBEDDED POINTERS are instances of provided classes (TSglQueLink, for example) accessed via offsets; the main collection logic is in separate classes, which use the thin template idiom to provide type safety. EPOC applications, and operating system components, use these classes extensively. The most common reason for preferring them over collections requiring heap memory is that operations using them cannot fail; this is a significant benefit in situations where failure handling is not provided.

The Smalltalk LinkedList class uses inheritance to mix in the pointers; the only things you can store into a LinkedList are objects that inherit from class Link (Goldberg and Robson 1983). Class Link contains two fields and appropriate accessors (previous and next) to allow double linking. Compared with other Smalltalk collections, for each element you save one word of memory by using concatenation instead of pointers, plus you save the memory overhead of creating a new object (two words or so) and the overhead of doing the allocation.

See also

You may be able to use FIXED ALLOCATION (226) to embed objects directly into other objects, rather than just EMBEDDING POINTERS to objects.

Pointer reversal was first described by Peter Deutsch (Knuth 1997) and Schorr and Waite (1967). EMBEDDED POINTERS and pointer reversal are used together in many implementations of GARBAGE COLLECTION (278) (Goldberg and Robson 1983, Jones and Lins 1996). Jiri Soukup (1994) discusses using preprocessors to implement linked data structures in much more detail.

Multiple Representations

- There are several possible implementations of a class, with different trade-offs between size and behaviour.

- Different parts of your system, or different uses of the class, require different choices of implementation. One size doesn't fit all.

- There are enough instances of the class to justify extra code to reduce RAM usage.

Often when you design a class, you find there can be several suitable representations for its internal data structures. For example, in the Strap-It-On's word processor (Word-O-Matic) a word may be represented as a series of characters, a bitmap, or a sequence of phonemes. Depending on the current output mechanism (a file, the screen, or the vocalizer) each of these representations might be appropriate.

Having to choose between several possible representations is quite common. Some representations may have small memory requirements, but be costly in processing time or other resources; others may be the opposite. In most cases you can examine the demands of the system and decide on a best SMALL DATA STRUCTURE (169). But what do you do when there's no single 'best' implementation?

Therefore: **Make each implementation satisfy a common interface.**

Design a common abstract interface that suits all the implementations without depending on a particular one, and ensure every implementation meets the interface (Figure 4.17). Access implementations via an ABSTRACT CLASS (Woolf 2000) or use ADAPTERS to access existing representations (Gamma et al. 1995) so clients don't have to be aware of the underlying implementation.

For example, Word-O-Matic defines a single interface Word, which is used by much of the word-processing code. Several concrete classes, StorableWord, ViewableWord, and SpokenWord, implement the Word interface. Each implementation has different internal data structures and different implementations of the operations that access those structures. The software creates whichever concrete class is appropriate for the current use of the Word object, but the distinction is only

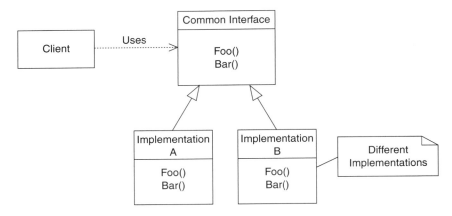

Figure 4.17 Using a common interface

significant when it comes to outputting the object. The multiple implementations are concealed from most of the client code.

Consequences

The system will use the most appropriate implementation for any task, reducing the *memory requirements* and *processing time* overheads that would be imposed by using an inappropriate representation. Code using each instance will use the common interface and need not know the implementation, *reducing programmer effort* on the client side and increasing *design quality* and *reusability*.

Representations can be chosen *locally* for each data structure. More memory-intensive representations can be used when more memory is available, adding to the *scalability* of the system.

However: The pattern can also increase total *memory requirements,* since the code occupies additional memory.

MULTIPLE REPRESENTATIONS increase *programmer effort* in the implementation of the object concerned, because multiple implementations are more *complex* than a single implementation, although this kind of complexity is often seen as a sign of *high-quality* design because subsequent changes to the representation will be easier. For the same reason, it increases *testing costs* and *maintenance costs* overall, because each alternative implementation must be tested and maintained separately.

Changing between representations imposes a *space and time* overhead. It also means *more complexity* in the code, and *more complicated testing* strategies, increasing *programmer effort* and making memory use *harder to predict*.

Implementation

There are a number of issues to take into account when you are using MULTIPLE REPRESENTATIONS.

1. Implementing the interface

In Java the standard implementation of dynamic binding means defining either a Java class or a Java interface. Which is more suitable? From the point of view of the client, it doesn't matter; either can define an abstract interface. Using a Java interface gives you more flexibility, because each implementation may inherit from other existing classes as required; however, extending a common superclass allows several implementations to inherit common functionality. In C++ there's only the one conventional option for implementing the common interface: making all implementations inherit from a base class that defines the interface.

There's a danger that clients may accidentally rely on features of a particular implementation — particularly non-functional ones — rather than of the common interface. D'Souza and Wills (1998) discuss design techniques to avoid such dependencies in components.

2. Binding clients to implementations

Sometimes you need to support several implementations, though a given client may only ever use one. For example, the C++ Standard Template Library (STL) iterator classes work on several STL collections, but any given STL iterator object works with only one (Stroustrup 1997, Austern 1998). In this case, you can statically bind the client code to use only the one implementation — in C++ you could store objects directly and use non-virtual functions. If, however, a client needs to use several different object representations interchangeably, then you need to use dynamic binding.

3. Creating dynamically bound implementations

The only place where you need to reference the true implementation classes in the code is where the objects are created. In many situations, it's reasonable to hard-code the class names in the client, as in the following C++ example:

```
CommonInterface *anObject = new SpecificImplementation(parameters);
```

If there's a good reason to hide even this mention of the classes from the client, then the ABSTRACT FACTORY pattern (Gamma et al. 1995) can implement a virtual constructor (Coplien 1994) so that the client can specify which object to create using just a parameter.

4. Changing between representations

In some cases, an object's representation needs to change during its lifetime, usually because a client needs some behaviour that is not supported well by the object's current representation. Changes to an object's representation can be explicitly requested by its client, or can be triggered automatically within the object itself. Changing representations automatically has several benefits: the client doesn't need knowledge of the internal implementation, improving encapsulation, and you can tune the memory use entirely within the implementation of the specific object, improving localization. Changing representations automatically requires dynamic binding, so clients will use the correct representation without being aware of it. In some situations, however, the client can have a better knowledge of optimization strategies than is available to the object itself, typically because the client is in a better position to know which operations will be required.

4.1. Changing representations explicitly.   It is straightforward for an object to let a client change its representation explicitly: the object should implement a conversion function (or a C++ constructor) that takes the common interface as parameter, and returns the new representation.

```
class SpecificImplementation : public CommonInterface {
public:
    SpecificImplementation(CommonInterface c) {
    // initialize this from c
    }
};
```

4.2. Changing representations automatically.   You can use the BRIDGE pattern to keep the interface and identity of the object constant when its internal structure changes (strictly speaking a *half bridge*, since it varies only the object implementation and not the abstraction it supports) (Gamma et al. 1995). The client sees only the bridge object, which delegates all its operations to an implementation object through a common interface (Figure 4.18).

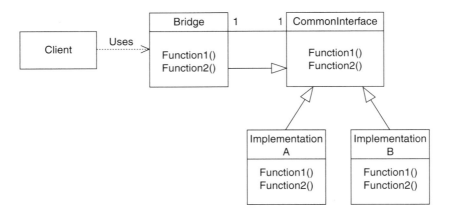

Figure 4.18   Using a bridge

The bridge class needs the same methods as the common interface; so it's reasonable (though unnecessary) in C++ and Java to make the bridge class derive from the common interface. Each implementation object will need a construction function taking the common interface as parameter. Of course, some implementations may store more or less data, so there may be special cases with more specific constructors.

Some languages make it simple to implement the bridge object itself. In Smalltalk, for example, you can override the DoesNotUnderstand: method to pass any unrecognized operation on to the implementation object (Lalonde 1994). In C++ you can implement operator->() to do the same (Coplien 1994), or alternatively you can avoid deriving the bridge class from the common interface and make all its functions non-virtual and inline.

Example

This Java example implements a Word object with two representations: as a simple string (the default), and as a string with an additional cached corresponding sound. Both these representations implement the basic Word interface, which can return either a string or sound value, and allows clients to choose the most appropriate representation.

```java
interface WordInterface {
    public byte[] asSound();
    public String asString();
    public void becomeSound();
    public void becomeString();
}
```

The most important concrete class is the Word class, which acts as a bridge between the word abstraction and its two representations, as a sound and as a text string.

```java
class Word implements WordInterface {
    private WordInterface rep;

    public byte[] asSound()       {return rep.asSound();}
    public String asString()      {return rep.asString();}
    public void becomeSound()     {rep.becomeSound();}
    public void becomeString()    {rep.becomeString();}
```

The constructor of the Word class must select an implementation. It uses the method become, which simply sets the implementation object.

```java
    public Word(String word) {
        become(new StringWordImplementation(this, word));
    }
    public void become(WordInterface rep) {
        this.rep = rep;
    }
```

The default implementation stores Words as a text string. It also keeps a pointer to its word **BRIDGE** object, and uses this pointer to automatically change a word's representation into the other format. It has two constructors: one, taking a string, is used by the constructor for the Word object; the other, taking a WordInterface, is used to create itself from a different representation.

```
class StringWordImplementation implements WordInterface {
    private String word;
    private Word bridge;

    public StringWordImplementation(Word bridge, String word) {
        this.bridge = bridge;
        this.word = word;
    }
    public StringWordImplementation(Word bridge, WordInterface rep) {
        this.bridge = bridge;
        this.word = rep.asString();
    }
```

It must also provide implementations of all the WordInterface methods. Note how it must change its representation to return itself as a sound; once the asSound method returns, this object will be garbage:

```
    public byte[] asSound()
    {
        becomeSound();
        return bridge.asSound();
    }
    public String asString() {return word;}

    public void becomeSound() {
        bridge.become(new SoundWordImplementation(bridge, this));
    }
    public void becomeString() {}
```

Finally, the sound word class is similar to the text version, but also caches the sound representation. Implementing the sound conversion function is left as an exercise for the reader!

```
class SoundWordImplementation implements WordInterface {
    private String word;
    private Word bridge;
    private byte[] sound;
```

```
SoundWordImplementation(Word bridge, WordInterface rep) {
   this.bridge = bridge;
   this.word = rep.asString();
   this.sound = privateConvertStringToSound(this.word);
}

public String asString() {return word;}
public byte[] asSound() {return sound;}
public void becomeString() {
   bridge.become(new StringWordImplementation(bridge, this));
}
public void becomeSound() {}
}
```

❖   ❖   ❖

Known uses

Symbian's EPOC C++ environment handles strings as *descriptors* containing a buffer and a length. Descriptors provide many different representations of strings: in ROM, in a fixed-length buffer, in a variable-length buffer and as a portion of another string. Each kind of descriptor has its own class, and users of the strings see only two base classes: one for a read-only string, the other for a writable string (Symbian 1999b).

Psion 5's Word Editor has two internal representations of a document. When the document is small the editor keeps formatting information for the entire document; when the document is larger than a certain arbitrary size, the editor switches to storing information for only the part of the document currently on display. The switch is handled internally in the editor's text view component; clients of the component (including other applications that need rich text) are unaware of the change in representation.

Smalltalk's collection classes also use this pattern: all satisfy the same protocol, so a user need not be aware of the particular implementation used for a given collection (Goldberg and Robson 1983). Java's standard collection classes have a similar design (Chan et al. 1998). C++'s STL collections also use this pattern: STL defines the shared interface using template classes; all the collection classes support the same access functions and iterator operations (Stroustrup 1997; Austern 1998).

Rolfe and Nolan's Lighthouse system has a 'Deal' class with two implementations: by default an instance contains only basic data required for simple calculations; on demand, it extends itself by reading the entire deal information from its database. Since clients are aware when they are doing more complex calculations, the change is explicit, implemented as a FattenDeal method on the object.

MULTIPLE REPRESENTATIONS can also be useful to implement other memory-saving patterns. For example, the LOOM Virtual Memory system for Smalltalk uses two different representations for objects: one for objects completely in memory, and a second for objects PAGED out to SECONDARY STORAGE (Kaehler and Krasner

1983). Format Software's PLUS application implements CAPTAIN OATES (57) for images using three representations, which change dynamically: a bitmap ready to `bitblt` to the screen, a compressed bitmap, and a reference to a representation in the database.

See also

The BRIDGE pattern describes how abstractions and implementations can vary independently (Gamma et al. 1995). The MULTIPLE REPRESENTATIONS pattern typically uses only half of the BRIDGE pattern, because implementations can vary (to give the multiple representations) but the abstraction remains the same.

Various different representations can use explicit PACKED DATA (174) or COMPRESSION (135), be stored in SECONDARY STORAGE (79), be READ-ONLY (65), or be SHARED (182). They may also use FIXED ALLOCATION (226) or VARIABLE ALLOCATION (236).

MEMORY ALLOCATION

Fixed Allocation

Variable Allocation

Memory Discard

Pooled Allocation

Compaction

Reference Counting

Garbage Collection

5

MEMORY ALLOCATION

How do you allocate memory to store your data structures?

- You're developing object-oriented software for a memory-constrained system.

- You've designed suitable data structures for each of your objects.

- You need to store these data structures in main memory.

- You need to recycle this memory once the objects are no longer required.

- Different classes — and different instances of a single class — have different allocation requirements.

When a system begins running, it sees only virgin memory space. A running program, particularly an object-oriented one, uses this memory as 'objects' or data structures, each occupying a unique and differently sized area of memory. These objects will change with time: some remain indefinitely; others last varying lengths of time; some are extremely transient. Computing environments need *allocation* mechanisms to call these structures into being from the primordial soup of system memory.

For example, the Strap-It-On PC uses objects in many different ways. User interface objects must be available quickly, with no awkward pauses. Transient objects must appear and disappear with minimum overhead. Objects in its major calculation engines must be provided and deallocated with minimum programmer effort. Objects in its real-time device drivers must be available within a fixed maximum time. Yet processing power is limited so, for example, an allocation technique that minimizes programmer effort can't possibly satisfy the real-time constraints. No single allocation approach suits all of these requirements.

At first glance, a particular environment may not appear to provide much of a choice, especially as many object-oriented languages, including Smalltalk and Java, allocate all objects dynamically (Goldberg and Robson 1983; Gosling et al. 1996; Egremont 1999). But in practice even these languages support a good deal of variation. Objects can exist for a long or short time (allowing runtime compiler optimizations); you can reuse old objects rather than creating new ones; or you can create all the objects you need at the start of the program. More low-level languages like C and C++ support even more possibilities. So what strategy should you use to store your objects?

> *Therefore:* **Choose the simplest allocation technique that meets your need.**

Each time you allocate an object, decide which technique is most suitable for allocating that object. Generally, you should choose the simplest allocation technique that will meet your needs, to avoid unnecessarily complicating the program, and also to avoid unnecessary work. The four main techniques for allocating objects that we discuss in this chapter are (in order from the simplest to the most complex):

FIXED ALLOCATION (226)   Pre-allocating objects as the system starts running.

MEMORY DISCARD (244)   Allocating transient objects in groups, often on the stack.

VARIABLE ALLOCATION (236)   Allocating objects dynamically as necessary from a heap.

POOLED ALLOCATION (251)   Allocating objects dynamically from pre-allocated memory space.

The actual complexity of these patterns does depend on the programming language you are using: in particular, in C or C++ MEMORY DISCARD is easier to use than VARIABLE ALLOCATION, while languages like Smalltalk and Java assume VARIABLE ALLOCATION as the default.

What goes up must come down; what is allocated must be deallocated. If you use any of the dynamic patterns (VARIABLE ALLOCATION, MEMORY DISCARD, or POOLED ALLOCATION) you'll also need to consider how the memory occupied by objects can be returned to the system when the objects are no longer needed. In this chapter we present three further patterns that deal with deallocation: COMPACTION (259) ensures the memory once occupied by deallocated objects can be recycled efficiently, and REFERENCE COUNTING (268) and GARBAGE COLLECTION (278) determine when shared objects can be deallocated.

Consequences

Choosing an appropriate allocation strategy can ensure that the program meets its *memory requirements*, and that its runtime demands for memory are *predictable*. Fixed allocation strategies can increase a program's *real-time responsiveness* and *time performance*, while variable strategies can ensure the program can *scale up* to take advantage of more memory if it becomes available, and avoid allocating memory that is unused.

However: Supporting more than one allocation strategy requires *programmer effort* to implement. The system developers must consider the allocation strategies carefully, which takes significantly more work than just using the default allocation technique supported by the programming language. This approach also requires *programmer discipline* since developers must ensure that they use suitable allocation strategies. Allocating large amounts of memory as a system begins executing can increase its *start-up time,* while relying on dynamic allocation can make memory use *hard to predict* in advance.

❖   ❖   ❖

Implementation

As with all patterns, the patterns in this chapter can be applied together, often with one pattern relying on another as part of its implementation, however, the patterns in this chapter can be applied in a particularly wide variety of permutations. For example, you could have a very large object allocated on the heap (VARIABLE ALLOCATION (236)), which contains an embedded array of sub-objects (FIXED ALLOCATION (226)) that are allocated internally by the large containing object (POOLED ALLOCATION (251)). Here, the FIXED ALLOCATION and POOLED ALLOCATION patterns are implemented within the large object, and each pattern is supported by other patterns in their implementation.

You can use different patterns for different instances of the same class. For example, different instances of an Integer class could be allocated on the heap (VARIABLE ALLOCATION), on the stack (MEMORY DISCARD (244)), or embedded in another object (FIXED ALLOCATION), depending on the requirements of each particular use.

You can also choose between different patterns depending on circumstance. For example, a Smalltalk networking application was required to support a guaranteed minimum throughput, but could improve its performance if it could allocate extra buffer memory. The final design pre-allocated a pool of five buffers (FIXED ALLOCATION); if a new work item arrived while all the buffers were in use, and more memory was available, the system dynamically allocated further buffers (VARIABLE ALLOCATION).

Here are some further issues to consider when designing memory allocation:

1. Fragmentation

Fragmentation is a significant problem with dynamic memory allocation. There are two kinds of fragmentation: *internal fragmentation*, when a data structure does not use all the memory it has been allocated; and *external fragmentation*, when memory lying between two allocated structures cannot be used, generally because it is too small to store anything else (Figure 5.1). For example, if you delete an object that occupies the space between two other objects, some of the deleted object's space will be wasted, unless

- the other objects are also deleted, giving a single contiguous memory space;
- you are able to move objects around in memory, to squeeze the unused space out from between the objects; or
- you are lucky enough to allocate another object that fills the unused space exactly.

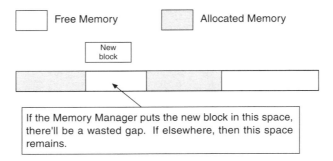

Figure 5.1   Fragmentation

Fragmentation is difficult to resolve because patterns that reduce internal fragmentation (say by allocating just the right amount of memory) typically increase external fragmentation because space is wasted between all the oddly sized allocated blocks of memory. Similarly, patterns that reduce external fragmentation (by allocating equally sized blocks of memory) increase internal fragmentation because some memory will be wasted within each block.

2. Memory exhaustion

No matter what allocation strategy you choose, you can never have enough memory to meet all eventualities: you may not pre-allocate enough objects using FIXED ALLOCATION; or a request for a VARIABLE ALLOCATION from heap or stack memory can fail; or the memory pools for POOLED ALLOCATION can be empty. Sooner or later you will run out of memory. When planning your memory allocation, you also need to consider how you will handle memory exhaustion.

2.1. Fixed-size client memories.   You can expose a fixed-size memory model directly to your users or client components. For example, many pocket calculators make users choose one of ten memories in which to save a value, with no suggestion that the system could have more memory; many components support up to a fixed number of objects in their interfaces (connections, tasks, operations, or whatever) and generate an error if this number is exceeded. This approach is easy to program, but it decreases the usability of the system, because it makes users, or client components, take full responsibility for dealing with memory exhaustion.

2.2. Signal an error.   You can signal a memory exhaustion error to the client. This approach also makes clients responsible for handling the failure, but typically leaves them with more options than if you provided a fixed number of user memories. For example, if a graphics editor program does not have enough memory to handle a large image, users may prefer to shut down other applications to release more memory in the system as a whole.

Signalling errors is more problematic internally, when one component sends an error to another. Although it is quite simple to notify client components of memory errors, typically by using exceptions or return codes, programming client components to handle errors correctly is much more difficult (see the PARTIAL FAILURE (48) pattern).

2.3. Reduce quality.   You can reduce the quantity of memory you need to allocate by reducing the quality of the data you need to store. For example, you can truncate strings and reduce the sampling frequency of sounds and images. Reducing quality can maintain system throughput, but is not applicable if it discards data that is important to users. Using smaller images, for example, may be fine in a network monitoring application, but not in a graphics manipulation program.

2.4. Delete old objects.   You can delete old or unimportant objects to release memory for new or important objects. For example, telephone exchanges can run out of memory when creating a new connection, but they can regain memory by terminating the connection that's been ringing for longest, because it's least likely to be answered (FRESH WORK BEFORE STALE (Meszaros 1996)). Similarly, many message logs keep from overflowing by storing only a set amount of messages and deleting older messages as new messages arrive.

2.5. Defer new requests.   You can delay allocation requests (and the processing that depends on them) until sufficient memory is available. The simplest and most common approach for this is for the system not to accept more input until the current tasks have completed. For example, many MS Windows applications change the pointer to a 'please wait' icon, typically an hourglass, meaning that the user can't do anything else until this operation is complete. Many communications systems have 'flow control' mechanisms to stop further input until the current input has been handled. Even simpler is batch-style processing, reading elements sequentially from a file or database and only reading the next when you've processed the previous one. More complicated approaches require concurrency in the system so that one task can block or queue requests being processed by another. Many environments support synchronization primitives such as semaphores, or higher-level pipes or shared queues that can block their clients automatically when they cannot fulfil a request. In single-threaded systems component interfaces can support callbacks or polling to notify their clients that they have completed processing a request. Doug Lea's book *Concurrent Programming in Java* (2000) discusses this in more detail, and the techniques and designs he describes are applicable to most object-oriented languages, not just Java.

2.6. Ignore the problem.   You can completely ignore the problem, and allow the program to malfunction. This strategy is, unfortunately, the default in many environments, especially where paged virtual memory is taken for granted. For example, the internet worm propagated through a bug in the UNIX `finger` demon where long messages could overwrite a fixed-sized buffer (Page 1988). This approach is trivial to implement, but can have extremely serious consequences: the worm that exploited the `finger` bug disabled much of the internet for several days.

A more predictable version of this approach is to detect the problem and immediately halt processing. While this will avoid the program running amuck through errors in memory use, it does not contribute to system stability or reliability in the long term.

❖   ❖   ❖

Specialized patterns

The following chapter explores seven patterns of memory allocation:

FIXED ALLOCATION (226) ensures you'll always have enough memory by pre-allocating structures to handle your needs, and by avoiding dynamic memory allocation during normal processing.

VARIABLE ALLOCATION (236) avoids unused empty memory space by using dynamic allocation to take memory from and return it to a heap.

MEMORY DISCARD (244) simplifies deallocating temporary objects by putting them in a temporary workspace and discarding the whole workspace at once.

POOLED ALLOCATION (251) avoids the overhead of variable allocation given a large number of similar objects, by pre-allocating them as required and maintaining a 'free list' of objects to be reused.

COMPACTION (259) avoids memory fragmentation by moving allocated objects in memory to remove the fragmentation spaces.

REFERENCE COUNTING (268) manages shared objects by keeping a count of the references to each shared object, and deleting each object when its reference count is zero.

GARBAGE COLLECTION (278) manages shared objects by periodically identifying unreferenced objects and deleting them.

Figure 5.2 shows the relationships between the patterns.

Possibly the key aspect in choosing a pattern is deciding which is more important: minimizing memory size or making memory use predictable. FIXED ALLOCATION will make memory use predictable, but generally leaves some memory unused, while VARIABLE ALLOCATION can make better use of memory but provides less predictability.

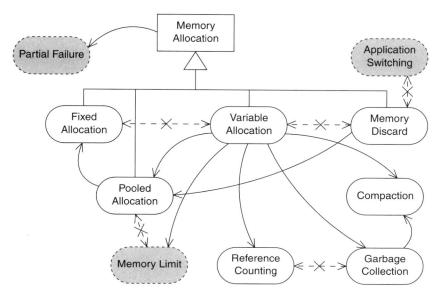

Figure 5.2 MEMORY ALLOCATION pattern relationships

See also

The SMALL DATA STRUCTURES (169) chapter explores patterns to determine the structure of the allocated objects. COMPRESSION (135) provides an alternative means to reduce the space occupied by RAM-resident objects.

The SMALL ARCHITECTURE (25) patterns describe how to plan memory use for the system as a whole, how memory should be communicated between components, and how to deal with memory exhaustion using PARTIAL FAILURE (48).

Kent Beck's *Smalltalk Best Practice Patterns* contains several patterns that describe how variables should be chosen to minimize object lifetimes (Beck 1997).

Fixed Allocation

Also known as: Static Allocation, Pre-Allocation

How can you ensure you will never run out of memory?

- You can't risk running out of memory.
- You need to predict the amount of memory your system will use exactly.
- You need to allocate memory quickly, or within a given time.
- Allocating memory from the heap has unacceptable overheads.

Many applications cannot risk running out of memory. For example, the Strap-It-On's Muon-based 'ET-Speak' communication system must be prepared to accept short messages from extra-terrestrials at any time; running out of memory while receiving a message could be a major loss to science. Many other systems have absolute limits to the memory available, and have no acceptable means for handling out-of-memory situations. For example, what can an anaesthetist do about a message from a patient monitor that has run out of internal memory? When users have no effective control over memory use, running out of memory can become a truly fatal program defect.

The usual object-oriented approach is to allocate objects dynamically on the heap whenever there's a need for them (Ingalls 1981). Indeed many OO languages, including Smalltalk and Java, allocate all objects from the heap. Using dynamic allocation, however, always risks running out of memory. If every component allocates memory at arbitrary times, how can you be certain that memory will never run out?

It's certainly possible to estimate a program's memory use when designing a **SMALL ARCHITECTURE** (25), but how can you be sure the estimates accurately reflect the behaviour of the finished system? Similarly, you can test the system with arbitrary combinations of data, but *'testing can be used to show the presence of bugs, but never to show their absence'* (Dijkstra 1972) so how can you be sure you've found the most pathological case?

Dynamic memory allocation has other problems. Some allocation algorithms can take unpredictable amounts of time, making them unsuitable for real-time systems. Virtually all allocation algorithms need a few extra bytes with each item to store the block size and related information. Memory can become fragmented as variable-sized memory chunks come and go, wasting further memory, and to avoid memory leaks you must be careful to deallocate every unused object.

Therefore: **Pre-allocate objects during initialization.**

Allocate fixed amounts of memory to store all the objects and data structures you will need before the start of processing. Forbid dynamic memory allocation during the execution of the program. Implement objects using fixed-sized data structures such as arrays or pre-allocated collection classes.

Design your objects so that you can assign them to new uses without having to invoke their constructors — the normal approach is to write separate initialization functions and dummy constructors. Alternatively (in C++) keep the allocated memory unused until it's needed and construct objects in this memory.

As always, you shouldn't 'hard-code' the numbers of objects allocated (Plum and Saks 1991) — even though this will be fixed for any given program run. Use named constants in code or system parameters in the runtime system so that the numbers can be adjusted when necessary.

So, for example, the ET-Speak specification team has agreed that it would be reasonable to store only the last few messages received and to set a limit to the total storage ET-Speak can use. The ET-Speak programmers allocated a fixed buffer for this storage, and made new incoming messages overwrite the oldest messages.

Consequences

FIXED ALLOCATION means you can *predict the system's memory use* exactly: you can tell how much memory your program will need at compile time. The *time required* for any memory allocation operation is constant and small. These two features make this pattern particularly suitable for *real-time* applications.

In addition, fixed allocation minimizes *space overhead* for using pointers, and *global overhead* for a garbage collector. Using FIXED ALLOCATION *reduces programmer effort* when there's no need to check for allocation failure. It makes programs *easier to test* (they either have enough memory or they don't) and often makes programs more reliable as there is less to go wrong.

Fixed memory tends to be allocated at the start of a process and never deallocated, so there will be little *external fragmentation*.

However: The largest liability of FIXED ALLOCATION is that to handle expected worst case loads, you have to allocate more memory than necessary for average loads. This will increase the program's *memory requirements*, as much of the memory is unused due to *internal fragmentation,* particularly in systems with many concurrent applications.

To use FIXED ALLOCATION, you have to find ways to limit or defer demands on memory. Often you will have to limit throughput, so that you never begin a new task until previous tasks have been completed; and to limit capacity, imposing a fixed maximum size or number of items that your program will store. Both these reduce the program's *usability*.

Pre-allocating the memory can increase the system's *start-up time* — particularly with programming languages that don't support static data.

In many cases FIXED ALLOCATION can increase *programmer effort*; the programmer is forced to write code to deal with the fixed size limit, and should at least think about how to handle the problem. It can also make it harder to take advantage of more memory should it become available, reducing the program's *scalability.*

Nowadays programs that use fixed-size structures are sometimes seen as *lower-quality designs*, although this probably says more about fashion than function!

Implementation

This pattern is straightforward to implement:

- Design objects that can be pre-allocated.
- Allocate all the objects you need at the start of the program.
- Use only the pre-allocated objects, and ensure you don't ever need (or create) more objects than you've allocated.

1. Designing fixed allocation objects

Objects used for the FIXED ALLOCATION pattern may have to be designed specifically for the purpose. With FIXED ALLOCATION, memory is allocated (and constructors invoked) only at the very start of the system; any destructor will be invoked only when the system terminates (if then). Rather than using constructors and destructors normally, you'll need to provide extra pseudo-constructors and pseudo-destructors that configure or release the pre-allocated objects to suit their use in the program.

```
class FixedAllocationThing {
public:
    FixedAllocationThing() {}

    Construct() { . . . }
    Destruct()  { . . . }
};
```

By writing appropriate constructors you can also design classes so that only one (or a certain number) of instances can be allocated, as described by the SINGLETON pattern (Gamma et al. 1995).

2. Pre-allocating objects

Objects using FIXED ALLOCATION need to be pre-allocated at the start of the program. Some languages (C++, COBOL, FORTRAN etc.) support fixed allocation directly, so that you can specify the structure statically at compile time so the memory will be set up correctly as the program loads. For example, the following defines some buffers in C++:

```
struct Buffer { char data[1000]; };
static Buffer AllBuffers[N_BUFFERS_REQUIRED];
```

Smalltalk permits more sophisticated FIXED ALLOCATION, allowing you to include arbitrarily complicated allocated object structures into the persistent Smalltalk image loaded whenever an application starts.

In most other OO languages, you can implement FIXED ALLOCATION by allocating all the objects you need at the start of the program, calling new as normal. Once objects are allocated you should never call new again, but use the pre-existing objects instead, and call their pseudo-constructors to initialize them as necessary. To support this pattern, you can design objects so that their constructors (or calls to new) signal errors if they are called once the pre-allocation phase has finished.

Pre-allocating objects from the system heap raises the possibility that even this initial allocation could fail due to insufficient memory. In this situation there are two reasonable strategies you can adopt. You can regard this as a fatal error and terminate the program; at this point termination is usually a safe option, as the program has not yet started running and it's unlikely to do much damage. Alternatively, you can write the code so that the program can continue in the reduced space, as described in the PARTIAL FAILURE (48) pattern.

3. Library classes

It's straightforward to avoid allocation for classes you've written: just avoid heap operations such as new and delete. It's more difficult to avoid allocation in library classes, unless the libraries have been designed so that you can override their normal allocation strategies. For example, a Java or C++ dynamic vector class will allocate memory whenever it has insufficient capacity to store an element inserted into it.

Most collection classes separate their size (the number of elements they currently contain) from their capacity (the number of elements they have allocated space for); a collection's size must be less than or equal to its capacity. To avoid extra allocation, you can pre-allocate containers with sufficient capacity to meet their needs (see HYPOTH-A-SIZED COLLECTION (Auer and Beck 1996)). For example, the C++ Standard Template Library precisely defines the circumstances when containers will allocate memory, and also allows you to customize this allocation (Austern 1998).

Alternatively, you can use EMBEDDED POINTERS (198) to implement relationships between objects, thus removing the need for library collection classes to allocate memory beyond your control.

4. Embedded objects

A very common form of FIXED ALLOCATION in object-oriented programs is *object embedding* or *inlining*: one object is allocated directly within another object. For example, a Screen object owning a Rectangle object might embed the Rectangle in its own data structure rather than having a pointer to a separate object (Figure 5.3).

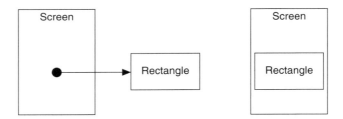

Figure 5.3   Embedded objects

C++ and Eiffel support inlining directly (Stroupstrup 1997; Meyer 1992). In other languages you can inline objects manually by refactoring your program, moving the fields and methods from the internal object into the main object and rewriting method bodies as necessary to maintain correctness (Fowler 1999).

In languages, such as Java and Smalltalk, that do not support embedded objects intrinsically you won't be able to refer to the embedded object or pass it as an argument to other objects in the system. For example, you might implement a Rectangle using two point objects as follows:

```
class Point {                           class Rectangle {
    private int x;                          private Point topLeft;
    private int y;                          private Point bottomRight;
    // methods omitted                      // etc.
}                                       }
```

But you could avoid the need to allocate the two Point objects by making the two Point objects inline, at the cost of not being able to use the Point objects directly:

```
class InlinedRectangle {
    private int xTopLeft;
    private int yTopLeft;
    private int xBottomRight;
    private int yBottomRight;
    // ...
}
```

Embedding objects removes the time and space overheads required by heap allocation: the main object and the embedded object are just one object as far as the runtime system is concerned. The embedded object no longer exists as a separate entity, however, so you cannot change or replace the embedded object and you cannot use subtype polymorphism (virtual function calls or message sends).

5. Deferring commitment to fixed allocation

Sometimes you need to make the decision to use FIXED ALLOCATION later in the project, either because you are unsure it will be worth the effort, or because you used variable allocation but discovered memory problems during performance testing. In that case you can use Pooled Allocation (251) to give a similar interface to variable allocation but from a pre-allocated, fixed-size pool.

Example

This example implements a message store as a fixed-size data structure, similar to the circular buffer used in the ET-Speak application. The message store stores a fixed number of fixed-size messages, overwriting old messages as new messages arrive.

Figure 5.4 shows an example of the message store, handling the text of Hamlet's most famous soliloquy:

To be, or not to be, that is the question.
Whether 'tis nobler in the mind to suffer the slings and arrows of outrageous fortune,
Or to take arms against a sea of troubles and by opposing end them?
To die, to sleep — no more;
And by a sleep to say we end the heart-ache and the thousand natural shocks
    That flesh is heir to.
'Tis a consummation devoutly to be wished.

The figure shows the store just as the most recent message ('tis a consummation ...' is just about to overwrite the oldest ('To be, or not to be ...').

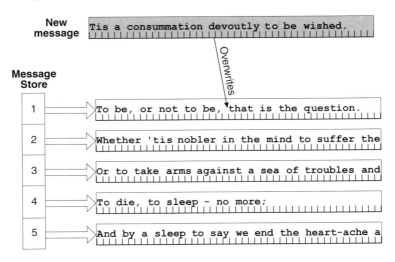

Figure 5.4   Circular buffer message store

1. Java implementation

The basic MessageStore class stores a two-dimensional array of messages, an array of message lengths, the index of the oldest message in the store, and a count of the number of messages in the store. It's impossible to avoid memory allocation using the existing versions of the Java String and StringBuffer classes (Chan et al. 1998), so we have implemented the store using character arrays. A more robust implementation would create a FixedMemoryString class to make it easier to manipulate these character arrays, or else modify the StringBuffer class to allow clients to use it without memory allocation.

```java
class MessageStore {
    protected char[][] messages;
    protected int[] messageLengths;
    protected int messageSize;
    protected int oldestMessage;
    protected int size;
    public int messageSize() {return messages[0].length;}
    public int capacity() {return messages.length;}
```

The MessageStore constructor has two initialization parameters: the number of messages to store (capacity) and the maximum size of each message (maximumMessageLength). The constructor allocates all the memory ever used; no other method allocates memory either explicitly or through library operations.

```java
public MessageStore(int capacity, int messageSize) {
    this.messageSize = messageSize;
    messages = new char[capacity][messageSize];
    messageLengths = new int[capacity];
    oldestMessage = size = 0;
}
```

The most important method acceptMethod adds a new message into the store. This method silently overwrites earlier messages received and truncates messages that are longer than the chunkSize. Note that this message accepts a character array and length as parameters, to avoid the allocation implicit in using Java Strings.

```java
public void acceptMessage(char[] msg, int msgLength) {
    int nextMessage = (oldestMessage + size) % capacity();

    messageLengths[nextMessage] = Math.min(msgLength, messageSize);
    System.arraycopy(msg, 0, messages[nextMessage], 0,
                     messageLengths[nextMessage]);
    if (size == capacity()) {
        oldestMessage = (oldestMessage + 1) % capacity();
    } else {
        size++;
    }
}
```

The getMessage method retrieves a message from a message store. Again, to avoid using the Java String classes the client must pass in a pre-allocated buffer and the method returns the length of the string copied into the buffer (see lending in the SMALL INTERFACES (38) pattern).

```
public int getMessage(int i, char[] destination) {
   int msgIndex = (oldestMessage + i) % capacity();
   System.arraycopy( messages[msgIndex], 0, destination, 0,
                     messageLengths[msgIndex]);
   return messageLengths[msgIndex];
}
```

2. C++ implementation

C++ does less memory allocation than Java, so the same example in C++ looks more conventional than the Java example. The main difference is that all the messages are stored inside one large buffer (messageBuffer) rather than as a two-dimensional array.

```
class MessageStore {
private:
   char* messageBuffer;
   int oldestMessageNumber;
   int nMessagesInStore;
   int maxMessageLength;
   int maxMessagesInStore;
```

The constructor is straightforward:

```
public:
   MessageStore(int capacity, int maxMsgLength)
      : maxMessagesInStore(capacity),
        maxMessageLength(maxMsgLength),
        oldestMessageNumber(0),
        nMessagesInStore(0) {
           messageBuffer = new char[]Capacity() * MessageStructureSize()];
      }
```

Note that MessageStructureSize() is one byte larger than maxMessageLength to cope with the null character '\0' on the end of every C++ string:

```
int NMessagesInStore()     { return nMessagesInStore; }
int Capacity()             { return maxMessagesInStore; }
int MessageStructureSize() { return maxMessageLength+1; }
```

The AcceptMessage function copies a new message from a C++ string:

```
void AcceptMessage(const char* newMessageText) {
   int nextMessage = (oldestMessageNumber + NMessagesInStore()) % Capacity();
   int newMessageLength = strlen(newMessageText);
   int nBytesToCopy = min(newMessageLength,maxMessageLength)+1;
```

```
    strncpy(MessageAt(nextMessage), newMessageText, nBytesToCopy);
    MessageAt(nextMessage)[maxMessageLength] = '\0';
    if (NMessagesInStore() == Capacity()) {
      oldestMessageNumber = (oldestMessageNumber + 1) % Capacity();
    } else {
      nMessagesInStore++;
    }
  }
```

Accessing a message is easy: we simply return a pointer directly into the message buffer ('Borrowing' — see SMALL INTERFACES (25)). Calling GetMessage with index 0 returns the oldest message, 1 the next oldest, etc.

```
const char* GetMessage(int i) {
    int messageIndex = (oldestMessageNumber + i) % Capacity();
    return MessageAt(messageIndex);
}
```

We use an auxiliary function to locate each message buffer:

```
private:
  char * MessageAt(int i) {
      return messageBuffer + i*MessageStructureSize();
  }
}
```

❖   ❖   ❖

Known uses

Many procedural languages support only fixed allocation, so most FORTRAN and COBOL programs use only this pattern, allocating large arrays and never calling new or malloc. Nowadays, most popular languages support VARIABLE ALLOCATION (236) by default, so it can be hard to revert to FIXED ALLOCATION. Many real-time systems use this pattern too: dynamic memory allocation and compaction can take an unpredictable amount of time. The book *Real-Time Specification for Java* supports FIXED ALLOCATION directly, by allowing objects to be allocated from an ImmutableMemory area (Bollella et al. 2000).

Safety-critical systems frequently use this pattern, since dynamic memory allocation systems can fail if they run out of memory. Indeed the UK's Department of Defence regulations for safety-critical systems permitted only Fixed Allocation, although this has been relaxed recently in some cases (Matthews 1989; Ministry of Defence 1997). For example, in a smart mobile phone the telephone application must always be able to dial the emergency number (112, 999 or 911). A smart phone's telephone application typically pre-allocates all the objects it needs to make such a call — even though all its other memory allocation is dynamic.

Strings based on fixed-size buffers use this pattern. EPOC, for example, provides a template class `TBuf<int s>` representing a string up to *s* characters in length (Symbian 1999b). Programmers must either ensure than no strings can ever be allowed to overflow the buffer, or else truncate strings where necessary.

See also

VARIABLE ALLOCATION (236) saves memory by allocating only enough memory to meet immediate requirements, but requires more effort and overhead to manage and makes memory requirements harder to predict.

POOLED ALLOCATION (251) can provide memory for a larger number of small objects, by allocating space for a fixed-size number of items from a fixed-sized pool. Pooled allocation can also provide the same interface as variable allocation while allocating objects from a fixed-size memory space.

If you cannot inline whole objects into other objects, you may be able to use EMBEDDED POINTERS (198) as an alternative.

MEMORY LIMIT (32) can offer a more flexible approach to the same problem by permitting dynamic allocation while limiting the total memory size allocated to a particular component.

READ-ONLY MEMORY (65) is static by nature and always uses FIXED ALLOCATION.

Variable Allocation

Also known as: Dynamic Allocation

How can you avoid unused empty space?

- You have varying or unpredictable demands on memory.

- You need to minimize your program's memory requirements, or

- You need to maximize the amount of data you can store in a fixed amount of memory.

- You can accept the overhead of heap allocation.

- You can handle the situations where memory allocation may fail at any arbitrary point during the processing.

You have a variable amount of data to store. Perhaps you don't know how much data to store, or how it will be distributed between the classes and objects in your system.

For example, the Strap-It-On's famous Word-O-Matic word processor stores part of its current document in main memory. The amount of memory this will require is unpredictable, because it depends upon the size of the document, the screen size resolution, and the fonts and paragraph formats selected by the user. To support a voice output feature beloved by the marketing department, Word-O-Matic also saves the vocal emotions for each paragraph; some documents use no emotions, but others require the complete emotional pantechnicon: joy, anger, passion, despair, apathy. It would be very difficult indeed to pre-allocate suitable data structures to handle Word-O-Matic's requirements, because this would require balancing memory between text, formats, fonts, emotions, and everything else. Whatever choices you made, there would still be a large amount of memory wasted most of the time.

Writing a general-purpose library is even more complex than writing an application, because you can't make assumptions about the nature of your clients. Some clients may have fixed and limited demands; others might legitimately require much more, or have needs that vary enormously from moment to moment.

So how can you support flexible systems while minimizing their use of memory?

Therefore: **Allocate and deallocate variable-sized objects as and when you need them.**

Store the data in different kinds of objects, as appropriate, and allocate and free them dynamically as required. Implement the objects using dynamic structures such as linked lists, variable-length collections and trees.

Ensure objects that are no longer needed are returned for reuse, either by making explicit calls to release the memory, or by clearing references so that objects will be recovered by REFERENCE COUNTING (268) or a GARBAGE COLLECTION (278).

For example, Word-O-Matic dynamically requests memory from the system to store the user's documents. To produce voice output Word-O-Matic just requests more memory. When it no longer needs the memory (say because the user closes a document) the program releases the memory back to the Strap-It-On system for other applications to use. If Word-O-Matic runs out of memory, it suggests the user free up memory by closing another application.

Consequences

Variable-size structures avoid unused empty space, thus *reducing memory requirements* overall and generally *increasing design quality.* Because the program does not have assumptions about the amount of memory built into it directly, it is more likely to be *scalable*, able to take advantage of more memory should it become available.

A heap makes it easier to define interfaces between components; one component may allocate objects and pass them to another, leaving the responsibility for freeing memory to the second. This makes the system easier to program, improving the *design quality* and making it *easier to maintain*, because you can easily create new objects or new fields in objects without affecting the rest of the allocation in the system.

Allocating memory throughout a program's execution (rather than all at the beginning) can decrease a program's *start-up time.*

However: There will be a *memory overhead* to manage the dynamically allocated memory; typically a two-word header for every allocated block. Memory allocation and deallocation require *processor time*, and this cost can be *global* to the language run-time system, the operating system or even, in the case of the ill-fated Intel 432, in hardware. The memory required for typical and worst-case scenarios can become *hard to predict.* Because the objects supplied by the heap are of varying size, heaps tend to get *fragmented,* adding to the *memory overhead* and *unpredictability,*

Furthermore, you must be prepared to handle the situation where memory runs out. This may happen *unpredictably* at any point where memory is allocated; handling it *adds additional complexity* to the code and requires additional *programmer effort* to manage, and time and energy to *test properly.* Finally, of couse, it's impossible to use variable allocation in *read-only memory.*

❖   ❖   ❖

Implementation

Using this pattern is trivial in most object-oriented languages; it's what you do by default. Every OO language provides a mechanism to create new objects in heap memory, and another mechanism (explicit or implicit) to return the memory to the heap, usually invoking an object cleanup mechanism at the same time (Ingalls 1981).

1. Deleting objects

It's not enough just to create new objects, you also have to recycle the memory they occupy when they are no longer required. Failing to dispose of unused objects causes *memory leaks*, one of the most common kinds of bugs in object-oriented programming. While a workstation or desktop PC may be able to tolerate a certain amount of memory leakage, systems with less memory must conserve memory more carefully.

There are two main kinds of techniques for managing memory: *manual* and *automatic*. The manual technique is usually called *object deletion*; example mechanisms are C++'s delete keyword and C's free library call. The object is returned to free memory immediately during the operation. The main problem with manual memory management is that it is easy to forget to delete objects: forgetting to delete an object results in a memory leak. A more dramatic problem is to delete an object that is still in use; this can cause your system to crash, especially if the memory is then reallocated to some other object.

In contrast, automatic memory management techniques such as REFERENCE COUNTING (268) and GARBAGE COLLECTION (278) do not require programs to delete objects directly; rather they work out automatically which objects can be deleted, by determining which objects are no longer used in the program. This may happen some time after the object has been discarded. Automatic management prevents the bugs caused by deleting objects that are still in use, since an object still referenced will never be deleted. They also simplify the code required to deal with memory management. Unfortunately, however, it's quite common to have collections, or static variables, still containing references to objects that are no longer actually required. Automatic techniques can't delete these objects, so they remain — they are memory leaks. It remains the programmer's responsibility to ensure this doesn't happen.

2. Signalling allocation failure

VARIABLE ALLOCATION is flexible and dynamic, so it can tune a system's memory allocation to suit the instantaneous demands of the program. Unfortunately, because it is dynamic the program's memory use is unpredictable, and it can fail if the system has insufficient memory to meet a program's request. Allocation failures need to be communicated to the program making the request.

2.1. Error codes.   Allocation functions (such as new) return an error code if allocation fails. This is easy to implement: C's malloc, for example, returns a null pointer on failure. This approach requires programmer discipline and leads to clumsy application code, since you must check for allocation failure every time you allocate some memory. Furthermore, every component interface must specify mechanisms to signal that allocation has failed. In practice, this approach, although simple, should be used as a last resort.

2.2. Exceptions.   Far easier for the programmer allocating memory is to signal failure using an exception. The main benefit of exceptions is that the special case of allocation failure can be handled separately from the main body of the application, while still ensuring that the allocation failure does not go unnoticed. Support for exceptions can increase code size, however, and make it more difficult to implement code in intermediate functions that must release resources as a result of the exception.

2.3. Terminating the program.   Ignoring allocation failure altogether is the simplest possible approach. If failure does happen, therefore, the system can try to notify the user as appropriately, then abort. For example, many MS Windows programs put up a dialog box on heap failure, then terminate. This approach is clearly only suitable when there is significantly more memory available than the application is likely to need — in other words, when you are not in a memory-limited environment. Aborting the program is acceptable in the one case where you are using the system heap to implement FIXED ALLOCATION (226) by providing a fixed amount of memory before your program has begun executing, because you cannot tolerate failure once the program has actually started running.

3. Avoiding fragmentation

Fragmentation can be a significant problem with VARIABLE ALLOCATION from a heap for some applications. Often, the best way to address fragmentation is not to worry about it until you suspect that it is affecting your program's performance. You can detect a problem by comparing the amount of memory allocated to useful objects with the total memory available to the system (see the MEMORY LIMIT (32) pattern for a way of counting the total memory allocated to objects). Memory that is not in use but cannot be allocated may be due to fragmentation.

3.1. Variable-sized allocations.   Avoid interspersing allocations of very large and small objects. For example, a small object allocated between two large objects that are then freed will prevent the heap manager combining the two large empty spaces, making it difficult to allocate further larger blocks (Figure 5.5). You can address this by having two or more heaps for different-sized objects: Microsoft C++, for example, uses one heap for allocations of less than about 200 bytes, and a second heap for all other allocations (Microsoft 1997a).

3.2. Transient objects.   Operating systems can often reclaim unused memory from the end of the heap, but not from the middle (Figure 5.6). If you have a transient need for a very large object, avoid allocating further objects until you've deallocated it.

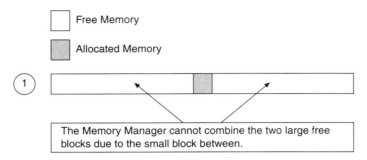

Figure 5.5   Interspersed large and small objects

Otherwise, you may leave a very large hole in the heap, which never gets filled and cannot be returned to the wider system until your application terminates. For the same reason, be careful of reallocating buffers to increase their size; this leaves the memory allocated to the old buffer unused in the middle of the heap. Use the MEMORY DISCARD (244) pattern to provide specialized allocation for transient objects.

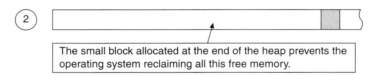

Figure 5.6   Transient objects

3.3. Grouping allocations.   Try to keep related allocations and deallocations together, in preference to interspersing them with unrelated heap operations (Figure 5.7). This way, the allocations are likely to be contiguous, and the deallocations will free up all of the contiguous space, creating a large contiguous area for reallocation.

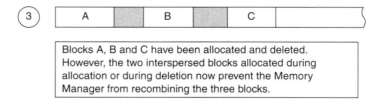

Figure 5.7   Unrelated interspersed objects

4. Standard allocation sizes

Normally applications tell the heap the sizes of the objects they need to allocate, and the heap allocates memory to store those objects. Another way around fragmentation is for the heap to specify the sizes of memory blocks available to the application. This works if you can afford to waste unused memory inside small blocks (internal fragmentation), if all the objects you allocated have the same size (**POOLED ALLOCATION** (251)), or the application can support non-contiguous allocation. For example, if you can use ten 1K memory blocks rather than one 10K block, the heap will be much more likely to be able to meet your requirements when memory is low.

6. Implementing a heap

A good implementation of a heap has to solve a number of difficult problems:

- how to represent an allocated cell;
- how to manage the 'free list' of blocks of deallocated memory;
- how to ensure requests for new blocks reuse a suitable free block;
- how to prevent the heap becoming fragmented into smaller and smaller blocks of free memory by combining adjacent free blocks (Figure 5.8).

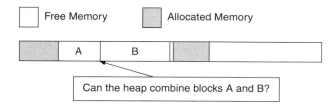

Figure 5.8   Combining adjacent free blocks

Knuth (1997) and Jones and Lins (1996) describe many implementations of memory heaps and garbage collectors that address these problems; Goldberg and Robson (1983) present a detailed example in Smalltalk. In practice, however, you'll almost always be better off buying or reusing an existing heap implementation. Libraries for low-level memory management, such as Doug Lea's malloc (Lea 2000), are readily available.

Example

We can implement a Message Store using **VARIABLE ALLOCATION** from the Java heap. The implementation of this version is much simpler, even though we've kept the strange character-array interface for compatibility with the **FIXED ALLOCATION** (226) version. Because we're able to allocate objects on the heap at any time, we can use library routines that allocate heap memory, and we can rely on the Java built-in memory failure exceptions and garbage collection to deal with resource limitations and object deletion.

The HeapMessageStore class simply uses a Java vector to store messages:

```
class HeapMessageStore {
    protected Vector messages = new Vector();
```

To accept a message, we simply add a string into the vector.

```
public void acceptMessage(char[] msg, int msgLength) {
    messages.addElement(new String(msg, 0, msgLength));
}
```

Of course, these allocations could fail if there is not enough memory, propagating exceptions into the client code.

To return a message, we can copy the string into the array provided by the client, keeping the same interface as the FIXED ALLOCATION version:

```
public int getMessage(int i, char[] destination) {
    String result = (String) messages.elementAt(i);
    result.getChars(0, result.length(), destination, 0);
    return result.length();
}
```

Or more simply we could just return the string — if the rest of the system permitted, we could add messages by storing a string directly as well:

```
public String getMessage(int i) {
    return (String) messages.elementAt(i);
}
```

Finally, we now need to provide a way for clients to delete messages from the store, since they are no longer overwritten automatically:

```
public void deleteMessage(int i) {
    messages.removeElementAt(i);
}
```

This relies on Java's GARBAGE COLLECTION (278) to clean up the String object and any objects in the internal implementation of the Vector.

Known uses

Virtually all object-oriented programming languages support this pattern by encouraging the use of dynamically allocated memory and by providing libraries based on variable allocation. The vast majority of C++, Smalltalk, and Java applications use this pattern by default. Other languages that encourage dynamic memory allocation also encourage this pattern; hence most C, Pascal, and Lisp programs use this pattern too. Most environments provide dynamically allocated strings, which use variable-length data structures, and dynamic languages like Smalltalk and Java provide built-in garbage collectors to manage dynamically varying storage requirements.

See also

COMPACTION (259) can reduce the memory overhead from fragmentation, usually at a cost in time performance. If the memory runs out, the program should normally suffer only a PARTIAL FAILURE (48). Using FIXED ALLOCATION (226) avoids the overhead, unpredictability, and complexity of a variable-sized structure at the cost of often allocating more memory than is actually required. MULTIPLE REPRESENTATIONS (209) can switch between different variable-sized structures for particular cases. You can limit the memory allocated to specific components by imposing a MEMORY LIMIT (32).

The HYPOTH-A-SIZE collection pattern optimizes allocation of variable-sized structures (Auer and Beck 1996).

Exceptional C++ (Sutter 2000), *Advanced C++* (Coplien 1994), and *More Effective C++* (Meyers 1996) describe various programming techniques to ensure objects are deleted correctly in C++.

Doug Lea describes the design of his memory allocator, malloc, in *A Memory Allocator* (Lea 2000). Many versions of the UNIX system use this allocator, including Linux. Paul Wilson and Mark Johnston have conducted several surveys of the performance of memory that demonstrate that standard allocation algorithms (such as Doug Lea's) are suitable for most programs (Johnstone and Wilson 1998).

Lycklama (1999) describes several situations where unused Java objects will not be deleted, and techniques for avoiding them.

Memory Discard

Also known as: Stack Allocation, Scratchpad

How can you allocate temporary objects?

- You are doing OO programming with limited memory.

- You need transient objects that all last only for a well-defined time.

- You don't want temporary allocations to interfere with the allocation of permanent objects.

- You don't want the complexity of implementing garbage collection or the overhead of heap allocation.

- These objects don't own non-memory resources, or have simple mechanisms to free them.

Dynamic allocation techniques can impose significant overheads. For example, the designers of the Strap-It-On's 'Back Seat Jet Pilot' application fondly hoped to connect the Strap-It-On to the main control system of a commercial jet plane, allowing passengers to take over in an emergency! The method that calculates the control parameters uses a large number of temporary objects and must execute about 50 times a second. If the objects were allocated from the Strap-It-On's system heap, the cycle time would be too slow, and the jet would crash immediately.

Similar (but less far-fetched, perhaps) situations are common in programming. You often need a set of transient objects with lifetimes that are closely linked to the execution of the code, the most common example being objects that last for the duration of a method invocation.

FIXED ALLOCATION (226) is unsuitable for temporary objects because, by definition, it allocates space permanently and requires you to know exactly which objects will be required in advance. VARIABLE ALLOCATION (236) isn't suitable for allocating such transient objects either, as it can be relatively slow and lots of temporary objects can fragment the heap.

Therefore: **Allocate objects from a temporary workspace and discard it on completion.**

Use a program stack frame, a temporary heap, or a pre-allocated area of memory as a temporary workspace to store transient objects. Allocate objects from this memory area by incrementing an appropriate pointer. Deallocate all the objects simultaneously by discarding or resetting the memory area. If necessary keep a list of other resources owned by the transient objects and release these explicitly.

For example, the Back Seat Jet Pilot application pre-allocates a buffer (FIXED ALLOCATION), and allocates each temporary object by incrementing a pointer within this buffer. On return from the calculation method, the pointer is reset to the start of the buffer, effectively discarding all of the temporary objects. This made the calculation of the jet plane controls quite fast enough, so that when the aviation authorities banned Back Seat Jet Pilot on safety grounds the designers were triumphantly able to convert it to create the best-selling Strap-Jet Flight Simulator.

Consequences

Both memory allocation and deallocation are very fast, improving the system's *time performance*. The time required is fixed, making it suitable for *real-time* systems. Initializing the memory area is fast, so *start-up time* costs are minimal. The temporary workspace doesn't last long, which avoids *fragmentation*.

The basic pattern is easy to program, requiring little *programmer effort*. By quarantining transient objects from other memory allocations, this pattern can make the memory consumption of the whole system *more predictable,* ensuring that transient objects remain a strictly *local* affair.

However: *Programmer discipline* is required to allocate transient objects from the temporary workspace, and to manage any external resources owned by the objects, and to ensure that the transient objects are not used after the workspace has been discarded or recycled. In particular, if the temporary objects use objects from external libraries, these may allocate normal heap memory, or operating system handles.

Because this pattern increases the program's complexity, it also increases its *testing cost*. Languages that rely on automatic memory management generally do not support the MEMORY DISCARD pattern directly: the point of automatic memory management is that it discards the objects for you.

Implementation

Here are some issues to consider when implementing MEMORY DISCARD.

1. Stack allocation

In languages that support it, such as C++ and Pascal, stack allocation is so common that we take it for granted; generally, stack allocation is the most common form of MEMORY DISCARD. Objects are allocated on the program stack for a method or function call, and deallocated when the call returns. This is very easy to program, but supports only objects with the exact lifetime of the method.

Some C and C++ environments even allow variable-sized allocation on the stack. Microsoft C++, for example, supports _alloca to allocate memory that lasts only till the end of the function (Microsoft 1997a):

```
void* someMemory = _alloca(100); // Allocates 100 bytes on the stack
```

GNU G++ has a similar facility (Stallman 1999). These functions are not standard, however, and no form of stack allocation is possible in standard Java or Smalltalk.

2. Temporary heaps

You can allocate some memory permanently (FIXED ALLOCATION) or temporarily (VARIABLE ALLOCATION), and create your objects in this area. If you will delete the transient objects en masse when you delete the whole workspace, you can allocate objects simply by increasing a pointer into the temporary workspace: this should be almost as efficient as stack allocation. You can then recycle all the objects in the heap by resetting the pointer back to the start of the workspace, or just discard the whole heap when you are done.

A temporary heap is more difficult to implement than stack allocation, but has the advantage that you can control the lifetime and size of the allocated area directly.

2.1. Using operating system heaps in C++.
Although there are no standard C++ functions that support more than one heap, many environments provide vendor-specific APIs to multiple heaps. EPOC, for example, provides the following functions to support temporary heaps (Symbian 1999b):

UserHeap::ChunkHeap	Creates a heap from the system memory pool.
RHeap::SwitchHeap	Switches heaps, so that all future allocations for this thread come from the heap passed as a parameter.
RHeap::FreeAll	Efficiently deletes all objects allocated in a heap.
RHeap::Close	Destroys a heap.

MS Windows CE and other Windows variants provide the functions (Microsoft 97):

HeapCreate	Creates a heap from the system memory pool.
HeapAlloc, HeapFree	Allocates and releases memory from a heap passed as a parameter.
HeapDestroy	Destroys a heap.

PalmOs is designed for much smaller heaps than either EPOC or CE, and doesn't encourage multiple dynamic heaps. Of course, Palm applications do **APPLICATION SWITCHING** (84), so discard all their dynamic program data regularly.

2.2. Using C++ placement new. If you implement your own C++ heap or use the Windows CE heap functions, you cannot use the standard version of the operator new, because it allocates memory from the default heap. C++ includes the placement new operator that constructs an object within some memory that you supply (Stroustrup 1997). You can use the placement new operator with any public constructor:

```
void* allocatedMemory = HeapAlloc(temporaryHeap, sizeof(MyClass));
MyClass* pMyClass = new(allocatedMemory) MyClass;
```

Placement new is usually provided as part of the C++ standard library, but if not it's trivial to implement:

```
void* operator new(size_t /*heapSizeInBytes*/, void* memorySpace) {
    return memorySpace;
}
```

3. Releasing resources held by transient objects

Transient objects can own resources such as heap memory or external system objects (e.g. file or window handles). You need to ensure that these resources are released when the temporary objects are destroyed. C++ guarantees to invoke destructors for all stack-allocated objects whenever a C++ function exits, either normally or via an exception. In C++ *'resource de-allocation is finalization'* (Stroustrup 1995) so you should release resources in the destructor. The C++ standard library includes the auto_ptr class that mimics a pointer, but deletes the object it points to when it is itself destructed, unless the object has been released first. (See **PARTIAL FAILURE** (48) for more discussion of auto_ptr.)

It's much more complex to release resources held by objects in a temporary heap, because the heap generally does not know the classes of the objects that are stored within it. Efficient heap designs do not even store the number of objects they contain, but simply the size of the heap and a pointer to the next free location.

If you do keep a list of every object in a temporary heap, and can arrange that they all share a common base class, you can invoke the destructor of each object explicitly:

```
object->~BaseClass();
```

But it's usually simpler to ensure that objects in temporary heaps do not hold external resources.

When resources can be **SHARED** (182), so that there may be other references to the resources in addition to the transient ones, simple deallocation from the destructor may not be enough, and you may need to use **REFERENCE COUNTING** (268) or even **GARBAGE COLLECTION** (278) to manage the resources.

4. Dangling pointers

You have to be very careful about returning references to discardable objects. These references will be invalid once the workspace has been discarded. Accessing objects via such *dangling pointers* can have unpredictable results, especially if the memory that was used for the temporary workspace is now being used for some other purpose, and it takes care and programmer discipline to avoid this problem.

Example

This C++ example implements a temporary heap. The heap memory itself uses FIXED ALLOCATION (226); it's allocated during the heap object initialization and lasts as long as the heap object. It supports a Reset() function that discards all the objects within it. The heap takes its memory from the system-wide heap so that its size can be configured during initialization.

Using such a heap is straightforward, with the help of another overloaded operator new. For example, the following creates a 1,000-byte heap, allocates an object on it, then discards the object. The heap will also be discarded when theHeap goes out of scope. Note that the class IntermediateCalculationResult may not have a destructor.

```
TemporaryHeap theHeap(1000);
IntermediateCalculationResult* p =
          new(theHeap) IntermediateCalculationResult;
theHeap.Reset();
```

The overloaded operator new is, again, simple:

```
void * operator new (size_t heapSizeInBytes, TemporaryHeap& theHeap) {
   return theHeap.Allocate(heapSizeInBytes);
}
```

1. TemporaryHeap **implementation**

The TemporaryHeap class records the size of the heap, the amount of memory currently allocated, and keeps a pointer (heapMemory) to that memory.

```
class TemporaryHeap {
private:
   size_t nBytesAllocated;
   size_t heapSizeInBytes;
   char* heapMemory;
```

The constructor and destructor for the heap class are straightforward; any allocation exceptions will percolate up to the client:

```
TemporaryHeap::TemporaryHeap(size_t heapSize)
   : heapSizeInBytes(heapSize) {
   heapMemory = new char[heapSizeInBytes];
   Reset();
}
TemporaryHeap::~TemporaryHeap() {
   delete[] heapMemory;
}
```

The function to allocate memory from the `TemporaryHeap` increases a count and throws the `bad_alloc` exception if the heap is full.

```
void * TemporaryHeap::Allocate(size_t sizeOfObject) {
   if (nBytesAllocated + sizeOfObject >= heapSizeInBytes)
      throw bad_alloc();

   void *allocatedCell = heapMemory + nBytesAllocated;
   nBytesAllocated += sizeOfObject;
   return allocatedCell;
}
```

The `Reset` function simply resets the allocation count.

```
void TemporaryHeap::Reset() {
   nBytesAllocated = 0;
}
```

❖   ❖   ❖

Known uses

All object-oriented languages use stack allocation for function return addresses and for passing parameters. C++ and Eiffel also allow programmers to allocate temporary objects on the stack (Stroustrup 1997; Meyer 1992). The Real-time Specification for Java will support **MEMORY DISCARD** by allowing programmers to create `ScopedMemory` areas that are discarded when they are no longer accessible by real-time threads (Bollella et al. 2000).

In Microsoft Windows CE, you can create a separate heap, allocate objects within that heap, and then delete the separate heap, discarding every object inside it (Boling 1998). PalmOs discards all memory chunks owned by an application when the application exits (Palm 2000).

Recently, some Symbian developers were porting an existing handwriting recognition package to EPOC. For performance reasons it had to run in the Window Server, a process that must never terminate. Unfortunately, the implementation, though otherwise good, contained small memory leaks — particularly following memory exhaustion. Their solution was to run the recognition software using a separate heap, and to discard the heap when it got too large.

Regions are a compiler technique for allocating transient objects that last rather longer than stack frames. Dataflow analysis identifies objects to place in transient regions; the regions are allocated from a stack that is independent of the control stack (Tofte 1998).

The *Generational Copying* GARBAGE COLLECTORS (Jones and Lins 1996; Ungar 1984) used in modern Smalltalk and Java systems provide a form of memory discard. These collectors allocate new objects in a separate memory area (the *Eden* space). When this space becomes full, an angel with a flaming sword copies any objects inside it that are still in use out of Eden and into a more permanent memory area. The Eden space is then reset to be empty, discarding all the unused objects. Successively larger and longer-lived memory spaces can be collected using the same technique, each time promoting objects up through a cycle of reincarnation, until permanent objects reach the promised land that is never garbage collected, where objects live for ever.

See also

APPLICATION SWITCHING (84) is a more coarse-grained alternative, using process termination to discard both heap and executable code. DATA FILES (92) often uses stack allocation or a temporary workspace to process each item in turn from secondary storage. The discarded memory area may use either FIXED ALLOCATION (226), or VARIABLE ALLOCATION (236).

POOLED ALLOCATION (251) is similar to MEMORY DISCARD (244), in that both patterns allocate a large block of memory and then apportion it between smaller objects; POOLED ALLOCATION, however, supports deallocation.

Pooled Allocation

Also known as: Memory Pool

How can you allocate a large number of similar objects?

- Your system needs a large number of small objects.

- The objects are all roughly the same size.

- The objects need to be allocated and released dynamically.

- You don't, can't, aren't allowed to, or won't use VARIABLE ALLOCATION (236).

- Allocating each object individually imposes a large overhead for object headers and risks fragmentation.

Some applications use a large number of similar objects, and allocate and deallocate them often. For example, Strap-It-On's Alien Invasion game needs to record the positions and states of lots of graphical sprites that represent invading aliens, asteroids, and strategic missiles fired by the players. You could use VARIABLE ALLOCATION to allocate these objects, but typical memory managers store object headers with every object; for small objects these headers can double the program's *memory requirements*. In addition, allocating and deallocating small objects from a shared heap risks fragmentation and increases the time overhead of managing large numbers of dynamic objects.

You could consider using the FLYWEIGHT pattern (Gamma et al. 1995), but this does not help with managing data that is intrinsic to objects themselves. COMPACTION (259) can reduce fragmentation but imposes extra overheads in memory and time performance. So how can you manage large numbers of small objects?

Therefore: **Pre-allocate a pool of objects, and recycle unused objects.**

Pre-allocate enough memory to hold a large number of objects at the start of your program, typically by using FIXED ALLOCATION (226) to create an array of the objects. This array becomes a *pool* of unused, uninitialized, objects (Figure 5.9). When the application needs a new object, choose an unused object from the pool and pass it to the program to initialize and use it. When the application is finished with the object, return the object to the pool.

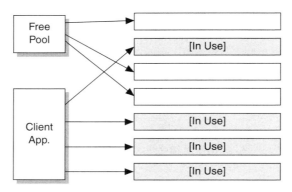

Figure 5.9   Pooled allocation

In practice, objects do not have to be physically removed and reinserted into the pool (this will be difficult in languages like C++ when the objects are stored directly within the pool array using FIXED ALLOCATION (226)). Instead you'll need to track which pool objects are currently in use and which are free. A linked list (using EMBEDDED POINTERS (198)) of the free objects will often suffice.

For example, the Strap-It-On uses a pool of sprite objects to support the Alien Invasion game. This pool is allocated at the start of the program and holds enough objects to represent all the sprites that can be displayed on the Strap-It-On's high-resolution 2" screen. No extra memory is required for each object by the memory manager or runtime system. All unused sprites are kept on a free list, so a new sprite can be allocated or deallocated using just two assignments.

Consequence

By reducing memory used for object headers and lost to fragmentation, POOLED ALLOCATION lets you store more objects in less memory, reducing the *memory requirements* of the system as a whole. Simultaneously, by allocating a fixed-sized pool to hold all these objects, you can *predict* the amount of memory required exactly. Objects allocated from a pool will be close together in memory, reducing the need for PAGING (119) overhead in a paged system. Memory allocation and deallocation is fast, increasing *time performance* and *real-time responsiveness*.

However: The objects allocated to the pool are never returned to the heap, so the memory isn't available to other parts of the application, potentially increasing overall *memory requirements*. It takes *programmer effort* to implement the pool, *programmer discipline* to use it correctly and further effort to *test* that it all works. A fixed-size pool can decrease your program's *scalability*, making it harder to take advantage of more memory should it become available, and also reduce your *maintainability*, by making it harder to subclass pooled objects. Preallocating a pool can increase your system's *startup time*.

❖   ❖   ❖

Implementation

POOLED ALLOCATION combines features of FIXED ALLOCATION (226) and VARIABLE ALLOCATION (236). The pool itself is typically statically allocated (so the overall memory consumption is predictable) but objects within the pool are allocated dynamically. Like FIXED ALLOCATION, the pooled objects are actually preallocated and have to be initialized before they are used (independently of their constructors). Like VARIABLE ALLOCATION, requests to allocate new objects may be denied if the pool is empty, so you have to handle memory exhaustion; and you have to take care to release unused objects back to the pool.

Here are some issues to consider when using POOLED ALLOCATION:

1. Reducing memory overheads

One reason to use POOLED ALLOCATION is to reduce the amount of memory required for bookkeeping in a variable allocation memory manager: POOLED ALLOCATION needs to keep less information about every individual object allocated, because each object is typically the same size and often the same type. By comparing memory manager overheads with the objects' size, you can evaluate if POOLED ALLOCATION makes sense in your application. Removing a two-word header from a three-word object is probably worthwhile, but removing a two-word header from a two-kilobyte object is not (unless there are millions of these objects and memory is very scarce).

2. Variable-sized objects

POOLED ALLOCATION works best when every object in the pool has the same size. In practice, this can mean that every object in the pool should be the same class, but this greatly reduces the flexibility of a program's design.

If the sizes of objects you need to allocate are similar, although not exactly the same, you can build a pool capable of storing the largest size of object. This will suffer from internal fragmentation, wasting memory when smaller objects are allocated in a larger space, but this fragmentation is bounded by the size of each pool entry (unlike external fragmentation, which can eventually consume a large proportion of a heap).

Alternatively, you can use a separate pool for each class of object you need to allocate. Per-class pools can further reduce memory overheads because you can determine the pool to which an object belongs (and thus its class) by inspecting the object's memory address. This means that you do not need to store a class pointer (Goldberg and Robson 1983) or vtbl pointer (Ellis and Stroustrup 1990) with every object, rather one pointer can be shared by every object in the pool. A per-class pool is called a *Big Bag of Pages* or *BiBoP* because it is typically allocated contiguous memory pages so that an object's pool (and thus class) can be determined by fast bit manipulations on its address (Steele 1977; Dybvig 1994).

3. Variable-size pools

If your pool is a FIXED ALLOCATION you have to determine how big the pool should be before your program starts running, and you have no option but to fail a request for a new object when the pool is empty. Alternatively, when the pool is empty you could use VARIABLE ALLOCATION and request more memory from the system. This has the advantage that pooled object allocation will not fail when there is abundant memory in the system, but of course it makes the program's memory use more difficult to predict. Flexible pools can provide guaranteed performance when memory is low (from the FIXED ALLOCATION portion) while offering extra performance when resources are available.

4. Making pools transparent

Sometimes it can be useful for objects that use POOLED ALLOCATION to present the same interface as VARIABLE ALLOCATION. For example, you could need to introduce pooled allocation into a program that uses VARIABLE ALLOCATION by default (because the programming language uses VARIABLE ALLOCATION by default).

In C++ this is easy to implement; you can overload operator new to allocate an object from a pool, and operator delete to return it. In Smalltalk and Java this approach doesn't work so seamlessly: in Smalltalk you can override object creation, but in Java you cannot reliably override either creation or deletion. In these languages you will need to modify clients to allocate and release objects explicitly.

C++ has a further advantage over more strongly typed languages such as Java. Because we can address each instance as an area of raw memory, we can reuse the objects differently when the client does not need them. In particular, as Figure 5.10 shows, we can reuse the first few bytes of each element as an EMBEDDED POINTER (198) to keep a free list of unallocated objects.

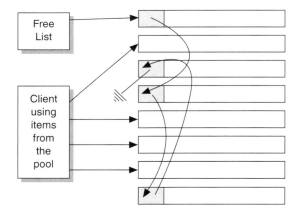

Figure 5.10   Reusing object memory to implement a free list

The following code uses this technique to implement a C++ class, TreeNode, representing part of a tree data structure. Clients use instances of the class as though allocated from the system heap:

```
TreeNode* node = new TreeNode;
delete node;
```

Internally the class uses a static pointer, freeList, to the start of the free list. Each TreeNode object is small so we don't want the overhead of heap allocation for each one separately. Instead we allocate them in blocks, of size BLOCK_SIZE:

```
class TreeNode {
private:
   enum { BLOCK_SIZE = 10 };
   static void* freeList;

   TreeNode* leftNode;
   TreeNode* rightNode;
   void* data;
// etc.
};
```

(The implementation of a TreeNode to give a tree structure using these data members is left as an exercise for the reader.) TreeNode has one static function to allocate new objects when required and add them all to the free list:

```
/* static */
void* TreeNode::freeList = 0;

/* static */
void TreeNode::IncreasePool() {
   char* node = new char[BLOCK_SIZE * sizeof(TreeNode)];
   for (int i = 0; i<BLOCK_SIZE; i++)
     AddToFreeList(node + (i * sizeof(TreeNode)));
}
```

To make the POOLED ALLOCATION look like VARIABLE ALLOCATION, TreeNode must implement the operators new and delete. There's one caveat for these implementations: any derived class will inherit the same implementation. So, in operator new, we must check the size of the object being allocated to ensure that we only use this implementation for objects of the correct size, otherwise we allocate the object from the system heap.

```
void* TreeNode::operator new(size_t bytesToAllocate) {
   if (bytesToAllocate != sizeof(TreeNode))
     return ::operator new(bytesToAllocate);
   if (freeList == 0)
     IncreasePool();
```

```
        void *node = freeList;
        freeList = *((void**)node);
        return node;
    }
```

Operator delete is straightforward (or as straightforward as these operators can ever be). We check that the object is a suitable size to be allocated from the pool, and if so, return it to the free list; otherwise we return it to the heap.

```
    void TreeNode::operator delete(void* node, size_t bytesToFree) {
        if (bytesToFree != sizeof(TreeNode))
          ::operator delete(node);
        else
          AddToFreeList( node );
    }
```

AddToFreeList uses the first few bytes of the object as the list pointer:

```
    void TreeNode::AddToFreeList(void* node) {
        *((void**)node) = freeList;
        freeList = node;
    }
```

Example

As a contrast to the C++ and Java syntax, here we present a simple Smalltalk implementation of **POOLED ALLOCATION**. The class allocates a fixed number of pooled objects when the system starts up and stores them in the class-side array Pool. Objects are allocated from the Pool as if it were a stack; the class variable PoolTopObject keeps track of the top of the stack.

```
    Object subclass: #PooledObject
      instanceVariableNames:"
      classVariableNames:
        'Pool PoolTopObject'
      poolDictionaries: "
```

The class method buildPool initializes all the objects in the pool, and need be called only once on initialization of the system. Unlike other Smalltalk class initialization functions, this isn't really a 'compile-time-only' function; a previous execution of the system could have left objects in the pool, so we'll need to call this function to restore the pool to its initial state.

```
    buildPool: poolSize
      'Puts poolSize elements in the pool'
      | newObject |
      Pool := Array new: poolSize.
      (1 to: poolSize) do:
```

```
        [ :i | Pool at: i put: PooledObject create. ].
    PoolTopObject = 1.
    ^ Pool
```

We need a `create` class method that `buildPool` can call to create new instances.

```
create
    "Allocates an uninitialized instance of this object"
    ^ super new
```

We can then define the `PooledObject` class `new` method to remove and return the object at the top of the pool.

```
new
    "Allocate a new object from the Pool"
    | newObject |
    newObject := Pool at: PoolTopObject.
    Pool at: PoolTopObject put: nil.
    PoolTopObject := PoolTopObject + 1.
    ^ newObject
```

Clients of the pooled object must send the `free` message to a pooled object when they no longer need it. This requires more discipline than standard Smalltalk programming, which uses GARBAGE COLLECTION (278) or REFERENCE COUNTING (268) to recycle unused objects automatically.

```
free
    "Restores myself to the pool"
    self class free: self
```

The real work of recycling an object is done by the class method `free:` which pushes an object back into the pool.

```
free: aPooledObject
    "Return a pooled object to the pool"
    PoolTopObject := PoolTopObject − 1.
    Pool at: PoolTopObject put: aPooledObject.
```

Known uses

Many operating systems use POOLED ALLOCATION, and provide parameters that administrators can set to control the size of the pools for various operating system resources, such as IO buffers, processes, and file handles. VMS, for example, pre-allocates these into fixed-size pools, and allocates each type of object from the corresponding pool (Kenah and Bate 1984). UNIX uses a fixed-size pool of process objects (the process table) (Goodheart and Cox 1994) and even MS-DOS provides a configurable pool of file IO buffers, specified in the configuration file CONFIG.SYS.

EPOC's Database Server uses a variable-sized pool to store blocks of data read from a database, and EPOC's Socket service uses a fixed-size pool of buffers (Symbian 1998).

NorTel's Smalltalk implementation of telephone exchange software uses pools of Call objects to avoid the real-time limitations of heap allocation in critical parts of the system.

See also

Memory pools are often allocated using FIXED ALLOCATION (226), although they can also use VARIABLE ALLOCATION (236). MEMORY DISCARD (244) also allocates many smaller objects from a large buffer; it can handle variable-sized objects, though they must all be deleted simultaneously.

MEMORY LIMIT (32) has a similar effect to POOLED ALLOCATION as both can cap the total memory used by a component.

Compaction

Also known as: Managed Tables, Memory Handles, Defragmentation

How do you recover memory lost to fragmentation?

- You have a large number of variable-sized objects.

- Objects are allocated and deallocated randomly.

- Objects can change in size during their lifetimes.

- Fragmentation wastes significant amounts of memory space.

- You can accept a small overhead in accessing each object.

External fragmentation is a major problem with VARIABLE ALLOCATION (236). For example, the Strap-It-On's voice input decoder has up to a dozen large buffers active at any time, each containing a logical word to decode. They account for most of the memory used by the voice decoder component and can vary in size as decoding progresses. If they were allocated directly from a normal heap, there'd be a lot of memory lost to fragmentation. If objects shrink, more space is wasted between them; one object cannot grow past the memory allocated to another object, but allocating more free memory between objects to leave them room to grow just wastes more memory (Figure 5.11).

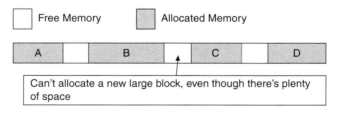

Figure 5.11 The effect of allocating large buffers

Fragmentation occurs because computer memory is arranged linearly and accessed through pointers. Virtual memory (see PAGING (119)) implements this same linear address space. When you allocate objects in memory you record this allocation and ownership using a pointer: that is, an index into this linear address space.

Therefore: **Move objects in memory to remove unused space between them.**

Space lost by external fragmentation can be recovered by moving allocated objects in memory so that objects are allocated contiguously, one after another: all the previously wasted space is collected at one end of the address space, so moving the objects effectively moves the unused spaces between them (Figure 5.12).

A	B	C	D	

Figure 5.12   Result of compaction

The main problem with moving objects is ensuring that any references to them are updated correctly: once an object has been moved to a new location, all pointers to its old location are invalid. While it is possible to find and update every pointer to every moved object, it is generally simpler to introduce an extra level of indirection. Rather than having lots of pointers containing the memory address of each object, pointers refer to a *handle for this object*. A handle is a unique pointer to the actual memory address of an object: when you move the allocated object in memory you update the handle to refer to the object's new location, and all other pointers can still access the object correctly.

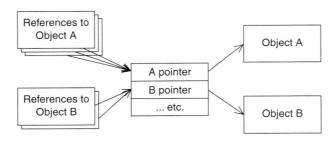

Figure 5.13   Handles

In Figure 5.13, if you copy object A to a different location in memory and update the 'A pointer' handle, all external references to object A will remain the same but accesses through them will find the new location.

Thus the Strap-It-On's voice input decoder maintains a large contiguous memory area for buffers, and uses a simple algorithm to allocate each buffer from it. Each buffer is accessed through a handle. When there's insufficient contiguous space for a new buffer or when an existing buffer needs to grow, even though there's sufficient total memory available, the software moves buffers in memory to free up the space and adjusts the handles to refer to the new buffer locations.

Consequences

You have little or no memory wastage due to external *fragmentation*, reducing the program's *memory requirements* or increasing its capacity within a fixed amount of memory. Compacting data structures can *scale up* easily should more memory become available.

However: You'll need additional code to manage the handles; if the compiler doesn't do this for you, this will require *programmer effort* to implement. Indirect access to objects requires *programmer discipline* to use correctly, and indirection and moving objects increases the program's *testing cost*.

There will be a small additional *time overhead* for each access of each object. Compacting many objects can take a long time, *reducing time performance*. The amount of time required can be *unpredictable*, so standard compaction is often unsuitable for *real-time* applications, although there are more complex incremental compaction algorithms that may satisfy real-time constraints; such algorithms impose a further *runtime* overhead.

❖   ❖   ❖

Implementation

Here are some further issues to consider when implementing the COMPACTION pattern.

1. Compaction without handles

You can compact memory without using explicit handles, provided that you can move objects in memory and ensure they are referenced at their new location.

EPOC's Packed Array template class, `CArrayPakFlat`, is one example of this approach (Symbian 1999b). A Packed Array is a sequential array of items; each element in the packed array contains its size, allowing you to locate the position of the next one (Figure 5.14). Inserting or deleting an element involves moving all the subsequent elements; the entire array is reallocated and copied if there is insufficient space. The template specialization `CArrayPak<TAny>` even allows variable-sized elements.

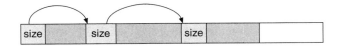

Figure 5.14 Packed array

Locating an element by index is slow, though the implementation optimizes for some situations by caching the last item found.

Text editors that use an insertion cursor can also use compaction. Text only changes at the cursor position; text before and after the cursor is static. So you can allocate a large buffer, and store the text before the cursor at the start of the buffer and the text after the cursor at the end. Text is inserted directly at the cursor position, without needing to reallocate any memory (Figure 5.15); however, when the cursor is moved, each character it moves past must be copied from one end of the buffer to the other.

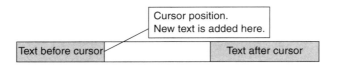

Figure 5.15   Text insertion

In this case, the indirection is simply the location of the text following the cursor. You store a static pointer to this, so any part of the application can locate it easily.

2. Object tables

If many objects are to be compacted together, an *object table* gives better random access performance at a cost of a little more memory. An object table contains all the handles allocated together. Object tables make it easy to find every handle (and thus every object) in the system, making compaction easier. You can store additional information, along with the handle in each *object table entry*, such as a class pointer for objects, count fields for REFERENCE COUNTING (268), mark bits for GARBAGE COLLECTION (278), and status bits or disk addresses for PAGING (119).

3. Optimizing access to objects.

Using a direct pointer to an object can temporarily increase execution speed compared with indirection through a handle or object table for every access. But, consider the following:

```
SomeClass* p = handle.GetPointer();          // 1
p->FunctionWhichTriggersCompaction();        // 2
p->AnotherFunction();                        // 3. p is now invalid!
```

If the function in line 2 triggers compaction, the object referred to by handle may have moved, making the pointer p invalid. You can address this problem explicitly by allowing handles to *lock* objects in memory while they're being accessed; objects may not be moved while they are locked. Locking does allow direct access to objects, but requires *programmer discipline* to unlock objects that are not needed immediately, space in each handle to store a lock bit or lock count, and a more complex compaction algorithm that avoids moving locked objects. The PalmOs and MacOS operating systems support lockable handles to most memory objects, so that their system heaps can be compacted (Apple 1985; Palm 2000).

4. Compacting objects

In the simplest approach, objects are stored in increasing order of memory location. You can compact the objects by copying each one in turn to the high water mark of the ones already compacted (Figure 5.16).

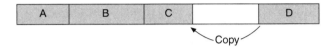

Figure 5.16   Compacting objects stored in increasing order of memory location

This approach works well when there is already a logical order on the objects, such as the elements of a sequence. If the sequence is compacted whenever an object is deleted, half the objects will be copied on average.

This does not work so well when objects are not stored in the correct order. In that case a better approach is simultaneously to sort and compact objects by copying them into a different memory space (Figure 5.17). Copying GARBAGE COLLECTION (278) algorithms, for example, copies old objects into a new memory space. Unused objects are not copied, but are discarded when the old space is reused.

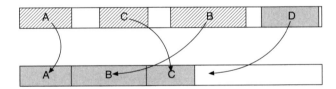

Figure 5.17   Copying objects that are not stored in the correct order

5. Compacting on demand

Persistent or long-lived objects can be compacted occasionally, often on user command. One way to implement this is to store all the persistent objects on SECONDARY STORAGE (79), reordering them (as described above) as they are stored, and then read them back in. If the objects are compacted rarely, you can use direct pointers for normal processing, since the time cost of finding and changing all the pointers is paid rarely and under user control.

5.1 C++ Handle *classes*

C++'s operator overloading facilities allow us to implement an object with semantics identical to a pointer (Coplien 1994), but which indirects through the object table. Here's an example of a template class that we can use in place of a pointer to an object of class T. The Handle class references the object table entry for the underlying object (hence tableEntry is a pointer to a pointer) and redefines all the C++ pointer operations to indirect through this entry.

```
template <class T> class Handle {
public:
    Handle(T** p) : tableEntry(p) {}
    T* operator->() const { return ptr(); }
    T& operator*() const { return *ptr(); }
    operator T*() const { return ptr(); }
private:
    T* ptr() const { return *tableEntry; }
    T** tableEntry;
};
```

Example

The following Java example extends the MessageStore example described in the FIXED ALLOCATION (226) and VARIABLE ALLOCATION (236) patterns. This version uses memory COMPACTION to permit variable-size messages without wasting storage memory. Instead of storing each message in its own separate fixed-size buffer, it uses a single buffer to store all the messages, and keeps just the lengths of each message. We've implemented this using FIXED ALLOCATION, avoiding new outside the constructor.

Figure 5.18 shows the new message format.

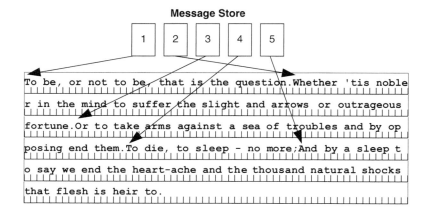

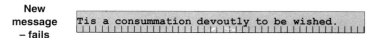

Figure 5.18 Using memory compaction for variable-size messages

The CompactingMessageStore class has a messageBuffer to store characters, an array of the lengths of each message, and a count of the number of messages in the store.

```
class CompactingMessageStore {
    protected char[] messageBuffer;
    protected int[] messageLengths;
    protected int numberOfMessages = 0;
```

The constructor allocates the fixed-sized arrays.

```
public CompactingMessageStore(int capacity, int totalStorageCharacters) {
    messageBuffer = new char[totalStorageCharacters];
    messageLengths = new int[capacity];
}
```

We can calculate the offset of each message in the buffer by summing the lengths of the preceding messages:

```
protected int indexOfMessage(int m) {
    int result = 0;
    for (int i = 0; i < m; i++) {
        result += messageLengths[m];
    }
      return result;
}
```

Adding a new message is simple: we just copy the new message to the end of the buffer. In this implementation, overflow throws an exception rather than overwriting earlier messages as in the FIXED ALLOCATION example.

```
public void acceptMessage(char[] msg, int msgLength) {
    int endOffset = indexOfMessage(numberOfMessages);

    try {
      messageLengths[numberOfMessages] = msgLength;
      System.arraycopy(msg, 0, messageBuffer,
                       endOffset, msgLength);
    }
    catch (ArrayIndexOutOfBoundsException e) {
      throw new OutOfMemoryError("Message store overflow");
    }
    numberOfMessages++;
}
```

Retrieving a message is straightforward:

```
public int getMessage(int i, char[] destination) {
    System.arraycopy(messageBuffer, indexOfMessage[i],
                     destination, 0, messageLengths[i]);
    return messageLengths[i];
}
```

The interesting point is what happens when we remove messages from the buffer. To keep everything correct, we have to copy all the messages after the one we've removed forward in the buffer, and move the elements of the messageLengths array up one slot:

```
public void deleteMessage(int i) {
    int firstCharToMove = indexOfMessage(i+1);
    int lastCharToMove = indexOfMessage(numberOfMessages);

    System.arraycopy(messageBuffer, firstCharToMove,
                     messageBuffer, indexOfMessage(i),
                     lastCharToMove – firstCharToMove);
    System.arraycopy(messageLengths, i+1, messageLengths, i,
                     numberOfMessages – i – 1);
    numberOfMessages ––;
}
```

❖   ❖   ❖

Known uses

EPOC's Font & Bitmap Server manages large bitmaps **Shared** between several processes. It keeps the data areas of large bitmaps (> 4Kb) in a memory area with no gaps in it — apart from the unused space at the top of the last page. When a bitmap is deleted the Server goes through its list of bitmaps and moves their data areas down by the appropriate amount, thereby compacting the memory area. The Server then updates all its pointers to the bitmaps. Access to the bitmaps is synchronized between processes using a mutex (Symbian 1999b).

The Palm and Macintosh memory managers both use handles into a table of master pointers to objects so that allocated objects can be compacted (Palm 2000; Apple 1985). Programmers have to be disciplined to lock handles while using the objects to which they refer.

The Sinclair ZX-81 (also known as the Timex Sinclair TS-1000) was based on compaction. The ZX-81 supported an interactive BASIC interpreter in 1K of RAM; the interpreter tables were heavily compacted, so that if you used lots of variables you could have only a few lines of program code, and vice versa. The pinnacle of compaction was in the screen memory: if the screen was blank, it would shrink so that only the end-of-line characters were allocated. Displaying text on the screen caused more screen memory to be allocated, and everything else in memory would be moved to make room.

See also

FIXED ALLOCATION (226) and POOLED ALLOCATION (251) are alternative ways to solve the same problem. By avoiding heap allocation during processing, they avoid fragmentation altogether.

PAGING (119), REFERENCE COUNTING (268), and GARBAGE COLLECTION (278) can all use COMPACTION and object tables.

Many garbage collectors used for dynamic languages such as Lisp, Java, and Smalltalk use COMPACTION, with or without object tables and handles. Jones and Lins (1996) present the most important algorithms. The Smalltalk *Blue Book* (Goldberg and Robson 1983) includes a full description of a Smalltalk interpreter that uses COMPACTION with an object table.

Reference Counting

- You are **SHARING** (182) objects in your program.

- The shared objects are transient, so their memory has to be recycled when they are no longer needed.

- Interactive response is more important than overall performance.

- The space occupied by objects must be retrieved as soon as possible.

- The structure of shared objects does not form cycles.

Objects are often **SHARED** (182) across different parts of components, or between multiple components in a system. If the shared objects are transient, then the memory they occupy must be recycled when they are no longer used by any client. Detecting when shared objects can be deleted is often very difficult, because clients may start or stop sharing them at any time.

For example, the Strap-It-On wrist-mounted PC caches bitmaps displayed in its user interface, so that each bitmap is stored only once, no matter how many windows it is displayed in. The bitmaps are cached in a hash table that maps from bitmap IDs to actual bitmap objects. When a bitmap is no longer required it should be deleted from the cache; in Figure 5.19, bitmap B is no longer required and can be deleted.

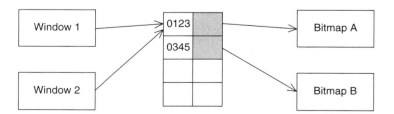

Figure 5.19   Bitmaps cached in a hash table

The traditional way to manage memory for bitmaps displayed in windows is to allocate bitmaps when windows are opened, and deallocate bitmaps when windows are closed. This doesn't work if the bitmaps are cached, because caching aims to use a pre-existing bitmap, if one exists, and to deallocate bitmaps only when all windows that have used them are closed. Deleting a shared bitmap when its first window closes could mean that the bitmap was no longer available to other windows that need it.

Therefore: **Keep a count of the references to each shared object, and delete each object when its count is zero.**

Every shared object needs to have a reference count field which stores the number of other objects that point to it. A reference count must count all references to an object, whether from shared objects, temporary objects, or permanent objects, and references from global, local, and temporary variables. The invariant behind reference counting is that an object's reference count field is an accurate count of the number of references to the object. When an object's reference count is zero it has no references from the rest of the program; there is no way for any part of the program to regain a reference to the object, so the object can be deleted. In Figure 5.20 object C has a zero reference count and can be deleted.

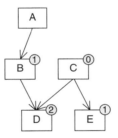

Figure 5.20 Reference counts

When an object is allocated, no other objects or variables can refer to it so its reference count is zero. When a reference to the object is stored into a variable or into a field in another object, the object's reference count must be incremented, and similarly when a reference to an object is deleted, the object's reference count must be decremented. When an object's reference count gets back to zero, the object can be deleted and the memory it occupies can be recycled.

There are a couple of important points to this algorithm. First, an assignment to a variable pointing to reference-counted objects involves two reference count manipulations: the reference count of the old contents of the variable must be decremented, and then the reference count of the new contents of the variable must be incremented. Second, if an object itself contains references to reference-counted objects, when the object is deleted all the reference counts of objects to which it referred must be decremented recursively. After all, a deleted object no longer exists so it cannot exercise any references it may contain. In Figure 5.20, once C has been deleted, object E can be deleted and object D will have a reference count of one.

For example, the Strap-It-On associates a reference count with each bitmap in the cache. When a bitmap is allocated, the reference count is initialized to zero. Every window that uses a bitmap must first send `attach` to the bitmap to register itself; this increases the bitmap's reference count. When a window is finished with a bitmap, it must send `release` to the bitmap; `release` decrements the reference count. When a bitmap's reference goes back to zero, it must have no clients and so deallocates itself.

Consequences

Like other kinds of automatic memory management, REFERENCE COUNTING increases the program's *design quality*: you no longer need to worry about deleting dynamically allocated objects. Memory management details do not have to clutter the program's code, making the program easier to read and understand, increasing *maintainability*. Memory management decisions are made *globally*, and *implicitly* for the whole system, rather than *locally* and *explicity* for each component. REFERENCE COUNTING also decreases coupling between components in the program, because one component does not need to know the fine details of memory management implemented in other components. This also makes it easier to reuse the component in different contexts with different assumptions about memory use, further improving the system *maintainability*.

The overhead of REFERENCE COUNTING is distributed throughout the execution of the program, without any long pauses for running a garbage collector. This provides smooth and predictable performance for interactive programs, and improves the *real-time responsiveness* of the system.

REFERENCE COUNTING works well when memory is low, because it can delete objects as soon as they become unreachable, recycling their memory for use in the rest of the system. Unlike many forms of GARBAGE COLLECTION (278), REFERENCE COUNTING permits shared objects to release external resources, such as file streams, windows, or network connections.

However: REFERENCE COUNTING requires *programmer discipline* to correctly manipulate reference counts in programs. If a reference to an object is created without incrementing the object's reference count, the object could be deallocated, even though the reference is in use.

REFERENCE COUNTING does not guarantee that memory the program no longer needs will be recycled by the system, even if reference counts are managed correctly. REFERENCE COUNTING deletes objects which are unreachable from the rest of the program. *Programmer discipline* is required to ensure that objects which are no longer required are no longer reachable, but this is easier than working out when shared objects can be manually deleted.

Reference count manipulations impose a large *runtime* overhead because they occur on every pointer write; this can amount to 10 or 20 per cent of a program's running time. Allocating memory for reference count fields can increase the *memory requirements* of reference-counted objects. REFERENCE COUNTING also increases the program's *memory requirements* for stack space to hold recursive calls when deleting objects.

Finally, REFERENCE COUNTING doesn't work for *cycles* of shared objects.

❖   ❖   ❖

Implementation

Reference count manipulations and recursive deletion are basically local operations, affecting single objects and happening at well-defined times with respect to the execution of the program. This means that programmers are likely to feel more "in control" of REFERENCE COUNTING than other GARBAGE COLLECTION techniques. This also means that REFERENCE COUNTING is comparatively easy to implement; however, there are a number of issues to consider when using reference counting to manage memory.

1. Deleting compound objects

Shared objects can themselves share other objects. For example, Strap-It-On's bitmap cache could be extended to cache compound figures, where a figure can be made up of a number of bitmaps or other figures (see Figure 5.21, where Figure A includes Figure B).

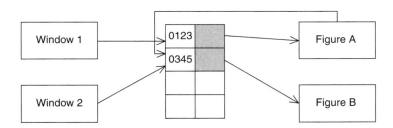

Figure 5.21   Sharing shared objects

When a reference-counted object is deleted, if it refers to other reference-counted objects, their reference counts must also be decremented. In Figure 5.21, if Figure A is destroyed, it should decrease the reference count for Figure B.

Freeing reference-counted objects is a recursive process: once an object's reference count is zero, it must reduce the reference counts of all the objects to which it refers; if those counts also reach zero, the objects must be deleted recursively. Recursive freeing makes REFERENCE COUNTING's performance unpredictable (although long pauses are very rare) and also can require quite a large amount of stack memory. The memory requirements can be alleviated by threading the traversal through objects' existing pointers using pointer reversal (see the **EMBEDDED POINTERS** (198) pattern), and the time performance by queuing objects on deletion and recycling them on allocation. This is *lazy deletion* — see Jones and Lins (1996) for more details.

2. Cycles

Objects can form any graph structure and these structures may or may not have cycles (where you can follow references from one object back to itself through the graph). In Figure 5.22, the structure in the left illustration is acyclic; in the right illustration, C and E form a cycle.

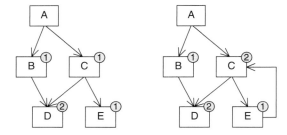

Figure 5.22 Cyclic and acyclic graphs

REFERENCE COUNTING doesn't work for cycles of shared objects, and such cycles can be quite common: consider doubly linked lists, skip lists, or trees with both upward and downward pointers. If two (or more) objects point to each other, then both of their reference counts can be non-zero, even if there are no other references to the two objects. In Figure 5.23, objects C and E form a cycle. They will have reference counts of one, even though they should be deleted because they are not accessible from any other object. In fact they would never be deleted by reference counting, even if every other object was removed.

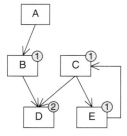

Figure 5.23 Reference counting doesn't work for a cycle of shared objects

2.1 Breaking cycles. One way of dealing with cycles is to require programmers to break cycles explicitly; that is, before deleting the last external reference to a cyclic structure of objects, programmers should overwrite at least one of the references that creates the cycle with `nil`. For example, you could remove the pointer from E to C in Figure 5.23. After this, the object structure no longer contains a cycle, so it can be recycled when the last external reference to it is also removed. This requires programmer discipline to remember to `nil` out the references that cause cycles.

2.2 Garbage collectors. You can also implement a GARBAGE COLLECTOR as a backup to REFERENCE COUNTING, because garbage collectors can reclaim cyclic structures. The collection can run periodically and/or whenever reference counting cannot reclaim enough memory. A garbage collector requires more programmer effort than reference counting, and computation must be stopped when it runs, costing processing time and decreasing interactive responsiveness and therefore usability.

2.3 Cycle-aware reference counting. Alternatively, there are more complex versions of the basic REFERENCE COUNTING algorithm that can handle cyclic structures directly, but they are not often worth the implementation effort (Jones and Lins 1996).

3. Allocating the reference count field

Each reference-counted object needs a reference count field which imposes a size overhead. In theory a reference count field needs to be large enough to count references from every other pointer in the system, requiring at least enough space for a full pointer to store the count.

In practice, most objects are pointed to by only a few other objects, so reference counts can be made much smaller, perhaps only one byte. Using a smaller reference count can save a large amount of memory, especially if the system contains a large number of small objects and has a large word size. Smaller reference counts raise the possibility that the counts can overflow. The usual solution is called *sticky* reference counts: once a count field reaches its maximum value it can never be decreased again. Sticky counts ensure that objects with many references will never be recycled incorrectly, by ensuring they will *never* be collected, at least by REFERENCE COUNT-ING. A backup GARBAGE COLLECTOR can correct sticky reference counts and collect once widely shared objects that have since become garbage.

4. Extensions

Because REFERENCE COUNTING is a simple but inefficient algorithm, it lends itself to extensions and optimizations.

4.1 Keeping objects with a zero reference count. If the objects represent external resources and are held in a cache, it may sometimes make sense to keep objects even if their reference count is zero. This applies if the items are expensive to re-create, and there's a reasonable chance that they may be needed again. In this case, you use reference counts as a guide in most situations, but you can implement CAPTAIN OATES (57) and delete unused objects when the memory cost of keeping them outweighs the cost of re-creating them later.

4.2 Finalization. Unlike more efficient forms of garbage collection, REFERENCE COUNTING explicitly deletes unreachable objects. This makes it easy to support *finalization*, that is, allowing objects to execute special actions just before they are about to be deleted. An object's finalization action is executed once its reference count reaches zero but before decrementing the objects it references and before recycling its memory. Finalization code can increase an object's reference count, so deletion should only proceed if the reference count is still zero after finalization.

4.3 Optimizations. Reference counting imposes an overhead on every pointer assignment or copy operation. You can optimize code by avoiding increment and decrement operations when you are *sure* an object will never be deallocated due to a given reference, typically because you have at least one properly reference-counted valid reference to the object. More sophisticated REFERENCE COUNTING schemes, such as *deferred reference counting* (Jones and Lins 1996; Deutsch and Bobrow 1976), can provide the benefits of this optimization without the difficulties, though with a slightly increased runtime overhead and substantially more programmer effort.

Example

This C++ example implements an object large enough to justify sharing and therefore reference counting. A ScreenImage contains a screen display of pixels. We might use it as follows:

```
{
    ScreenImage::Pointer image = new ScreenImage;
    image->SetPixel(0, 0);
    // And do other things with the image object...
}
```

When the image goes out of scope at the terminating brace, the ScreenImage object will be deleted, unless there are other ScreenImage::Pointer objects referencing it. The implementation of ScreenImage must have a reference count somewhere. This implementation puts it in a base class, ReferenceCountedObject.

```
typedef char Pixel;

class ScreenImage : public ReferenceCountedObject {
    Pixel pixels(SCREEN_WIDTH * SCREEN_HEIGHT);
```

The reference counting pointer template class requires a lot of typing to use; for convenience we define a typedef for it:

```
public:
    typedef ReferenceCountingPointer<ScreenImage> Pointer;
```

And here are a couple of example member functions:

```
    void SetPixel(int i, Pixel p) { pixels(i) = p; }
    Pixel GetPixel(int i) { return pixels(i); }
};
```

1. Implementation of ReferenceCountedObject

The class ReferenceCountedObject contains the reference count, and declares member functions to manipulate it. The DecrementCount operation can safely delete the object, since it doesn't access its this pointer afterwards. Note the virtual destructor, so that deletion invokes the correct destructor for the derived class.

```
class ReferenceCountedObject {
private:
    int referenceCount;
public:
    void IncrementCount() { referenceCount++; }
    void DecrementCount() { if (-- referenceCount == 0) delete this; }
protected:
    ReferenceCountedObject() : referenceCount(0) {}
    virtual ~ReferenceCountedObject() {}
};
```

2. Implementation of the smart pointer ReferenceCountingPointer

This is another example of the C++ Smart Pointer idiom. It uses the pointer operator (–>) to make an instance have the same semantics as a C++ pointer, and manages the reference counts:

```
template <class T> class ReferenceCountingPointer {
private:
    T* pointer;
    void IncrementCount() { if (pointer) pointer->IncrementCount(); }
    void DecrementCount() { if (pointer) pointer->DecrementCount(); }
```

To keep the reference counts correct, it needs all the 'Canonical Class Form' (Ellis and Stroustrup 1990): default constructor, copy constructor, assignment operator, and destructor:

```
public:
    ReferenceCountingPointer() : pointer(0) {}
    ReferenceCountingPointer(T* p)
        : pointer(p) { IncrementCount(); }
```

```
ReferenceCountingPointer(const ReferenceCountingPointer<T>& other)
    : pointer(other.pointer) { IncrementCount(); }
~ReferenceCountingPointer() { DecrementCount(); }
```

The assignment operator is particularly complicated, since it may cause the object originally referenced to be deleted. Note how, as always, we have to check for self-assignment and to return a reference to *this (Meyers 1992).

```
const ReferenceCountingPointer<T>&
operator=(const ReferenceCountingPointer<T>& other) {
    if (this != &other) {
        DecrementCount();
        pointer = other.pointer;
        IncrementCount();
    }
    return *this;
}
```

The 'smart' operations, though, are simple enough:

```
T* operator->() const { return pointer; }
T& operator*() const { return *pointer; }
```

And finally we need a couple more operators if we want to use the smart pointers in STL collections, since some STL implementations require a comparison operator (Austern 1998):

```
bool operator<(const ReferenceCountingPointer<T>& other) const {
    return pointer < other.pointer;
}
bool operator==(const ReferenceCountingPointer<T>& other) const {
    return pointer == other.pointer;
}
```

Known uses

REFERENCE COUNTING is part of the GARBAGE COLLECTION (278) implementation provided in some language environments. These implementations are invisible to the programmer, but improve the time performance of memory management by deferring the need for a GARBAGE COLLECTION process. The limbo language for programming embedded systems used REFERENCE COUNTING, because it doesn't pause computation, and because it allows external objects (menus and popup windows, for example) to be deleted immediately they are no longer used (Pike et al. 1997). Smalltalk-80 and VisualWorks\Smalltalk prior to version 2.5 similarly used REFERENCE COUNTING for reasons of interactive performance (Goldberg and Robson 1983; ParcPlace 1994).

Microsoft's COM framework has a binary API based on Microsoft C++'s VTBL implementation. COM uses REFERENCE COUNTING to allow several clients to share a single COM object (Box 1998).

UNIX directory trees provide a good example of a directed acyclic graph. The UNIX ln command allows you to create *hard links*, alternative names for the same file in different directories. A file is not deleted until there are no hard links left to it. Thus each UNIX low-level file object (inode) contains a reference count of the number of links to it, and the ln command will fail if you try to use it to create a cycle (Kernighan and Pike 1984).

See also

Modern memory management research has focused on GARBAGE COLLECTION (278) rather than REFERENCE COUNTING, to improve a system's overall time performance (Jones and Lins 1996).

The particular implementation we've used in the example section is the COUNTED POINTER idiom described by Buschmann et al. (1996) and Coplien (1994).

Garbage Collection

Also known as: Mark-sweep Garbage Collection, Tracing Garbage Collection

How do you know when to delete shared objects?

- You are SHARING (182) objects in your program.

- The shared objects are transient, so their memory has to be recycled when they are no longer needed.

- Overall performance is more important than interactive or real-time responsiveness.

- The structure of the shared objects does form cycles.

You are SHARING (182) dynamically allocated objects in your program. The memory occupied by these objects needs to be recycled when they are no longer needed. For example, the Strap-It-On's DailyFreudTimer application implements a personal scheduler and psychoanalyst using complex artificial intelligence techniques. DailyFreudTimer needs many dynamically allocated objects to record potential time schedules and psychological profiles modelling the way you spend your week. As it runs, DailyFreudTimer continually creates new schedules, evaluates them, and then rejects low-rated schedules in favour of more suitable ones, discarding some (but not all) of the objects it has created so far. The application often needs to run for up to an hour before it finds a schedule which means you do all you need to do this week, and also that you are in the right psychological state at the right time to perform each task.

Objects are often shared within components, or between multiple components in a system. Determining when shared objects are no longer used by any client can be very difficult, especially if there are a large number of shared objects. Often, too, the structure of those objects forms cycles, making REFERENCE COUNTING (268) invalid as an approach.

Therefore: **Identify unreferenced objects, and deallocate them.**

To do GARBAGE COLLECTION, you suspend normal processing in the system, and then follow all the object references in the system to identify the objects that are still reachable. Since any other objects in the system cannot now be referenced, it follows that they'll never be accessible in future (from where could you obtain their references?). In fact, these unreferenced objects are garbage, so you can deallocate them.

To find all the referenced objects in the system, you'll need to start from all the object references available to the running system. The places to start are called the *root set:*

- global and static variables,
- stack variables,
- references saved by external libraries.

Starting from these, you can traverse all the other *active* objects in your runtime memory space by following all the object references in every object you encounter. If you encounter the same object again, there's no need to examine its references a second time, of course.

There are two common approaches to removing the inactive objects:

- *Mark-sweep garbage collectors* visit all the objects in the system, deallocating the inactive ones.
- *Copying garbage collectors* copy the active objects to a different area, discarding the inactive ones.

For example, Strap-It-On implements mark-sweep collection for its schedule and profile objects in the DayFreudTimer. It keeps a list of every such object, and associates a mark bit to each. When DayFreudTimer runs out of memory, it suspends computation and invokes a GARBAGE COLLECTION. The collector traces every active object from a set of roots (the main `DayFreudTimerApplication` object), recursively marks the objects it finds, and then sweeps away all unmarked objects.

Consequences

GARBAGE COLLECTION can handle every kind of memory structure. In particular, it can collect structures of objects containing cycles with no special *effort* or *discipline* on behalf of the programmer. There's generally no need for designers to worry about object ownership or deallocation, and this improves *design quality* and thus the *maintainability* of the system. Similarly, it reduces the impact of *local* memory-management choices on the *global* system.

GARBAGE COLLECTION does not impose any time overhead on pointer operations, and has negligible memory overhead per allocated object. Overall it is usually more *time efficient* than REFERENCE COUNTING, since there is no time overhead during normal processing.

However: GARBAGE COLLECTION can generate big pauses during processing. This can disrupt the *real-time response* of the system, and in user interface processing tends to impact the *usability* of the system. In most systems it's difficult to *predict* when GARBAGE COLLECTION will be required, although special-purpose real-time algorithms may be suitable. Garbage objects are collected some time after they become unreachable, so there will always appear to be less free memory available than with other allocation mechanisms.

Compared with REFERENCE COUNTING, most garbage collectors will need more free space in the heap (to store garbage objects between collection phases), and will be less efficient when the application's memory runs short. Garbage collectors also have to be able to find the global root objects of the system, to start the mark phase traversal, and to find all outgoing references from an object. In contrast, REFERENCE COUNTING only needs to track pointer assignments.

Finally, the recursive mark phase of a mark-sweep collector needs stack space to run, unless pointer reversal techniques are used (see the EMBEDDED POINTER (198) pattern).

❖   ❖   ❖

Implementation

Garbage collectors still have been used in production systems since the late 1960s, but people are afraid of them. Why? Perhaps the most important reason is the illusion of control and efficiency afforded by less sophisticated forms of memory management, such as static allocation, manually deallocated heaps, or stack allocation, especially as many (badly tuned) garbage collectors can impose random pauses in a program's execution. Stack allocation took quite some time to become as accepted as it is today (many FORTRAN and COBOL programmers still shun stack allocation), so perhaps GARBAGE COLLECTION will be as slow to make its way into mainstream programming.

In systems with limited memory, garbage collectors have even less appeal than REFERENCE COUNTING and other more positive forms of memory management. But if you have complex linked structures, a simple garbage collector will be at least as efficient and reliable as manual deallocation code.

We can present only a brief overview of garbage collection in the space of one pattern. *Garbage Collection,* by Richard Jones with Raphael Lins (1996), is the standard reference on GARBAGE COLLECTION, and well worth reading if you are considering implementing a GARBAGE COLLECTOR.

1. Programming with Garbage Collection

Programming with GARBAGE COLLECTION is remarkably like programming without GARBAGE COLLECTION, except that it is easier, because you don't have to worry about explicitly freeing objects, juggling reference counts, or breaking cycles. It is quite possible to control the lifetimes of objects in a garbage-collected system just as closely as in a manually managed system, following three simple insights:

• If new is never called, objects are never allocated.

• If objects never become unreachable, they will never be deallocated.

- If objects are never allocated or deallocated, the garbage collector should never run.

The first point is probably the most important: if you don't allocate objects you should not need any dynamic memory management. In languages that are habitually garbage collected it can be difficult to find out when objects are allocated; for example, some libraries will allocate objects willy-nilly when you do not expect them to. Deleting objects in garbage-collected systems can be difficult: you must find and break every pointer to the object you wish to delete (Lycklama 1999).

2. Finalization and weak references

Certain kinds of object may own, and thus need to release, non-memory resources such as file handles, graphics resources, or device connections. These objects need to implement *finalization* methods to do this release.

Finalization can be quite hard to implement in many garbage collectors. You generally don't want the main sweeping thread to be delayed by calling finalization, so you have to queue objects for processing by a separate thread. Even if supported well, finalization tends to be unreliable because the precise time an object is finalized depends purely on when the garbage collector runs.

Some garbage collectors support *weak references*, references that are not traced by the collector. Unlike normal references, an object pointed to by a weak reference will become garbage unless at least one normal reference also points to the object. If the object is deleted, all the weak references are usually automatically replaced with some `nil` value. Weak references can be useful when implementing caches, since if memory is low, unused cached items will be automatically released.

3. Mark-sweep Garbage Collection

A mark-sweep GARBAGE COLLECTOR works by stopping the program, marking all the objects that are in use, and then deleting all the unused objects in a single clean sweep. Mark-sweep GARBAGE COLLECTION requires only one mark bit per object in the system. This bit can often be PACKED (174) within some other field in the object — perhaps the first pointer field since this bit is only ever set during the GARBAGE COLLECTION phases; during the main computation this bit is always zero.

When an object is allocated, its mark bit is clear. Computation proceeds normally, without any special actions from the garbage collector: object references can be exchanged, fields can be assigned to, and, if their last reference is assigned to another object or to nil, objects may become inaccessible. When memory is exhausted, however, the main program is paused, and the marking and sweeping phases of the algorithm are executed.

Figure 5.24 shows a system with five objects. Object A is the root of the system, and objects B and D are accessible from it. Objects C and E are not accessible from A, and so strictly are garbage. However they make up a 'cycle', so REFERENCE COUNTING could not delete them.

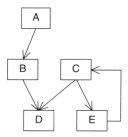

Figure 5.24   Before garbage collection

Mark-sweep GARBAGE COLLECTION proceeds in two phases. First, the mark phase recursively traces every inter-object reference in the program, beginning from a root set, such as all global variables and all variables active on the stack. When the mark phase reaches an unmarked object, it sets the object's mark bit, and recursively visits all the object's children. After the mark phase, every object reachable from the root set is marked: objects unreachable from the root set are unmarked.

Figure 5.25 shows the state of the objects after the mark phase. The marked objects are shown with shaded backgrounds. A, B and D are marked because they are reachable from the root of the system. C and E are not marked.

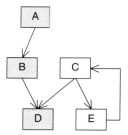

Figure 5.25   After the mark phase

Second, the *sweep* phase visits every object on the heap: that is, every object active at the end of the last sweep phase plus every object allocated since then. Whenever the sweep phase finds a marked object, it clears its mark bit (to be ready for the next mark phase). Whenever the sweep phase finds an unmarked object, it recycles the memory used by that object, running the object's finalization code, if it has any.

Considering the example, the sweep phase visits every object in an arbitrary order, deleting those that do not carry the mark. So after the sweep phase only objects A, B and D remain; the unmarked C and E objects have been deleted (Figure 5.26).

Mark-sweep works because it explicitly interprets the idea of an *active* or *live* object. Live objects must be reachable either directly from the root set (global variables, stack variables, and perhaps references saved by external libraries), or via chains of references through objects starting from the root set. The mark phase marks just those objects that meet this criterion, and then the sweep phase eliminates all the garbage objects that do not.

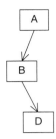

Figure 5.26 After the sweep phase

4. Copying garbage collectors

Modern workstation garbage collectors are typically based on object copying, rather than mark-sweep, thus implementing a form of COMPACTION (259). A simple copying collector allocates twice as much virtual memory as it needs, in two *hemispheres*. While the system is running, it uses only one of these hemispheres, called the fromspace, containing all the existing objects packed together at one end. New objects are allocated following directly after the old objects, simply by incrementing a pointer (just as cheaply as stack allocation). When the fromspace is full, the normal program is paused, and all fromspace objects are traversed recursively, beginning from the roots of the system.

A copying collector's traversal differs from a marking collector's. When a copying collector reaches an object in fromspace for the first time (note that by definition, a reachable object is not garbage) it copies that object into the other hemisphere (the *tospace*). It then replaces the fromspace object with a forwarding pointer to the tospace version. If the copy phase reaches a forwarding pointer, that pointer must come from an object already copied into the tospace, and the tospace object's field is updated to follow the forwarding pointer into the tospace. Once no more objects can be copied, the tospace and fromspace are (logically) swapped, and the system continues to execute.

More sophisticated copying collectors allocate two hemispheres for only the recently created objects, moving longer-lived objects into a separate memory space (Ungar 1984; Hudson and Moss 1992).

Copying collectors have a number of advantages over mark-sweep collectors. Copying collectors avoid fragmentation, because the act of copying also compacts all the active objects. More importantly, copying collectors can perform substantially better because they have no sweep phase. The time required to run a copying collector is based on copying all live objects, rather than marking live objects, plus sweeping through every object on the heap, allocated and garbage. On the other hand, copying collectors move objects around as the program runs, costing processing time; require more virtual memory than a simpler collector; and are more difficult to implement.

Example

This example illustrates a `CollectableObject` class that supports mark-sweep GARBAGE COLLECTION. Every object to be garbage collected must derive from `CollectableObject`. The static method `CollectableObject::GarbageCollect` does the GARBAGE COLLECTION.

For example, we might implement a `Node` class with `left` and `right` pointers. `Node` derives from `CollectableObject`, and every instance must be allocated on the heap:

```
class Node : public CollectableObject {
private:
    Node* left;
    Node* right;
public:
    Node(Node* l = 0, Node* r = 0) : left(l), right(r) {}
    ~Node() {}
    void SetLinks(Node* l, Node* r) { left = l; right = r; }
```

The only special functionality `Node` must provide is a mechanism to allow the GARBAGE COLLECTOR to track all its references. This implementation uses a TEMPLATE METHOD, `GetReferences`, declared in the base class (Gamma et al. 1995). `GetReferences` must call `HaveReference` for each of its references. For convenience a call to `HaveReference` with a null pointer has no effect.

```
private:
    void GetReferences() {
        HaveReference(left);
        HaveReference(right);
    }
};
```

Then we can allocate `Node` objects into structures, and they will be garbage collected. This implementation of mark-sweep garbage collection uses the normal `delete` calls, invoking `Node`'s destructor as normal. For example, we might set up the structure shown in Figure 5.27.

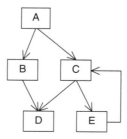

Figure 5.27 Example structure

```
Node* E = new Node(0, 0);
Node* D = new Node(0, 0);
Node* C = new Node(D, E);
Node* B = new Node(0, D);
Node* A = new Node(B, C);
E->SetLinks(0, C);
```

An initial garbage collection will have no effect:

```
CollectableObject::GarbageCollect(A);
```

However, when we remove the reference from A to C, a second garbage collection will delete C and E:

```
A->SetLinks(B, 0);
CollectableObject::GarbageCollect(A); // Deletes C and E
```

Finally, we can do a garbage collection with a null root node, to delete all the objects:

```
CollectableObject::GarbageCollect(0);
```

1. Implementation of the Garbage Collector

The garbage collector uses a single class, CollectableObject. Every CollectableObject maintains one extra field, the markBit for use by the collector. Every CollectableObject enters a collection allCollectableObjects, so that they can be found during the sweep phase.

```
class CollectableObject {
friend int main();
private:
    bool markBit;
public:
    CollectableObject();
    virtual ~CollectableObject();
    virtual void GetReferences() = 0;
    void HaveReference(CollectableObject* referencedObject);
private:
    void DoMark();
```

2. The Garbage Collection functions

The main garbage collector functionality is implemented as static functions and members in the CollectableObject class. We use a doubly-linked list, or deque, for the collection of all objects, since this is very efficient at adding entries, and at removing them via an iterator:

```
    typedef deque<CollectableObject*> Collection;
    static Collection allCollectableObjects;
public:
    static void GarbageCollect(CollectableObject* rootNode);
private:
    static void MarkPhase(CollectableObject* rootNode);
    static void SweepPhase();
};
```

The main `GarbageCollect` function is simple:

```
/*static*/
void CollectableObject::GarbageCollect(CollectableObject* rootNode) {
    MarkPhase(rootNode);
    SweepPhase();
}
```

The mark phase calls `DoMark` on the root object, if there is one; this will recursively call `DoMark` on all other active objects in the system:

```
/*static*/
void CollectableObject::MarkPhase(CollectableObject* rootNode) {
    if (rootNode)
        rootNode->DoMark();
}
```

The sweep phase is quite straightforward. We simply run down every object, and delete them if they are unmarked. If they are marked, they are still in use, so we simply reset the mark bit in preparation for subsequent mark phases:

```
/*static*/
void CollectableObject::SweepPhase() {
    for (Collection::iterator iter = allCollectableObjects.begin();
            iter != allCollectableObjects.end(); ) {
        CollectableObject* object = *iter;
        if (!object->markBit) {
            iter = allCollectableObjects.erase(iter);
            delete object;
        } else {
            object->markBit = false;
            ++iter;
        }
    }
}
```

3. Member functions for `CollectableObject`

The constructor for `CollectableObject` initializes the mark bit to unmarked, and adds itself to the global collection:

```
CollectableObject::CollectableObject()
   : markBit(false) {
   (void) allCollectableObjects.push_back(this);
}
```

We also need a virtual destructor, as derived instances will be destructed as instances of `CollectableObject`.

```
/*virtual*/
CollectableObject::~CollectableObject( ) {}
```

The `DoMark` function recursively sets the mark bit on this object and objects it references:

```
void CollectableObject::DoMark() {
   if (!markBit) {
      markBit = true;
      GetReferences();
   }
}
```

And similarly the `HaveReference` function is invoked by the `GetReferences` functions in derived classes:

```
void CollectableObject::HaveReference(CollectableObject* referencedObject) {
   if (referencedObject != NULL)
      referencedObject->DoMark();
}
```

A more robust implementation would replace the recursion in this example with iteration, to avoid the problems of stack overflow. A more efficient implementation might use **POOLED ALLOCATION** (251) of the `CollectableObjects`, or might use an **EMBEDDED POINTER** (198) to implement the `allCollectableObjects` collection.

Known uses

Any dynamic language with real pointers needs some form of **GARBAGE COLLEC-TION** — Lisp, Smalltalk, Modula-3, and Java are just some of the best-known garbage-collected languages. **GARBAGE COLLECTION** was originally specified as part of Ada, although this was subsequently deferred, and has been implemented many times for C++ and even for C (Jones and Lins 1996).

Mark-sweep garbage collectors are often used as a backup to reference counted systems, as in some implementations of Smalltalk, Java, and Inferno (Goldberg and Robson 1983; Pike 1997 et al.). A mark-sweep collector is executed periodically or when memory is low, to collect cycles and objects with many incoming references that would be missed by reference counting alone.

See also

REFERENCE COUNTING (268) is an alternative to this pattern that imposes a high overhead on every pointer assignment, and cannot collect cycles of references.

Systems that make heavy use of SHARING (182) may benefit from some form of GARBAGE COLLECTION. GARBAGE COLLECTION can also be used to unload PACKAGES (108) from SECONDARY STORAGE (79) automatically when they are no longer required.

Garbage Collection (Jones and Lins 1996) is a very comprehensive survey of a complex field. Richard Jones' *Garbage Collection* web page (Jones 2000) and the *Memory Management Reference Page* (Xanalys 2000) contain up-to-date information about GARBAGE COLLECTION. Paul Wilson (1994) has also written a critical overview of GARBAGE COLLECTION techniques.

A DISCUSSION OF FORCES

Forces in this book

Forces related to non-functional requirements

Architectural impact

Development process

APPENDIX

A DISCUSSION OF FORCES

How do you find the patterns relevant to your specific system?

If you're working on a project, the chances are you're already asking yourself 'Which of the patterns in this book might I apply to my project?'

No serious software product ever had (or will have) as its mission purely to save memory. If it did, the solution would be simple: write no code! But all real software has other aims and other constraints. In the words of the patterns community (Coplien 1996; Vlissides 1998) you have other *forces* acting on you and your project. Each pattern provides a solution to a problem in the context of the forces acting on you as you make the decision.

A pattern's forces capture the problem's considerations and the pattern's consequences, to help you to decide when to use that pattern rather than another. Each pattern's initial problem statement identifies the major force driving that pattern, and discusses other forces affecting the solution. Then the pattern's consequences section identifies how the pattern affects the configuration of the forces.

Some forces may be *resolved* by the pattern, that is, the pattern solves that aspect of the problem, and these forces form a pattern's positive benefits. Other forces may be *exposed* by the pattern, that is, applying the pattern causes additional problems, and these forces form a pattern's liabilities. You can then use further patterns to resolve the exposed forces, patterns that in their turn expose further forces, and so on.

This Appendix answers the question above by asking in return 'What other constraints and requirements do you have?', or,

What are your most important forces?

Identifying your forces can lead you to a set of patterns that you may — or may not — choose to use in your system.

Forces in this book

For all the patterns in this book the most important force is the software's memory requirements. But there are other important forces. The list below summarizes most of the forces we've identified. In each case, a positive answer to the question generally means a benefit to the project.

The forces are in three categories:

- Non-functional requirements
- Architectural impact on the system
- Effect on the development process

Tables A1, A2 and A3 give a brief summary of each force. The rest of this Appendix examines each force in more detail, exploring the patterns that resolve and that expose each one.

Table A1   Forces expressing non-functional requirements

Memory requirements	Does the pattern reduce the overall memory use of the system?
Memory predictability	Does the pattern make the memory requirements predictable?
Scalability	Does the pattern increase the range of memory sizes in which the program can function?
Usability	Does the pattern tend to make it easier for users to operate the system?
Time performance	Does the pattern tend to improve the runtime speed of the system?
Real-time response	Does the pattern support fixed and predictable maximum response times?
Start-up time	Does the pattern reduce the time between a request to start the system and its beginning to run?
Hardware and O/S cost	Does the pattern reduce the hardware or operating system support required by the system?
Power consumption	Does the pattern reduce the power consumption of the resulting system?
Security	Does the pattern make the system more secure against unauthorized access or viruses?

Table A2   Forces expressing architectural impact

Memory waste	Does the pattern reduce the amount of memory in use but serving no purpose?
Fragmentation	Does the pattern reduce the amount of memory lost through fragmentation?
Local vs. global	Does the pattern tend to help encapsulate different parts of the application, keeping them more independent of each other?

Table A3   Forces representing the effect on the development process

Programmer effort	Does the pattern reduce the total programmer effort to produce a given system?
Programmer discipline	Does the pattern remove restrictions on programming style, so that programmers can pay less attention to detail in some aspects of programming?
Maintainability and design quality	Does the pattern encourage better design quality? Will it be easier to make changes to the system later on?
Testing costs	Does the pattern reduce the total testing effort for a typical project?
legal restrictions	Will implementing the pattern be free from legal restrictions or licensing costs?

The table in the back cover summarizes a selection of the most important of these forces, illustrating how they apply to each of the patterns in the language. Each cell contains '☺' if the pattern normally has a beneficial effect in that respect (a 'yes' answer to the questions in the tables), or '☹' if the pattern's effect is detrimental. A '☺' indicates that the pattern usually has an effect, but whether it is positive or negative depends on circumstances.

The remainder of this Appendix examines each force in more detail. For each force, we indicate the patterns that best resolve it, and the patterns that regrettably often expose it.

Forces related to non-functional requirements

The forces in this section concern the delivered system. How will it behave? Will it satisfy the clients' needs by being sufficiently reliable, fast, helpful and, long-lived?

Memory requirements

Does the pattern reduce the overall memory use of the system?

The single most important force in designing systems for limited memory is, unsurprisingly enough, the memory requirements of the resulting system — the amount of memory the system requires to do its job.

Patterns that resolve this force

- All the patterns in this book (Chapters 1 to 5) resolve this force in one way or another.

Memory predictability

Does the pattern make the memory requirements predictable?

Minimizing a program's absolute memory requirements is all very well, but often it is more useful to know in advance whether a given program design can cope with its expected load, precisely what its maximum load will be, and whether it will exhaust the memory available to it. Often, increased memory requirements or reduced program capacity is better than random program crashes. In order to be able to determine that a program can support its intended load, or that it will not run out of memory and crash, you need to be able to audit the program to predict the amount of memory that it will require at runtime.

Predictability is particularly important for systems that must run unattended, where behaviour must be guaranteed and reliability is essential. In particular, life-critical systems must have predictable requirements. See, for example, the discussion in the FIXED ALLOCATION (226) pattern.

Patterns that resolve this force

- FIXED ALLOCATION (226) ensures that your memory requirements do not change while the code is running. You can calculate memory requirements exactly during the design phase.
- EMBEDDED POINTERS (198) allow you to easily calculate memory requirements for linked collections of objects.
- PARTIAL FAILURE (48) permits pre-defined behaviour when memory runs out.
- A MEMORY LIMIT (244) puts a constraint on the amount of memory used by any particular component.
- DATA FILES (92) and APPLICATION SWITCHING (84) handle only a certain amount of data at a time, potentially removing the chance of memory exhaustion.
- CAPTAIN OATES (57) releases memory from lower-priority tasks, making it possible to have high-priority tasks that complete reliably.

Patterns that expose this force

- VARIABLE ALLOCATION (236) encourages a component to use unpredictable amounts of memory.
- GARBAGE COLLECTION (278) makes it more difficult to determine in advance precisely when unused memory will be returned to the system.
- COMPRESSION (135) (especially ADAPTIVE COMPRESSION (160)) reduces the absolute memory requirements for storing the compressed data, but by an unpredictable amount.
- COPY-ON-WRITE (191) obscures the amount of memory required for an object — memory only needs to be allocated when an object is first modified.
- MULTIPLE REPRESENTATIONS (209) means that the amount of memory allocated to store an object can vary considerably, and in some uses, dynamically.

Scalability

Does the pattern increase the range of memory sizes in which the program can function?

Moore's Law (1997) states that hardware capacity increases exponentially. As a result, the amount of memory available tends to increase over time (or, rarely, the same devices can be sold more cheaply) (Smith 1999). So long-lasting software needs to be scalable to take advantage of more memory if it is available.

Furthermore, different users may have different amounts of money to spend, and different perceptions of the importance of performance and additional functionality. Such user choices require scalable software too.

Patterns that resolve this force

- VARIABLE ALLOCATION (236) adjusts the memory allocated to a structure to fit the number of objects the structure actually contains, limited only by the available memory.
- PAGING (119) and other SECONDARY STORAGE (79) patterns allow a program access to more apparent RAM, by storing temporarily unneeded information on secondary storage. Adding more RAM improves the time performance of the system without affecting the functionality.
- MULTIPLE REPRESENTATIONS (209) allows the system to size its objects according to the available memory.

Patterns that expose this force

- Designing a SMALL ARCHITECTURE (25) requires you to make components responsible for their own memory use and accepting this responsibility can sometimes increase the complexity and decrease the performance of each component. The components bear these costs even when more memory become available.
- FIXED ALLOCATION (226) (and POOLED ALLOCATION (251) from a fixed-sized pool) require you to commit to the size of a data structure early, often before the program is run or before the data structure is used.
- SMALL DATA STRUCTURES (169), especially PACKED DATA (174), trade time performance to reduce memory requirements. It can be hard to redesign data structures to increase performance if more memory is available.

Usability

Does the pattern tend to make it easier for users to operate the system?

Designing systems that use limited amounts of memory requires many compromises, and often these reduce the usability — ease of use, ease of learning, and users' speed, reliability and satisfaction — of the resulting system (Shneiderman 1997).

Usability is a complex, multifaceted concern, and we address it in this book only in so far as the system usability is directly affected by the memory constraints.

Patterns that resolve this force

- PARTIAL FAILURE (48) ensures that the system can continue to operate in low-memory conditions.
- CAPTAIN OATES (57) allows the system to continue to support users' most important tasks by sacrificing less important tasks.
- Other ARCHITECTURAL (25) patterns can make help make a system more consistent and reliable, and thus more usable.
- Using SMALL DATA STRUCTURE (169) can increase the amount of information a program can store and manipulate, to users' direct benefit.

- PAGING (119) makes the system's memory appear limitless, so users do not need to be concerned about running out of memory.

Patterns that expose this force

- SECONDARY STORAGE (79) patterns make users aware of different kinds of memory.
- APPLICATION SWITCHING (84) makes users responsible for changing between separate applications, even though they may not see any reason for the separation of the system.
- FIXED ALLOCATION (226) can make a system's memory capacity (or lack of it) directly and painfully obvious to the system's users.

Time performance

Does the pattern tend to improve the runtime speed of the system?

Being small is not enough; your programs usually have to be fast as well. Even where execution speed isn't an absolute requirement, there'll always be someone, somewhere, who wants it faster.

Patterns that resolve this force

- FIXED ALLOCATION (226) can assign fixed memory locations as the program is compiled, so they can be accessed quickly using absolute addressing.
- MEMORY DISCARD (244) and POOLED ALLOCATION (251) support fast allocation and deallocation.
- MULTIPLE REPRESENTATIONS (209) allows you to have memory-intensive implementation of some objects to give fast performance without incurring this overhead for every instance.
- EMBEDDED POINTERS (198) can support fast traversal and update operations on link-based collections of objects.
- Most GARBAGE COLLECTION (278) algorithms do not impose any overhead for memory management on pointer manipulations.

Patterns that expose this force

- VARIABLE ALLOCATION (236) and deallocation cost processing time.
- COMPRESSION, especially ADAPTIVE COMPRESSION (160), requires processing time to convert objects from smaller compressed representations to larger computable representations.
- COMPACTION (259) similarly requires processing time to move objects around in memory.

- Most SECONDARY STORAGE (79) patterns, especially PAGING (119), use slower secondary storage in place of faster primary storage.

- REFERENCE COUNTING (268) requires up to two reference count manipulations for *every* pointer manipulation.

- PACKED DATA (174) is typically slower to access than unpacked data.

- SMALL INTERFACES (38) pass small amounts of data incrementally, which can be much slower than passing data in bulk using large buffer structures.

- CAPTAIN OATES (57) can take time to shut down tasks or components.

- Indirect memory accesses via HOOKS (72) can reduce the system's time performance.

Real-time response

Does the pattern support fixed and predictable maximum response times?

Just as predictability of memory use — and the resulting stability, reliability, and confidence in a program's performance — can be as important or more important than the program's absolute memory requirements, so the predictability of a program's time performance can be more important than its absolute speed.

This is particularly important when dealing with embedded systems and communications drivers, which may have real-world deadlines for their response to external stimuli.

Patterns that resolve this force

- FIXED ALLOCATION (226), MEMORY DISCARD (244), and POOLED ALLOCATION (251) usually have a predictable worst-case performance.

- EMBEDDED POINTERS (198) can allow constant-time traversals between objects in linked data structures.

- SMALL INTERFACES (38) ensure that fixed amounts of data can be passed between components in fixed amounts of time.

- DIFFERENCE CODING (153) can compress and decompress simple data streams in fixed amounts of time per item.

- REFERENCE COUNTING (268) amortizes memory management overheads at every pointer manipulation, and so does not require random pauses during a system's execution.

Patterns that expose this force

- VARIABLE ALLOCATION (236) can require unpredictable amounts of time.

- The time required by most ADAPTIVE COMPRESSION (160) algorithms is dependent on the content of the information it is compressing.

- Some implementations of COMPACTION (259) may sporadically require a large amount of time to compact memory. If compaction is invoked whenever a standard allocator cannot allocate enough contiguous memory, then allocation will take varying amounts of time, and this performance will degrade as the free space decreases.
- Many SECONDARY STORAGE (79) patterns take extra time (randomly) to access secondary storage devices.
- COPY-ON-WRITE (191) requires time to make copies of objects being written to.

Start-up time

Does the pattern reduce the time between a request to start the system and its beginning to run?

Start-up time is another force that is related to execution time, but clearly independent of both absolute performance and real-time response. For embedded systems, and even more crucially for PDAs and mobile phones, the time between pressing the on switch and accomplishing useful work is vital to the usability and marketability of the system.

Patterns that resolve this force

- PACKAGES (108) and APPLICATION SWITCHING (84) allow a main module to load and start executing quickly; other modules load and execute later.
- READ-ONLY MEMORY (65) allows the CPU to access program code and resources immediately a program starts, without loading from secondary storage.
- SHARING (182) of executable code allows a new program to start up quickly if the code is already running elsewhere; SHARING (182) of data reduces initial allocation times.
- MEMORY DISCARD (244) can allocate objects quickly at the start of the program.
- VARIABLE ALLOCATION (236) defers allocation of objects until they are needed.
- COPY-ON-WRITE (191) avoids an initial need to allocate space and copy all objects that might possibly change; copying happens later as and when necessary.

Patterns that expose this force

- FIXED ALLOCATION (226) and POOLED ALLOCATION (251) require time to initialize objects or pools before the program begins running.
- COMPRESSION (135) can require time to uncompress code and data before execution.
- Initializing from DATA FILES (92) and RESOURCE FILES (101) on SECONDARY STORAGE (79) all takes time.

Hardware and operating system cost

Does the pattern reduce the hardware or operating system support required by the system?
Hardware or operating systems can provide facilities to directly support some of the patterns we have described here. Obviously, it makes sense to use these facilities when they are provided, if they address a need in your design. Without such support, you may be better off choosing an alternative pattern rather than expending the effort required emulating it yourself.

Patterns that expose this force

- CAPTAIN OATES (57) needs a mechanism for individual tasks within a system to determine the system's global memory use, and ideally a means to signal memory-low conditions to all programs.
- GARBAGE COLLECTION (278) is often provided in the virtual machines or interpreters for modern programming languages, or as libraries for languages like C++.
- RESOURCE FILES (101) and PACKAGES (108) need to load binary data such as executable files or font and icon files into running programs. This is easiest if implemented in the operating system.
- PAGING (119) is much more efficient if it uses the page and segment tables of your processor, and in practice this requires operating system support.
- Similarly, COPY-ON-WRITE (191) is implemented most efficiently if it can use hardware page table write protection faults.

Power consumption

Does the pattern reduce the power consumption of the resulting system?
Battery-powered systems, such as hand-helds, palmtop computers and mobile phones, need to be very careful of their power consumption. You can reduce power consumption by avoiding polling, avoiding long computations, and switching off power-consuming peripherals.

Patterns that resolve this force

- READ-ONLY MEMORY (65) often requires no power to remain valid.

Patterns that expose this force

- SECONDARY STORAGE (79) devices, such as battery-backed RAM and disk drives, consume power when they are accessed.
- COMPRESSION (135) algorithms need CPU power to compress and uncompress data.

- PAGING (119) is particularly bad, since it can require secondary storage devices to be running continuously on battery power.

Security

Does the pattern make the system more secure against unauthorized access or viruses?

Security is increasingly important, with the advent of the internet and private information being stored on insecure desktop or palmtop computers. As with forces like memory predictablity and real-time response, it is generally not enough to claim that a system is secure; you also need to be able to audit the implementation of the system to see how it is built.

Patterns that resolve this force

- Information stored in READ-ONLY MEMORY (65) cannot generally be changed so should remain sacrosanct.

Patterns that expose this force

- SECONDARY STORAGE (79) devices, especially if used by PAGING (119), may store unsecured copies of sensitive information from main memory.
- PACKAGES (108) can allow components of the system to be replaced or extended by other, insecure or hostile, versions.
- HOOKS (72) allow nominally read-only code and data to be changed, allowing the introduction of viruses.

Architectural impact

We can identify a different set of forces that affect the delivered system less directly — they're visible to the developers more than to the end-users.

Memory waste

Does the pattern reduce the amount of memory in use but serving no purpose?

Some design approaches waste memory. For example, low-priority tasks may keep unnecessary caches; fully featured, large, objects may be allocated where smaller and more Spartan versions would do; and allocated objects may sit around performing no useful purpose.

Clearly it's generally good to avoid such wasted memory, even if in some cases it's worth accepting the penalty in return for other benefits.

Patterns that resolve this force

- MULTIPLE REPRESENTATIONS (209) avoids unnecessarily memory-intensive instances of objects when a more limited representation will do the job.
- SHARING (182) and COPY-ON-WRITE (191) can prevent redundant copies of objects.
- PACKED DATA (174) reduces the amount of memory required by data strucutres.

Patterns that expose this force

- FIXED ALLOCATION (226) and POOLED ALLOCATION (251) tend to leave unused objects allocated.
- Objects allocated by VARIABLE ALLOCATION (236) can become memory leaks if they are no longer used and have not been explicitly deleted.
- REFERENCE COUNTING (268) and GARBAGE COLLECTION (278) can also have memory leaks — objects that are no longer in use, but are still reachable from the system root.

- MEMORY LIMITS (32) can waste memory by preventing components from using otherwise unallocated memory.
- ADAPTIVE COMPRESSION (160) often needs to uncompress large portions of data into memory, even when much of it isn't required.

Fragmentation

Does the pattern reduce the amount of fragmentation?

Fragmentation causes memory to be unusable because of the behaviour of memory allocators, resulting in memory that is allocated but can never be used (internal fragmentation) or that has been freed but can never be reallocated (external fragmentation). See MEMORY ALLOCATION (219) for a full discussion of fragmentation.

Patterns that resolve this force

- COMPACTION (259) moves allocated objects in memory to prevent external fragmentation.
- FIXED ALLOCATION (226) and POOLED ALLOCATION (251) avoid allocating variable-sized objects, also avoiding external fragmentation.
- MEMORY DISCARD (244) avoids fragmentation — stack allocation has no fragmentation waste and discarding a heap discards the fragmentation along with it.
- APPLICATION SWITCHING (84) can avoid fragmentation by discarding all the memory allocated by an application and starting over again.

Patterns that expose this force

- VARIABLE ALLOCATION (236) supports dynamic allocation of variable-sized objects, causing fragmentation dependent on your memory allocation algorithm.
- FIXED ALLOCATION (226) and POOLED ALLOCATION (251) generate internal fragmentation when they allocate variable-sized objects.

Local vs. global coupling

Does the pattern tend to help encapsulate different parts of the application, keeping them independent of each other?

Some programming concerns can be merely a local concern. For example, stack memory is local to the method that allocates it. The amount of memory is determined directly by that method and affects only invocations of that method and any method called from it.

In contrast, the amount of memory occupied by heap objects is a global concern. Methods can allocate many heap objects that exist after the method returns, and so the amount of memory allocated by such a method can affect the system globally. Some patterns can affect the balance between local and global concerns in a program, requiring local mechanisms to achieve global results or, on the other hand, imposing global costs to produce a local effect.

Patterns that resolve this force

- SMALL ARCHITECTURE (25) and SMALL INTERFACES (38) describe how program modules and their memory consumption can be kept strictly local.

- PACKED DATA (174) and other SMALL DATA STRUCTURES (169) can be applied to a local design for each structure, allowing redesign without affecting other components.

- MULTIPLE REPRESENTATIONS (209) can change data structure representations dynamically, without affecting the rest of the program.

- POOLED ALLOCATION (251) and MEMORY LIMITS (32) can localize the effects of dynamic memory allocation to within a particular module.

- MEMORY DISCARD (244) allows a set of local objects to be deleted simultaneously.

- PAGING (119) allows most system code to ignore issues of secondary storage.

- REFERENCE COUNTING (268) and GARBAGE COLLECTION (278) allow decisions about deleting objects shared globally also to be made globally.

Patterns that expose this force

- PARTIAL FAILURE (48) and CAPTAIN OATES (57) require local support within programs to provide support for graceful degradation globally throughout the program.

- VARIABLE ALLOCATION (236) shares memory between different components over time, so the local memory used by one component affects the global memory available for others.

- SHARING (182) potentially introduces coupling between every client object sharing a given item.

- EMBEDDED POINTERS (198) require local support within objects so that they can be members of external (global) collections.

Development process

The following forces concern the development process. How easy will it be to produce the system, to test it, to maintain it? Will you get management problems with individual motivation, with team co-ordination, or with the legal implications of using the techniques?

Programmer effort

Does the pattern reduce the total programmer effort to produce a given system?

The cost of programmer time far exceeds the cost of processor time for all but the most expensive supercomputers (and for all except the cheapest programmers) — unless the software is very widely used. Some patterns tend to increase implementation effort, while others can reduce it.

Patterns that resolve this force

- VARIABLE ALLOCATION (236) doesn't require you to predict memory requirements in advance.
- GARBAGE COLLECTION (278) means that you don't have to worry about keeping track of object lifetimes.
- HOOKS (72) allow you to customize code without having to rewrite it.
- MEMORY DISCARD (244) makes it easy to deallocate objects.
- PAGING (119) transparently uses secondary storage as extra memory.

Patterns that expose this force

- PARTIAL FAILURE (48) and CAPTAIN OATES (57) can require you to implement large amounts of checking and exception handling code.
- COMPRESSION (135) patterns (especially ADAPTIVE COMPRESSION ([160]) may require you to implement compression algorithms or learn library interfaces.

- COMPACTION (259) requires effort to implement data structures that can move in memory.
- Most SECONDARY STORAGE (79) patterns require programmers to move objects explicitly between primary and secondary storage.
- SMALL DATA STRUCTURES (169) can require you to re-implement parts of your program to optimize its memory use.
- EMBEDDED POINTERS (198) can require you to rewrite common collection operations for every new collection of objects.

Programmer discipline

Does the pattern remove restrictions on programming style, so that programmers can pay less attention to detail in some aspects of programming?

Some patterns depend upon you to pay constant attention to small points of detail, and carefully follow style rules and coding conventions. Following these rules requires a high level of concentration, and makes it more likely you will make mistakes. Of course, once learned the rules do not greatly reduce your productivity, or increase the overall effort you will need to make.

Some patterns (such as PAGING ((119)) reduce programmer discipline by using automatic mechanisms, but require effort to implement those mechanisms; others, such as REFERENCE COUNTING (268), require discipline to use but do not take much effort to implement.

Patterns that resolve this force

- GARBAGE COLLECTION (278) automatically determines which objects are no longer in use and so can be deleted, avoiding the need to track object ownership.
- PAGING (119) uses SECONDARY STORAGE (79) to increase the apparent size of main memory transparently, avoiding in many cases the discipline of PARTIAL FAILURE (48).
- COPY-ON-WRITE (191) means that clients can safely modify an object regardless of whether it is SHARED (182) or in READ-ONLY MEMORY (65).

Patterns that expose this force

- A SMALL ARCHITECTURE (25) requires discipline to keep system- and component-wide policies about memory use, and to use READ-ONLY MEMORY (65) and RESOURCE FILES (101) as appropriate.
- PARTIAL FAILURE (48) requires you to cater for memory exhaustion in almost all the code you write.
- CAPTAIN OATES (57) may require you to implement 'good citizen' code that doesn't add to your current component's apparent functionality.

- REFERENCE COUNTING (268) and COMPACTION (259) may require you to use special handle objects to access objects indirectly.

- POOLED ALLOCATION (251) and MEMORY DISCARD (244) require careful attention to the correct allocation, use, and deallocation of objects, to avoid dangling pointers or memory leaks.

- You have to include HOOKS (72) into the design and implementation of your components so that later users can customize each component to suit their requirements.

- Using COMPRESSION (135) routinely (say for all string literals) makes programming languages' literal facilities much harder to use.

- EMBEDDED POINTERS (198) require care when objects can belong to multiple collections.

Design quality and maintainability

Does the pattern encourage better design quality? Will it be easier to make changes to the system later on?

Some design and programming techniques make it easier for later developers to read, understand, and subsequently change the system.

Patterns that resolve this force

- Taking the time to design a SMALL ARCHITECTURE (25) and SMALL DATA STRUCTURES (169) increases the quality of the resulting system.

- HOOKS (72) allow a program's code to be extended or modified by end users or third parties, even if the code is stored in READ-ONLY MEMORY (65).

- PARTIAL FAILURE (48) supports failure modes other than memory exhaustion, such as network faults and disk errors.

- SMALL INTERFACES (38) reduce coupling between program components.

- MULTIPLE REPRESENTATIONS (209) allows the implementation of objects to change to suit the way they are used.

- SHARING (182) reduces duplication between (and within) the components of a system.

- RESOURCE FILES (101) and PACKAGES (108) allow a program's resources — literal strings, error messages, screen designs, and even executable components — to change without affecting the program's code.

- REFERENCE COUNTING (268), GARBAGE COLLECTION (278), and PAGING (119) allow you to make global strategic decisions about deleting objects or using secondary storage.

- APPLICATION SWITCHING (84) based on scripts can be very easily modified.

Patterns that expose this force

- FIXED ALLOCATION'S (226) fixed structures can make it more difficult to change the volume of data that can be processed by the program.
- Code and data stored in READ-ONLY MEMORY (65) can be very difficult to change or maintain.
- APPLICATION SWITCHING (84) can reduce a system's design quality when it forces you to split functionality into executables in arbitrary ways.
- PACKED DATA (174) structures can be hard to port to different environments or machines.
- Collections based on EMBEDDED POINTERS (198) are hard to reuse in different contexts.

Testing cost

Does the pattern reduce the total testing effort for a typical project?

It's not enough just to code up your program; you also have to make sure it works reliably (unless your product commands a monopoly in the market!). If you care about reliability, choose patterns that decrease the cost of testing the program, so that you can test more often and more thoroughly.

Patterns that resolve this force

- FIXED ALLOCATIONS (226) are always the same size independent of program loading, so they always run out of capacity at the same time. This simplifies exhaustion testing.
- READ-ONLY MEMORY (65) is easier to test because its contents cannot change.
- DATA FILES (92) and RESOURCE FILES (101) help testing because you can use versions of the files to set up different test scenarios.

Patterns that expose this force

- VARIABLE ALLOCATION (236), POOLED ALLOCATION (251), MEMORY DISCARD (244), MEMORY LIMIT (32), and MULTIPLE REPRESENTATIONS (209) require testing to check changes in their sizes and representations.
- PARTIAL FAILURE (48) and CAPTAIN OATES (57) have to be tested to check their behaviour both when memory is scarce and also when it is abundant.
- COMPRESSION (135) implementations should be tested to see that they perform in exactly the same way as implementations that don't use compression.
- Any kind of SHARING (182) (including HOOKS (72) and COPY-ON-WRITE (191)) has to be exhaustively tested from the perspective of all clients of any shared objects, and also for any potential interactions implicitly communicated between clients via the shared object.

Legal restrictions

Will implementing the pattern be free from legal restrictions or licensing costs?

Some programming techniques are subject to legal restrictions such as copyrights and patents. Choosing to use these techniques may require you to pay licence fees to the owner of the copyright or patent. Yet using third-party software or well-known techniques is a crucial component of good practice in software development — indeed, making existing practices better known is the aim of this book.

Alternatively, some free software (aka Open Source) licences, notably the GNU General Public License, may require you to release some or all of your software with similar licence conditions. However, the open source community is actively working to develop alternatives to proprietary techniques that can often be incorporated into all types of software without imposing onerous conditions on the software development.

Patterns that expose this force

- ADAPTIVE COMPRESSION (160) algorithms from third parties are often subject to copyright or patent restrictions.
- GARBAGE COLLECTION (278) and sophisticated VARIABLE ALLOCATION (236) libraries usually come as proprietary software.

REFERENCES

A

Adobe Systems Incorporated (1992) *TIFF (Tagged Image File Format) 6.0 Specification.* Adobe Systems Incorporated, Mountain View, California.

Adobe Systems Incorporated (1997) *Adobe FrameMaker 5.5 User Guide.* Adobe Systems Incorporated, Mountain View, California.

Adobe Systems Incorporated (1999) *Portable Document Format Reference Manual,* Version 1.3. Adobe Systems Incorporated, Mountain View, California.

Aho, A.V., Hopcroft, J. E. and Ullman, J. (1983) *Data Structures and Algorithms.* Addison-Wesley.

Alexander, C. (1979) *The Timeless Way of Building.* Oxford University Press, New York.

Alexander, C. Ishikawa, S., Silverstein, M., Jacobsen, M. Fiksdahl-King, I. and Angel. S. (1977) *A Pattern Language: Towns • Buildings • Construction.* Oxford University Press, New York.

Alpert, S.R., Brown, K. and Woolf, B. (1998) *The Design Patterns Smalltalk Companion.* Addison-Wesley Longman.

Apple Computer Inc. (1985) *Inside Macintosh,* Vols I and II. Apple Computer.

Auer, K. and Beck, K. (1996) Lazy optimization: Patterns for efficient Smalltalk programming. Chapter 2 in *Pattern Languages of Program Design 2* (J.M. Vlissides, J.O. Coplien and N.L. Kerth, eds). Addison-Wesley.

Austern, M.H. (1998) *Generic Programming and the STL: Using and Extending the C++ Standard Template Library.* Addison-Wesley.

B

Bachmann, G. (1999) *Palm Programming.* Macmillan Publishing Company.

Bass, L., Clements, P. and Kazman, R. (1998) *Software Architecture in Practice.* Addison-Wesley.

Beck, K. (1997) *Smalltalk Best Practice Patterns.* Prentice-Hall PTR.

Beizer, B. (1984) *Software System Testing and Quality Assurance.* Van Nostrard Reinhold.

Bell, T.C., Cleary, J.G. and Witten, I.H. (1990) *Text Compression*. Prentice Hall, New Jersey.

Berry, Buck, Mills, Stipe (1987) It's The End Of The World As We Know It (And I Feel Fine). Track 6 of *Document*. Capitol Records.

Binder, R. (2000) *Testing Object-Oriented Systems: Models, Patterns, and Tools*. Addison-Wesley, Reading, Massachusetts.

Blank, M.S. and Galley, S.W. (1980) How to Fit a Large Program Into a Small Machine. *Creative Computing*, July, 80–87. Available at `http://www.csd.uwo.ca/Infocom/Articles/small.html`

Blood P. and Patterson, A. (1992) *Rise Up Singing: The Group-Singing Song Book*. Sing Out! Publications.

Boling, D. (1998) *Programming Windows CE*. Microsoft Press.

Bollella, G., Brosgol, B., Dibble, P., Furr, S., Gosling, J., Hardin, D. and Turnbull, M. (2000) *Real-Time Specification for Java™*. The Real-Time for Java Experts Group: `http://www.rtj.org`. Addison-Wesley.

Booch, G. (1987) *Software Components with Ada*. Addison-Wesley.

Bosch, J. (2000) *Design and Use of Software Architectures: Adopting and evolving a product-line approach*. ACM Press. Pearson Education Limited, Harlow.

Boutell, E. (ed.) (1996) *PNG (Portable Network Graphics) Specification*, Version 1.0. W3C Recommendation. World Wide Web Consortium, Massachusetts Institute of Technology.

Box, D. (1998) *Essential COM*. Addison-Wesley.

Brokish, C.W. and Lewis, M. (1997) *A-Law and μ-Law Companding Implementations Using the TMS320C54x*. Application Note: SPRA163A, Digital Signal Processing Solutions, Texas Instruments Incorporated.

Brooks, Jr. F.P. (1982) *The Mythical Man-Month: Essays on Software Engineering*. Addison-Wesley.

Burrows, M. and Wheeler, D.J. (1994) *A Block-sorting Lossless Data Compression Algorithm*. SRC Research Report 124, Digital Systems Research Center, Palo Alto, May. `http://gatekeeper.dec.com/pub/DEC/SRC/research-reports/SRC-124.pdf`

Buschmann, F., Meunier, R., Rohnert, H., Sommerlad, P. and Stal, M. (1996) *Pattern-Oriented Software Architecture: A System of Patterns*. John Wiley & Sons, Chichester.

The BZIP2 Home Page: `http://sourceware.cygnus.com/bzip2/index.html`.

C

Card, R., Dumas, E. and Mével, F. (1998) *The LINUX KERNEL book*. English language edition. John Wiley & Sons, Chichester.

Cargill, T. (1996) Localized ownership: Managing dynamic objects in C++. Chapter 1 in *Pattern Languages of Program Design 2*. (J.M. Vlissides, J.O. Coplien and N.L. Kerth, eds). Addison-Wesley.

CCITT Recommendation G. 711 (1988) *Pulse code modulation (PCM) of voice frequencies*. International Telecommunication Union, Switzerland.

Chan, P., Lee, R. and Kramer, D. (1998) *The Java™ Class Libraries*, 2nd edn, Vol. 1, Addison-Wesley, Reading, Massachusetts.

Chappell, G. (1994) *DOS Internals*. Addison-Wesley, Reading, Massachusetts.

Chaudhri, A.B. and Loomis, M. (eds) (1997) *Object Databases in Practice*. Prentice Hall.

CompuServe Inc. (1990) *Graphics Interchange Format Programming Reference*, Version GIF89a. CompuServe Inc., Columbus, Ohio.

Connolly, T. and Begg, C. (1999) *Database Systems*. Addison-Wesley.

Coplien, J.O. (1994) *Advanced C++ Programming Styles and Idioms*. Addison-Wesley.

Coplien, J.O. (1996) *Software Patterns*. SIGS Press.

Coplien, J.O. (1999) *Multi-Paradigm Design for C++*. Addison-Wesley.

Cormen, T.H., Leiserson, C.E. and Rivest, R.L. (1990) *Introduction to Algorithms*. MIT Press.

Covey, S.R. (1990) *The 7 Habits of Highly Effective People: Powerful Lessons in Personal Change*. Fireside.

Cunningham, W. (1995) The CHECKS pattern language of information integrity. Chapter 10 in *Pattern Languages of Program Design* (J.O. Coplien and D.C. Schmidt, eds). Addison-Wesley.

Cyganski, D., Orr, J.A. and Vaz, R.F. (1998)   *Information Engineering Across the Professions*. http://ece.wpi.edu:8080/infoeng/textbook/main.html

D

Darragh, J.J., Witten I.H. and James, M.L. (1990) The Reactive Keyboard: A predictive typing aid. *IEEE Computer*. 23(11), November.

Date, C.J. (1999) *An Introduction to Database Systems*, 7th edn. Addison-Wesley.

Degener, J. (1994) Digital speech compression: Putting the GSM 06.10 RPE-LTP algorithm to work. *Dr Dobbs Journal*, December.

Deutsch, P. (1996) *DEFLATE Compressed Data Format Specification version 1.3*. Request for Comments: RFC 1951. Network Working Group.

Deutsch, P. and Bobrow, D. (1976) An efficient incremental automatic garbage collector. *Communications of the ACM*, 19(9), September.

Digital Equipment Corporation. (1975) *PDP-11 software handbook*. Digital Equipment Corporation, Maynard, Massachusetts.

Dijkstra, E.W. (1972) Notes on Structured Programming. Part I of *Structured Programming*. (O.- J. Dahl, E.W. Dijkstra, C.A.R. Hoare). Academic Press.

Drossopoulou, S., Wragg, D. and Eisenbach, S. (1998) What is Java binary compatibility? *Proc. 13th ACM Conference on Object-Oriented Programming, Systems, Languages, and Applications (OOPSLA)*, Vancouver, British Columbia, pp 341–358, ACM Press.

D'Souza, D.F. and Wills, A.C. (1998) *Objects, Components, and Frameworks With UML: The Catalysis Approach*. Addison-Wesley.

Dybvig, R.K., Eby, D. and Bruggeman, C. (1994) *Don't Stop the BIBOP: Flexible and Efficient Storage Management for Dynamically-Typed Languages*. Indiana University Computer Science Department Technical Report TR400.

E

Edwards, L. (1997) *Programming Psion Computers*. EMCC Software Limited, Carrington, Manchester.

Egremont III, C. (1998) *Mr Bunny's Guide to ActiveX*. Some Publishing Company, Reading, Massachusetts.

Egremont III, C. (1999) *Mr Bunny's Big Cup o' Java™*. Some Publishing Company, Reading, Massachusetts.

Ellis, M.A. and Stroustroup, B. (1990) *The Annotated C++ Reference Manual*. Addison-Wesley.

Elmasri R. and Navathe, S.B. (2000) *Fundamentals of Database Systems*, 3rd edn. Addison-Wesley.

Enea OSE Systems (2000). *Strength and Structure in Real-time Operating Systems*. White Paper, Enea OSE Systems AB, Täby, Sweden. See also http://www.enea.com/product/papers/strength.htm

F

Fielding, R., Gettys, J., Mogul, J., Frystyk, H., Masinter, L., Leach, P. and Berners-Lee, T. (1999) *Hypertext Transfer Protocol — HTTP/1.1*. Request for Comments: 2616. Network Working Group.

Fitzgerald, J. and Dennis, A. (1995) *Business Data Communications and Networking*, 5th edn. John Wiley & Sons, Chichester.

Folk, M.J. Zoellick, B. and Riccardi, G. (1998) *File Structures: An Object-Oriented Approach with C++*, 3rd edn. Addison-Wesley.

Foote, B. and Yoder, J. (2000) Big ball of mud. Chapter 29 in *Pattern Languages of Program Design 4* (N. Harrison, B. Foote and H. Rohnert, eds). Addison-Wesley Longman.

Fowler, M. (1997) *Analysis Patterns: Reusable Object Models*. Addison Wesley, Reading, Massachusetts.

Fowler, M. (1999) *Refactoring: Improving the Design of Existing Code*. Addison-Wesley Longman.

Fowler, M. with Scott, K. (1999) *UML Distilled, Applying the Standard Object Modelling Language*, 2nd edn. Addison-Wesley, Reading, Massachusetts.

G

Gage, P. (1997) Random access data compression. *C Users Journal*, 15(9), September.

Gamma, E., Helm, R., Johnson, R. and Vlissides R. (1995) *Design Patterns: Elements of Reusable Object-Oriented Software*. Addison-Wesley Longman, Reading, Massachusetts.

Gilly, D. and O'Reilly, T. (1990) *The X Window System in a Nutshell*, Version 11, Release 4. O'Reilly and Associates.

Goldberg, A. and Robson, D. (1983) *Smalltalk-80: The Language and its Implementation*. Addison-Wesley, Reading, Massachusetts.

Goldberg, A. and Rubin, K.S. *(1995) Succeeding With Objects: Decision Frameworks for Project Management.* Addison-Wesley.

Gonzalez, R.C. and Woods, R.E. (1992) *Digital Image Processing.* Addison-Wesley, Reading, Massachusetts.

Goodheart, B. and Cox, J. (1994) *The Magic Garden Explained: The Internals of Unix™ System V Release 4.* Prentice Hall.

Gosling, J., Joy, B. and Steele, G. (1996) *The Java™ Language Specification.* Addison-Wesley.

H

Hamacher, V.C., Vranesic, Z.G. and Zaky, S.G. (1984) *Computer Organization,* 2nd edn. McGraw-Hill.

Hayes, B. Collective Wisdom. (1998) *American Scientist,* March-April. See also: `http://setiathome.ssl.berkeley.edu`

Held, G. (1994) *The Complete Modem Reference,* 2nd edn. Wiley Professional Computing.

Henning, M. and Vinoski, S. (1999) *Advanced CORBA Programming with C++.* Addison-Wesley.

Hoare, C.A.R. (1972) Notes on Data Structuring. Part II of *Structured Programming* (O.-J. Dahl, E.W. Dijkstra, C.A.R. Hoare, eds). Academic Press.

Hoare, C.A.R. (1981) *The Emperor's Old Clothes.* 1980 Turing Award Lecture. *Comm. ACM,* 24(2), October.

Hogg, J. (1991) Islands: Aliasing protection in object-oriented languages. *Proc. ACM Conference on Object-Oriented Programming, Systems, Languages, and Applications (OOPSLA),* ACM Press.

Horspool, R.N. and Corless, J. (1998) Tailored compression of Java class files. *Software — Practice and Experience,* 28(12), 1253–1268, October.

Hudson, R.L. and Moss, J.E.B. (1992) Incremental collection of mature objects. *Proc. International Workshop on Memory Management.* LNCS #637. Springer-Verlag.

Huffman, D.A. (1952) A method for the construction of minimum-redundancy codes. *Proceedings of the Institute of Electrical and Radio Engineers,* 40(9).

Hunt, A. and Thomas, D. (2000) *The Pragmatic Programmer: from journeyman to master.* Addison-Wesley.

I

Ingalls, D. (1981) Design principles behind Smalltalk. *BYTE The Small Systems Journal,* 6(8), August.

ITU Recommendation T.87 (1998) *Lossless and near-lossless compression of continuous-tone still images — Baseline.* International Telecommunication Union, Switzerland.

J

Jackson, M. (1995) *Software Requirements & Specifications: a lexicon of practice, principles and prejudices*. ACM Press, Addison-Wesley.

Johnstone, M.S. and Wilson, P.R. (1998) The memory fragmentation problem: solved? *Proc. International Symposium on Memory Management*, Vancouver, British Columbia, October. ACM Press.

Jones, R. and Lins, R. (1996) *Garbage Collection: Algorithms for Automatic Dynamic Memory Management*. John Wiley & Sons, Chichester.

Jones, R. (2000) *The Garbage Collection Page*. http://www.cs.ukc.ac.uk/people/staff/rej/gc.html

K

Kaehler, T and Krasner, G. (1983) LOOM — Large Object-Oriented Memory for Smalltalk-80 Systems. Chapter 14 in *Smalltalk-80: Bits of History, Words of Advice* (G. Krasner, ed.) Addison-Wesley.

Keller, W and Coldewey, J. (1998) Accessing relational databases. Chapter 18 in *Pattern Languages of Program Design 3* (R. Martin, D. Riehle and F. Buschmann, eds). Software Patterns Series, Addison-Wesley.

Kenah, L.J. and Bate, S.F. (1984) *VAX/VMS internals and data structures*. Digital Press, Bedford Massachusetts.

Kernighan, B.W. and Ritchie, D.M. (1988) *The C Programming Language*. Prentice Hall.

Kernighan, B.W. and Pike, R. (1984) *The UNIX Programming Environment*. Prentice-Hall, Englewood Cliffs, New Jersey.

Kernighan, B.W. and Pike, R. (1999) *The Practice of Programming*. Addison-Wesley.

Kinnear, G.S. (1999) *The Compression Technology in Multimedia*. http://www.scit.wlv.ac.uk/~c9581158/index_main.html.

Knuth, D.E. (1997) *The Art of Computer Programming. Volume 1: Fundamental Algorithms,* 3rd edn. Addison-Wesley Longman.

Knuth, D.E. (1998) *The Art of Computer Programming. Volume 3: Sorting and Searching.* 2nd edn. Addison-Wesley Longman.

L

Lalonde, W. (1994) *Discovering Smalltalk*. Addison-Wesley.

Lamport, L. (1986) *LaTeX: A Document Preparation System*. Addison-Wesley.

Lea, D. (2000) *Concurrent Programming in Java™: Design Principles and Patterns,* 2nd edn. Addison-Wesley.

Lea, D. (2000) *A Memory Allocator*. http://gee.cs.oswego.edu/dl/html/malloc.html

Leffler, S.J., Mckusick, M.K., Karels, M.J. and Quarterman, J.S. (1989) *The Design and Implementation of the 4.3BSD UNIX Operating System*. Addison-Wesley.

Lewart, C.R. (1999) *The Ultimate Modem Handbook: Your Guide to Selection, Installation, Troubleshooting, and Optimization*. Prentice Hall Computer Books.

Limb, S. and Cordingley, P. (1982) *Captain Oates: Soldier and Explorer*. B.T. Batsford Ltd, London.

Lindholm, T. and Yellin, F. (1999) *The Java Virtual Machine Specification*. 2nd edn. Addison-Wesley, Reading, Massachusetts.

Lycklama, E. (1999) *Memory Leaks in Java*. Presentation at Java One, San Francisco, California. See also: http://www.klgroup.com/jprobe/javaonepres/

M

MacNeil, J. and Proudfoot, D. (1995) *Mem 2 — The Rainy Day Fund*. Pictorius Technical Note #30. Pictorius Incorporated, Halifax, Canada, August.

Matthews, S. (1989) UK Defense Software Standard. *The Risks Digest* (P.G. Neumann, moderator), 9(1) Thursday 6 July.

Meyer, B. (1992) *Eiffel: The Language*. Prentice Hall.

Meyer, B. (1997) *Object Oriented Software Construction,* 2nd edn. Prentice Hall PTR. Upper Saddle River, New Jersey.

Meyers, S. (1996) *More Effective C++: 35 New Ways to Improve your Programs and Designs*. Addison-Wesley Longman.

Meyers, S. (1998) *Effective C++: 50 Specific Ways to Improve your Programs and Designs,* 2nd edn. Addison-Wesley Longman.

Mezaros, G. (1996) A pattern language for improving the capacity of reactive systems. Chapter 35 in *Pattern Languages of Program Design 2* (J.M. Vlissides, J.O. Coplien and N.L. Kerth, eds). Addison-Wesley.

Meszaros, G. and Doble, J. (1998) A pattern language for pattern writing. Chapter 29 in *Pattern Languages of Program Design 3* (R. Martin, D. Riehle and F. Buschmann, eds). Software Patterns Series, Addison-Wesley.

Microsoft Corporation (1996) *Microsoft Visual C++ 5.0 Online Documentation*. Microsoft Corporation, Redmond, Washington.

Microsoft Corporation (1997a) *Microsoft Windows NT 4.0 Online Documentation*. Microsoft Corporation, Redmond, Washington.

Microsoft Corporation (1997b) *Microsoft Word SR-1 Online Documentation*. Microsoft Corporation, Redmond, Washington.

Microsoft Corporation (1998) *Microsoft Windows CE Programmer's Guide*. Microsoft Corporation, Redmond, Washington.

Ministry of Defence (1979) *DEF-STAN 00-55: Requirements for Safety-Related Software in Defence Equipment*. Ministry of Defence, United Kingdom.

Moore, G. (1997) An update on Moore's Law. Keynote address to Intel Developer Forum. See: http://www.intel.com/pressroom/archive/speeches/GEM93097.HTM

MP3 (1998) *Generic coding of moving pictures and associated audio information. Part 3: Audio.* ISO/IEC 13818-3. International Organization for Standardization (ISO), Switzerland.

MPEG (1998) *Generic coding of moving pictures and associated audio information. Part 1: Systems.* ISO/IEC 13818-1. International Organization for Standardization (ISO), Switzerland.

N

Noble, J. (1998) Classifying relationships between object-oriented design patterns. *Proc. Australian Software Engineering Conference (ASWEC)*, 98–107. IEEE CS Press.

Noble, J. (2000) Arguments and Results. Accepted for publication in the *Journal of Object-Oriented Systems*.

Noble, J. and Weir, C. (1998) The Proceedings of the Memory Preservation Society. *Proc. 3rd European Conference on Pattern Languages of Programming and Computing (EuroPLoP '98)* (J. Coldewey and P. Dyson, eds). Universtätsverlag Kontstanz.

Noble, J. and Weir, C. (2000) High level and process patterns from the Memory Preservation Society: Patterns for managing limited memory. Chapter 12 in *Pattern Languages of Program Design 4* (N. Harrison, B. Foote and H. Rohnert, eds). Addison-Wesley Longman.

Noble, J. Vitek, J. and Potter, J. (1998) Flexible alias protection. *Proc. European Conference on Object-Oriented Programming (ECOOP)*.

Norman, D. (1998) *The Invisible Computer: Why Good Products Can Fail, the Personal Computer Is So Complex, and Information Appliances Are the Solution.* MIT Press.

O

Orfali, R. Harkey, D. and Edwards, J. (1996) *Essential Distributed Objects Survival Guide.* John Wiley & Sons, Chichester.

Orwell, J. (1945) *Animal Farm.* Penguin, Harmondsworth.

Ousterhout, J.K. (1994) *Tcl and the Tk Toolkit.* Addison-Wesley.

P

Page, B. (1988) A report on the Internet worm. *The Risks Digest* (P.G. Neumann, moderator), 7(76), Saturday 12 Nov.

Palm Inc. (2000) *Palm OS SDK Reference.* Palm Inc., Santa Clara, California.

ParcPlace Systems (1994) *VisualWorks/Smalltalk User's Guide,* Version 2.0. ParcPlace Systems.

Petzold, C. (1998) *Programming Windows,* 5th book and CD edn. Microsoft Press.

Pike, R. and Thompson, K. (1993) Hello World. *Proc. of the Winter 1993 USENIX Conference,* pp. 43–50, San Diego.

Pike, R., Presotto, D., Dorward, S., Ritchie, D.M., Trickey, H. and Winterbottom, P. (1997)

The Inferno Operating System. *Bell Labs Technical Journal*, 2(1), Winter.

Plum, T. and Saks, D. (1991) *C++ Programming Guidelines*. Plum-Hall.

Potter, S. (1948) *The Theory and Practice of Gamesmanship, or The Art of Winning Games Without Actually Cheating*. Penguin.

Pree, W. (1995) *Design Patterns for Object-Oriented Software Development*. Addison-Wesley.

Prosise, J. (1999) *Programming Windows With MFC*. Microsoft Press.

Pryce, N. (2000) Abstract session: An object structured pattern. Chapter 7 in *Pattern Languages of Program Design 4* (N. Harrison, B. Foote, and H. Rohnert, eds). Addison-Wesley Longman.

Pugh, W. (1999) Compressing Java class files. *Proc. ACM SIGPLAN Conference on Programming Languages Design and Implementation (PLDI)*, 247–258. ACM Press.

R

Rhodes, N. and McKeehan, J. (1999) *Palm Programming: The Developer's Guide*. O'Reilly and Associates.

Riehle, D. (1997) Composite design patterns. *Proc. ACM Conference on Object-Oriented Programming, Systems, Languages, and Applications (OOPSLA)*. ACM Press.

RISC OS Ltd (2000) *RISC OS Programmers reference manuals*. RiscOs Ltd, Cyncoed, Cardiff. (See also www.riscos.com

Rising, L. (2000) *The Patterns Almanac 2000*. Addison-Wesley.

Ritchie, D.M. and Thompson, K. (1978) The Unix Time-Sharing System. *The Bell System Technical Journal*, 57(6), July–August.

Rogue Wave Software (1994) *Tools.h++*, Version 1.x. Rogue Wave Software, Boulder, Colorado.

S

Sane, S. and Campbell, R. (1996) Resource exchanger: A behavioral pattern for low-overhead concurrent resource management. Chapter 28 in *Pattern Languages of Program Design 2* (J.M. Vlissides, J.O. Coplien and N.L. Kerth, eds). Addison-Wesley.

Scheifler, R.W. and Gettys, J. (1986) The X Window System. *ACM Transactions on Graphics*, 5(2), April.

Schorr, H. and Waite, W. (1967) An efficient machine independent procedure for garbage collection in various list structures. *Communications of the ACM* 10(8), August.

Schumacher. E.F. (1989) *Small Is Beautiful: Economics As If People Mattered*. Harper Collins.

Scott, R.F. (1913) *Scott's Last Expedition: The Personal Journals of Captain R. F. Scott, R.N., C.V.O., on his Journey to the South Pole*. Elder & Co.

Sedgewick, R. (1988) *Algorithms*. Addison-Wesley.

Sedgewick, R. (1999) *Algorithms in C++: Fundamentals, Data Structures, Sorting, Searching*, 3rd edn. Addison-Wesley.

Shaw, M. and Garlan, D. (1996) *Software Architecture: Perspectives on an Emerging Discipline.* Prentice Hall, New Jersey.

Shlaer, S. and Mellor, S.J. (1991) *Object Lifecycles: Modeling the World in States.* Yourdon Press.

Shneiderman, B. (1997) *Designing the User Interface: Strategies for Effective Human–Computer Interaction,* 3rd edn. Addison-Wesley.

Simons, A.J.H. (1998) Borrow, copy or steal? Loans and larceny in the orthodox canonical form. *Proc. 13th ACM Conference on Object-Oriented Programming, Systems, Languages, and Applications (OOPSLA),* Vancouver, British Columbia, pp 65–83. ACM Press.

The *Small Memory Software* home page (2000): `http://www.smallmemory.com`

Smith, B. (1985) *The BBC Micro ROM Book: Sideways ROMs and RAMs.* Collins.

Smith, W.R. (1999) NewtonScript: Prototypes on the Palm. Chapter 6 in *Prototype-Based Programming: Concepts, Languages, and Applications.* (J.Noble, A. Taivalsaari and I. Moore, eds). Springer-Verlag.

Solari, S.J. (1997) *Digital Video and Audio Compression.* McGraw-Hill.

Soni, D., Nord, R.L. and Hofmeister, C. (1995) Software architecture in industrial applications. *Proc. 17th International Conference on Software Engineering,* Seattle, pp. 196–207. ACM Press.

Souku, P.J. (1994) *Taming C++: Pattern Classes and Persistence for Large Projects.* Addison-Wesley.

Stallman, R.M. (1984) Emacs: The extensible, customizable, self-documenting display editor. In *Interactive Programming Environments* (D.R. Barstow, H.E. Shrobe, and E. Sandewall, eds). McGraw-Hill, New York.

Stallman, R.M. (1999) *Using and Porting the GNU Compiler Collection (GCC).* Free Software Foundation, Boston, Massachusetts.

Steele, G.L. (1977) *Data Representation in PDP-10 MACLISP.* MIT AI MEMO 421.

Steiner, J.P. (1984) *The Standard BASIC Dictionary for Programming.* Prentice Hall, New Jersey.

Stroustrup, B. (1995) *The Design and Evolution of C++.* Addison-Wesley.

Stroustrup, B. (1997) *The C++ Programming Language,* 3rd edn. Addison-Wesley.

Sullivan, III, W.T., Werthimer, D., Bowyer, S., Cobb, J., Gedye, D. and Anderson, D. (1997) A new major SETI project based on Project Serendip data and 100,000 personal computers. *Astronomical and Biochemical Origins and the Search for Life in the Universe.* Proc. Fifth International Conference on Bioastronomy. IAU Colloq. No. 161C. (B. Cosmovici, S. Bowyer and D. Werthimer, eds). Editrice Compositori, Bologna, Italy. See also: `http://setiathome.ssl.berkeley.edu/`

Sutter, H. (2000) *Exceptional C++: 47 Engineering Puzzles, Programming Problems, and Solutions.* Addison-Wesley Longman.

Symbian Ltd. (1999a) *Exception handling in EPOC.* Tutorial, Symbian Ltd, London. See also: `http://developer.epocworld.com/techlibrary/Tutorials/excepthandling.htm`

Symbian Ltd (1999b) *EPOC Release 5 C++ SDK Documentation.* Symbian Ltd, London. See also: `http://www.symbiandevnet.com/techlibrary/documentation/ER5/CPP/sysdoc/index.html`

Symbian Ltd (2000) *The Theory of Binary Compatibility.* Symbian C++ Knowledgebase Article, Symbian Ltd, London. See also: `http://www.symbiandevnet.com/`

Szyperski, C. (1999) *Component Software: Beyond Object-Oriented Programming*. Addison-Wesley Longman, Harlow.

T

Tabor, S. (2000) *IS380 — Business Telecommunications Course*. See `http://telecomm.boisestate.edu/IS380.s00/`

Taivalsaari, A., Bush, B. and Simon, D. (1999) *The Spotless System: Implementing a Java™ System for the Palm Connected Organizer*. SMLI TR-99-73. Sun Microsystems Laboratories, Palo Alto, California.

Tannenbaum, A.S. (1992) *Modern Operating Systems*. Prentice Hall.

Tasker, M. (1999a) *Trap Cleanup: Memory management and cleanup*. Revision 1.0. Symbian Ltd, London: See also `http://www.symbian.com/technology/papers/memman/memman.html`

Tasker, M. (1999b) *Managing C++ APIs*. Revision 1.0. Symbian Ltd, London: See also `http://www.symbian.com/technology/papers/cppapi/cppapi.html`

Tasker, M., Allin, J., Dixon, J., Shackman, M., Richardson, T. and Forrest, J. (2000) *Professional Symbian Programming: Mobile Solutions on the EPOC Platform*. Wrox Press.

Thoelke, A. *DBMS Sharing: DBMS enhancements in EPOC R5*. Revison 0.1. Symbian Ltd, London. See also: `http://www.symbian.com/technology/papers/e5ndbms/e5ndbms.html`

Tofte, M. (1998) A brief introduction to regions. Invited Paper. *Proc. the 1998 ACM International Symposium on Memory Management*, Vancouver.

U

Ungar, D. (1984) Generation scavenging: A non-disruptive high-performance storage reclamation algorithm. *Proc. ACM Symposium on Practical Software Development Environments*, Pittsburg, April.

The Unicode Consortium. (1996) *The Unicode Standard*, Version 2.0. Addison-Wesley Developers Press, Reading, Massachusetts.

V

Vlissides, J. (1998) *Pattern Hatching*. Addison-Wesley Longman.

W

Wall, L., Christiansen, T., Schwartz, R.L. and Potter, S. (1996) *Programming Perl*, 2nd edn. O'Reilly & Associates.

Ward, B. (1999) *The Linux Kernel HOWTO*. The Linux Documentation Project. June. See also: `http://www.linuxdoc.org/`

Weir, C. (1995) Bullet-proofing your code: On error handling in C++ applications. *.EXE Magazine*, May.

Weir, C. (1996) Improve your sense of ownership: On managing associations in OO languages. *Report on Object Analysis and Design*, March.

Weir, C. (1998) Code that tests itself: Using conditions and invariants to debug your code. *C++ Report*, March.

Weir, C. (1998) Patterns for designing in teams. Chapter 18 in *Pattern Languages of Program Design 3* (R. Martin, D. Riehle and F. Buschmann, eds). Software Patterns Series, Addison-Wesley.

Wilson, P.R., Johnstone, M.S., Neely, M. and Boles, D. (1995) Dynamic Storage Allocation: A Survey and Critical Review. *Proc. International Workshop on Memory Management*, Kinross, Scotland, UK, September. Springer-Verlag.

Wilson, P.R. (1994) *Uniprocessor Garbage Collection Techniques*. University of Texas Technical Report. To appear in *ACM Computing Surveys*. See also `ftp://ftp.cs.utexas.edu/pub/garbage/bigsurv.ps`

Witten, I., Moffat, A. and Bell, T. (1999) *Managing Gigabytes*. Morgan Kaufmann.

Woolf, B. (2000) Abstract Class. Chapter 1 in *Pattern Languages for Program Design 4* (N. Harrison, B. Foote, H. Rohnert, eds). Addison-Wesley Longman.

X

Xanalys (2000) *The Memory Management Reference*. Xanalys Corporation. See also: `http://www.xanalys.com/software_tools/mm/`

Y

Yourdon, E. and Constantine, L.L. (1979) *Structured Design: Fundamentals of a Discipline of Computer Program and System Design*. Prentice Hall, New Jersey.

Z

Ziv, J. and Lempel, A. (1977) A universal algorithm for sequential data compression. *IEEE Transaction on Information Theory*, IT-23(3), May

INDEX

abstract class 209
Acorn Archimedes 37
adapters 209
adaptive compression 140, 160–6
    algorithms 103
    consequences 161–2
    implementation 162–3
    LZ compression 162–3, 164–5
    Move-To-Front (MTF) 161, 163–4
Adobe 159, 165
Aho, A.V. 173
Alexander, C. 1, 5, 11, 12
aliasing problems 185
Alien Invasion 251–2
allocating fields 273
Allocator template parameter 30
Alpert, S.R. 13, 190
Apple Macintosh 63, 262, 266
    MacOS 85, 86, 90
    resource files 106
application switching 4, 56, 82, 84–91
    communication between processes
        87–8
    consequences 85–6
    data management 88
    implementation 86–8
    known uses 90
    master programs 87
    program chaining 87
architectural strategies 26
architecture see small architecture
ASCII character set 137
Auer, K. 31, 170, 190, 229, 243
Austern, M.H. 200, 211, 215
autoloading packages 112

background processes 57, 60, 86
Bass, L. 25, 26, 31

batch processing see data files
Bate, S.F. 189, 196, 258
Beck, K. 12, 31, 170, 185, 190, 225, 229,
    243
Begg, T. 100, 184
Bell, TC. 136, 142, 166
'Big Bag of Pipes' 253
binary compatibility 113
BIOS (Basic Input Output System) 71
bit packing see packed data
bitmaps 268–9
bitwise operations 179
Blank, M.S. 131, 152
Blood, P. 137
Bobrow, D. 274
Boling, D. 37, 54, 60, 63, 249
Bollella, G. 37, 234, 249
Booch, G. 31
Boolean variables 176
borrowing memory 40, 42–3
Bosch, J. 25, 31
Boutell, E. 139, 159
Box, D. 110, 111, 112, 277
bridge pattern 212–13
Brokish, C.W. 138
Brooks, F.P. 26
buffers 228–9
Burrows, M. 166
Buschmann, F. 12, 13, 25, 31, 110, 193
BZip2 166

C++
    defining buffers 228–9
    deleting objects 238
    Handle classes 263–4
    memory allocation 233–4
    memory limit 35–7
    operating system heaps 246–7

C++ *cont.*
  placement new 247
  pooled allocation 254–6
  reference counting 274–6
  ScreenImage implementation 274–5
  smart pointer 275–6
  temporary heap implementation
    248–9
cache 185
cache release *see* Captain Oates
callback functions 29
Campbell, R. 42
Captain Oates 21, 32, 57–64
  consequences 59
  detecting low-memory conditions 60
  handling low-memory events 61
  implementation 59–61
  known uses 63–4
Card, R. 37, 131, 189
Cargill, T. 26, 31, 186
catch statement 52
chaining 86, 87, 94
Chan, P. 88, 99, 164, 166, 197, 215
Chappell, G. 71, 85, 118
Chaudhri, A.B. 131
class design 3
code segmentation 112
Coldewey, J. 100
COM framework 277
COMDAT folding 189
command scripts *see* application
  switching
common keyword 88
communicating memory exhaustion 51
communication between processes 87–8
compacting objects 263
compaction 21, 224, 259–67
  compacting objects 263
  consequences 261
  on demand 263
  implementation 261–4
  known uses 266
  object tables 262
  without handles 261–2
component design 25–7
  see also packages
compound patterns 12
compression 18, 20, 21, 79, 83, 135–42
  adaptive compression 140, 160–6
  consequences 136

decoding 141
difference coding 140, 153–9
encoding 141
implementation 136–9
known uses 141–2
lossy compression 138–9, 156
mechanical redundancy 137
processing and memory requirements
  140
and programming costs 141
and random access 141
ratios 137
resynchronization 141, 156
semantic redundancy 137–8
specialized patterns 139–41
table compression 140, 143–52
CompuServe 139, 159
configuration data 101–2
Connolly, T. 100, 184
Constantine, L.L. 40
control systems 6
Coplien, J.O. 4, 11, 39, 132, 193, 211,
  213, 243, 263, 291
copy-on-write 3, 172, 191–7
  consequences 192
  copying changes to objects 193–4
  delta objects 193–4
  implementation 192–4
  known uses 196–7
  proxy pattern 193
  writing to objects in ROM 194
copying garbage collectors 283
copying object changes 193–4
copying objects 182
CORBA 110
Cordingley, P. 59, 64
Corless, J. 166
Cormen, T.H. 173
Covey, S.R. 5
Cox, J. 83, 118, 131, 196, 258
Cunningham, W. 12, 56
cycles 272–3
Cyganski, D. 142, 152, 159

dangling pointers 248
Darragh, J.J. 72
data
  configuration data 101–2
  reducing quality of 223
Data Encryption Standard (DES) 69

data files 4, 82, 92–100
  consequences 93–4
  implementation 94–6
  incremental processing 94–5, 97
  indexes 96
  known uses 99
  random access 96
  subfile processing 95–6, 97
    multiple subfiles 98–9
data management 88, 123
data structures, see small data structures
data transfer 39, 40
Date, C.J. 96, 100, 184
DEC 114
Decoding within compression 141
defragmentation see compaction
Degener, J. 139
degraded modes 49, 53, 55
delaying allocation requests 223
delete operator 34, 255, 256
deleting objects 223, 238
  compound objects 271–2
  shared objects 186
delta coding 154, 155
delta objects 193–4
demand paging 120
design quality 307–8
design-level patterns 3
designing objects 228
detecting low-memory conditions 60
detecting memory exhaustion 51
Deutsch, P. 152, 165, 208, 274
device drivers 124
dialog editors 103
dictionaries 173
difference coding 140, 153–9
  consequences 154
  delta coding 154, 155
  implementation 154–7
  known uses 159
  lossy difference compression 156
  non-numeric data 157
  resynchronization 156
  run-length encoding 154, 155
Digital 86
Dijkstra, E.W. 226
Doble, J. 12
Drossopoulou, S. 113
D'Souza, D.F. 211
Dybvig, R.K. 253

dynamic allocation see variable
    allocation
dynamic loading see packages
dynamically linked libraries (DLL)
    110–11, 118

Eden space 250
Edwards, L. 106, 152
Egremont, C. 110, 219
Ellis, M.A. 67, 74, 253
Elmasri, R. 96, 100, 184
Emacs 76
embedded objects 229–30
embedded pointers 3, 172, 198–208
  consequences 200
  implementation 200–4
  inheritance 201
  inline objects 201–2
  known uses 208
  pointer differences 202
  pre-processing 202
  reuse 201–2
  traversals 203–4
embedded systems 6–7, 8–10, 71
encoding within compression 141
encryption algorithms 69
EPOC
  animated object example 115–17
  AppArc architecture 99
  Bitmap Server 70
  client-server interfaces 46
  data files 99–100
  embedded pointers 208
  file system 70
  Font and Bitmap Server 266
  low-memory conditions 61
  memory limit 35, 37
  packages 115–17
  Packed Array 261
  packed data 180–1
  partial failure 52–3, 55
  resource files 106
  Socket service 258
  string handling 215, 235
  Time World application 76
  TRAP harness macro 52–3
  updating ROM memory 77
  database server 258
error codes/signalling 222–3, 238–9
exceptions 239

exceptions *cont.*
　　catch statement 52
　　throw statement 52
exhaustion of memory *see* memory
　　exhaustion
extensions 273–4
external fragmentation 221, 227, 259–60

feast and famine *see* partial failure
Fielding, R. 166
file systems 80
　　read-only 69–70
filters *see* data files
Fitzgerald, J. 152
fixed allocation 3, 21, 220, 224, 226–35
　　consequences 227–8
　　deferring commitment 230–1
　　designing objects 228
　　embedded objects 229–30
　　implementation 228–31
　　known uses 234–5
　　library classes 229
　　pre-allocating objects 228–9
fixed-sized heap *see* memory limit
fixed-sized memories 222
flyweight pattern 185, 251
Folk, M.J. 96
font files 104, 185
Foote, B. 25
forces 5, 11–12, 18–20, 291–3
Format Software 216
Fowler, M. 13, 126, 184, 194
fragmentation 221–2, 227, 239–40,
　　259–60, 303–4

Gage, P. 152
Galley, S.W. 131, 152
games 106–7, 131
　　Alien Invasion 252
Gamma, E. ix, 4, 13, 39, 52, 53, 74, 77,
　　110, 111, 132, 164, 185, 190, 193,
　　194, 206, 211, 212, 216, 228, 251
garbage collection 21, 224, 250, 273,
　　278–88
　　consequences 279–80
　　copying 283
　　finalization 281
　　functions 285–7
　　'Generational Copying' 250
　　implementation 280–3

known uses 287
mark-sweep garbage collection 281–3
programming with 280–1
weak references 281
Garlan, D. 25, 31, 100
'Generational Copying' 250
GhostDetails object 39
GIF compression 139
Gilly, D. 29
Goldberg, A. 5, 141, 208, 215, 219, 253,
　　267, 276, 287
Gonzalez, R.C. 139, 159
Goodheart, B. 83, 118, 131, 196, 258
Gosling, J. 36, 181, 189, 219
graceful degradation *see* partial failure
grouping allocations 240
GSM compression 139

Hamacher, V.C. 118
hand-held/mobile projects 6, 8–10, 21–2
handles 261–2, 263–4
hardware constraints 8
hardware costs 300
Hayes, B. 57, 64
heaps 34–5, 246–9
Held, G. 152, 159
Henning, M. 110
'Hillside Group' 12
Hoare, C.A.R. 51, 173
Hogg, J. 183, 185
hooks 21, 72–7
　　consequences 73–4
　　implementation 74–5
Horspool, R.N. 166
Hudson, R.L. 283
Huffman coding 146–7, 152
Hunt, A. 31
hypoth-a-sized collection pattern 31,
　　229, 243

immutable objects 185
implementation guide 4–5
incremental interfaces 44–6
incremental processing 94–5, 97
indexes 96
Ingalls, D. 226, 238
inheritance 201
inline objects 201–2
inlining 229–30
Inter-Process Communication (IPC) 110

intercepting memory access 122–3
interfaces, *see* small interfaces
internal fragmentation 221, 227
interpreters 123
interrupt tables *see* hooks
invariants of components 51–2
iterative traversals 203–4
iterators 39, 45–6

Jackson, M. 11, 31
Java
    Compaction example 264–6
    compilation 99
    dynamically loaded packages 118
    fixed allocation example 231–3
    JAR format 166
    low-memory conditions 61
    memory discard 249
    memory exhaustion signal 53–4
    memory limit 36, 37
    multiple representations example
        213–15
    nibble coding example 149–51
    packing objects into basic types
        177–8
    and read-only memory 69
    releasing resources 52
    ROM Builder 67
    sequence compression example
        157–9
    serialization framework 88
    sharing example 187–9
    StringBuffer 197
    variable allocation example 241–2
    version control 113
    Zlib libraries 46, 164
Johnstone, M.S. 243
Jones, R. 179, 186, 208, 250, 267, 274,
    280, 287, 288
JPEG compression 139
jump tables *see* hooks

Kaehler, T. 131, 215–16
Keller, W. 100
Kenah, L.J. 189, 196, 258
Kernighan, B.W. 31, 87, 89, 90, 99, 277
Kinnear, G.S. 142, 159
Knuth, D.E. 96, 173, 198, 201, 208
Krasner, G. 131, 215–16

Lalonde, W. 213
Lamport, L. 99
language of pattern names 4, 12
LaTeX 186
lazy initialization 185
lazy loading *see* packages
Lea, D. 223, 243
Leffler, S.J. 83
legal restrictions 309
Lempel, A. 141, 162, 165
lending memory 40, 41–2
Lewart, C.R. 152
Lewis, M. 138
libraries, dynamically linked libraries
    (DLL) 110–11, 118
library classes 229
library functions 103
Limb, S. 59, 64
Lindholm, T. 37, 118, 141, 152
Lins, R. 179, 186, 208, 250, 267, 274,
    280, 287
Linux 165–6
Literals, sharing 186
loading packages 112
locality of reference 120, 124
LOOM 131, 215
Loomis, M. 131
lossy compression 138–9, 156
low-memory conditions 60
low-memory events 61
Lycklama, E. 243, 281
LZ compression 162–3, 164–5

Macintosh *see* Apple Macintosh
MacNeil, J. 54
mainframe computer projects 7, 8–10
maintainability 19, 307–8
managed tables *see* compaction
manual loading of packages 112
mark-sweep garbage collection 281–3
master documents 99
master programs 87
mathematical algorithms 69
Matthews, S. 234
mechanical redundancy 137
medical systems 6
memory allocation 3, 18, 20, 26–7,
    29–30, 219–25
    and compaction 21, 224, 259–67
    consequences 220–1

memory allocation *cont.*
  delaying allocation requests 223
  failure of 49
  fixed allocation 3, 21, 220, 224,
    226–35
  and fragmentation 221–2, 227,
    239–40, 259–60, 303–4
  garbage collection 21, 224, 250, 273,
    278–88
  memory discard 3, 220, 224, 244–50
  pooled allocation 21, 220, 224, 251–8
  and reference counting 21, 224,
    268–77
  specialized patterns 224
  variable allocation 3, 21, 220, 224,
    236–43
  see also memory exhaustion
memory constraints 8–10
memory discard 3, 220, 224, 244–50
  consequences 245
  dangling pointers 248
  implementation 245–8
  known uses 249–50
  releasing resources 247
  stack allocation 246
  temporary heaps 246–7
memory exhaustion 53–4, 171, 222–4
communicating 51
detecting 51
testing 46–7
memory limit 3, 32–7
application 33
consequences 33–4
implementation 34–5
intercepting memory management
    operations 34
known uses 37
using separate heaps 34–5
using separate processes 35
memory management unit (MMU) 123
memory partitions *see* memory limit
memory pool *see* pooled allocation
memory predictability 12, 19, 171,
    294–5
memory recycling 21
memory requirements 12, 19, 21, 294
memory reuse 21
memory strategy 29–30
memory waste 302–3
message logs 223

Meszaros, G. 12, 223
Meyer, B. 39, 47, 51, 56, 113, 230, 249
Meyers, S. 243
MFC framework 99
Microsoft 99, 114, 131, 166, 189, 239
  COM framework 277
  MS-DOS 85
  Windows
    low-memory conditions 60–1,
      63–4
    memory discard 249
    memory limits 37
    out-of-memory dialogue box 54
    program chaining 88–9
    resource files 103–4, 105–6
    run-length encoding 159
    script formats 90
    Task Manager 60
Ministry of Defence 234
mobile/hand-held projects 6, 8–10, 21–2
Moore's Law 295
Moss, J.E.B. 283
Move-To-Front (MTF) compression 161,
    163–4
MP3 compression 139
MPEG compression 139, 159
MS-DOS 85
multiple representations 53, 56, 209
  binding clients to implementations
    211
  changing between representations
    211–12
  consequences 210
  dynamically bound implementations
    211
  implementation 211–13
  and interfaces 211
  known uses 215–16

Navathe, S.B. 96, 100, 184
Netscape 55
new operator 34, 247, 255
NewtonScript 76, 197
nibble coding 145–6
Noble, J. 13, 17, 31, 47, 183, 185
normalization 184
  see also sharing
Norman, D. 6

Oates, Captain Lawrence 59

object tables 262
object-oriented databases 120
ObjectPLUS 63
objects
    compacting 263
    copying 182, 193–4
    deleting 223, 238
        compound 271–2
        shared 186
    delta objects 193–4
    embedded 201–2, 229–30
    immutable 185
    inlining see objects, embedded
    optimizing access 262
    pre-allocating 228–9
    variable-sized 253
    writing to objects in ROM 194
ObjectStore 131
operating systems
    costs 300
    heaps 246–7
O'Reilly, T. 29
Orfali, R. 110
Orwell, J. 57
Ousterhout, J.K. 90

packages 82, 108–18
    binary compatibility 113
    consequences 109
    dynamically linked libraries 110–11,
        118
    implementation 109–14
    implementing with code
        segmentation 112
    known uses 118
    loading 112
    optimizing 113–14
    processes as packages 110
    unloading 113
    version control 113
packed data 3, 13–14, 21, 172, 174–81
    compiler support 177
    consequences 176
    implementation 176–9
    known uses 180–2
packing pointers 178–9
Page, B. 223
page faults 122
page frames 122, 127–8
page replacement 123

page tables 120, 122
paging 82, 119–32
    consequences 121
    demand paging 120
    implementation 122–4
    intercepting memory access 122–3
    known uses 131
    object-oriented databases 120
    page replacement 123
    PageFile implementation 128–31
    program control of 124
    swapping 120
    thrashing 124
    working set size 124
Palm 80, 262, 266
PalmOS 85, 86, 90, 249
ParcPlace 276
partial failure 3, 48–56
    and application switching 56
    communicating memory exhaustion
        51
    consequences 50–1
    degraded modes 49, 53, 55
    detecting memory exhaustion 51
    implementation 51–4
    invariants of components 51–2
    known uses 55
    and multiple representations 53, 56
    rainy day funds 53–4
    releasing resources 52
    safety of systems 51–2
patch tables see hooks
Paterson, A. 137
patterns ix, 1–2, 11–23
    compound 12
    definition 11
    history of 12–13
    language of names 4, 12
    major techniques 16–17, 18
    specialized 16–17
PDF files 165
per-class pools 253
Petzold, C. 104, 106, 107, 118, 159
phases see application switching
PhotoShop 55
physical memory, types of 8
Pike, R. 31, 87, 89, 90, 99, 104, 152, 276,
        277, 287
pipes 99
placement new, see new operator

Plum, T. 227
PNG compression 139
pointers
    packing pointers 178–9
    smart pointer 275–6
    see also embedded pointers
polling 60, 62
pooled allocation 21, 220, 224, 251–8
    consequences 252
    implementation 253–6
    known uses 257–8
    reducing memory overheads 253
    transparent pools 254–6
    variable-sized objects 253
    variable-sized pools 254
Potter, S. ix
power consumption 300–1
PowerPoint 55
pre-allocating objects 228–9
pre-allocation *see* fixed allocation
pre-processing 202
predictability of memory use 12, 19,
    171, 294–5
Pree, W. 77
printer drivers 100, 118
problem solving 4
processes 84–6
    background 57, 60, 86
    communication between 87–8
    control systems 6
    and memory limits 35
    as packages 110
    swapping 123
program chaining see application
    switching
programmer discipline 306–7
programmer effort 19, 305–6
Prograph 54
projects
    strategy 5
    types 6–7
Prossie, J. 99
Proudfoot, D. 54
PROXY 110, 193
Pryce, N. 47
Psion 215
Pugh, W. 166

Quality, reducing data 223

rainy day funds 53–4
random access data files 96
random access memory 8, 21
read-only memory 4, 8, 21, 65–71, 83
    calling writable memory from 74
    consequences 66
    data included in code 67–9
    extending data in 75
    extending objects in 74
    implementation 66–70
    known uses 71
    and paging systems 71
    read-only file systems 69–70
    ROM Builder 67
    ROM Image 67
    static data structures 69
    storing executable code 66–7
    upgrading 72
    version control 70
    see also hooks
real-time response 19, 298–9
recycling 19, 22
reduction of waste 19, 22
redundancy, in data 136–9
reference counting 21, 224, 268–77
    allocating count fields 273
    consequences 270–1
    cycles 272–3
    deleting compound objects 271–2
    extensions 273–4
    finalization 274
    implementation 271–4
    known uses 276–7
    optimizations 274
regions 250
releasing resources 52
resource compilers 103
resource files 82, 101–7
    consequences 102
    dialog editors 103
    font files 104
    implementation 102–5
    inserting parameters into strings 105
    known uses 106
    library functions 103
    selecting variants 105
resynchronization, in decompression
    141, 156
reuse of products 19, 22
Reuters 152, 159

Riehle, D. 12
Rising, L. 13
Ritchie, D.M. 46
Robson, D. 141, 208, 215, 219, 253, 267, 276, 287
Rogue Wave 196
Rolfe and Nolan's Lighthouse system 215
ROM Builder 67
ROM Image 67
ROM memory *see* read-only memory
Rubin, K.S. 5
run-length encoding 154, 155

safety of systems 51–2
safety-critical systems 234
Saks, D. 227
Sane, S. 42
scalability 295–6
Schorr, H. 208
Scott, K. 126
Scott, R.F. 59, 64
scratchpad *see* memory discard
screensavers 64
scripting languages 90
secondary storage 8, 18, 19, 20, 21, 79–83
    application switching 4, 56, 82, 84–91
    consequences 80
    data files 4, 82, 92–100
    file system support 80
    implementation 81
    packages 82, 108–18
    paging 82, 119–32
    resource files 82, 101–7
    specialized patterns 81–2
security 301
Segewick, R. 173
segmentation 112
semantic redundancy 137–8
separate heaps 34–5
separate processes 35
servers 7, 8–10, 22–3
    see also EPOC
shared cache 185
sharing 3, 21, 32–3, 172, 182–90
    across components and processes 186
    aliasing problems 185
    consequences 183

deleting shared objects 186
immutable objects 185
implementation 184–6
known uses 189–90
lazy initialization 185
literals and strings 186
shared cache 185
Shaw, M. 25, 31, 100
Shlaer-Mellor methodology 69
signalling errors 222–3
Simons, A.J.H. 47
Sinclair ZX-81 266
single-user systems 7
singleton pattern 185, 228
small architecture 18, 20, 25–77
    architectural strategies 26
    callback functions 29
    Captain Oates 21, 32, 57–64
    component design 25–7
    consequences 27
    hooks 21, 72–7
    implementation 28–30
    interfaces 28, 38–47, 211
    known uses 31
    memory limit 3, 32–7
    memory strategy 29–30
    partial failure 3, 48–56
    read-only memory 4, 8, 21, 65–71, 83
    specialized patterns 30–1
    tailorability of memory use 28–9
small data structures 18, 20, 69, 169–73
    calculations and storage 172
    consequences 170–1
    copy-on-write 3, 172, 191–7
    embedded pointers 3, 172, 198–208
    exhaustion of memory 171
    flexibility and space 171
    implementation 171–2
    known uses 173
    multiple representations 173, 209–16
    packed data 3, 13–14, 21, 172, 174–81
    predictability of memory use 171
    sharing 3, 21, 172, 182–90
    specialized patterns 172–3
    static structures 69
small interfaces 28, 38–47, 211
    borrowing memory 40, 42–3
    consequences 39–40
    and data transfer 39, 40

small interfaces *cont.*
  designing 39
  exchanging memory across 40–4
  exhaustion testing 46–7
  implementation 40–6
  incremental 44–6
  iterators 39, 45–6
  known uses 46
  lending memory 40, 41–2
  multiple calls 44–5
  stealing memory 40, 43–4
Smalltalk 173, 186, 208, 215
  pooled allocation 256–7
  reference counting 276
smart pointer 275–6
smart-cards 6, 22
Smith, B. 70, 71
Smith, W.R. 76, 197, 295
software constraints 8
Solari, S.J. 142, 159
Solaris 113
Soni, D. 114
Soukup, P.J. 29, 208
Spookivity Database 39
stack
  allocation 246
    see also memory discard
  size 8
Stallman, R.M. 76, 112, 118, 177
start-up time 19, 299
state transition tables 69
static allocation *see* fixed allocation
static data structures 69
stealing memory 40, 43–4
Steele, G.L. 253
Steiner, J.P. 86, 88
storing executable code 66–7
strategy pattern 29
streaming 88
strings 105, 143, 148, 186
Stroustrup, B. 30, 31, 34, 36, 46, 52, 54,
  67, 74, 211, 215, 230, 247, 249, 253
subfile processing 95–6, 97
  multiple subfiles 98–9
Sullivan, W.T. 57, 64
Sun SparcWorks 114
Sutter, H. 47, 56, 243
swapping 120
Symbian *see* EPOC
Szyperski, C. 26, 110

table compression 140, 143–52
  compressing string literals 148
  consequences 144–5
  Huffman coding 146–7, 152
  implementation 145–8
  known uses 152
  nibble coding 145–6
  UTF8 encoding 148
Tabor, S. 152
Taivalsaari, A. 118
Tannenbaum, A.S. 83, 112, 123
Tasker, M. 37, 43, 53, 55, 56, 112, 116
Tektronix 12
temporary files *see* data files
temporary heaps 246–7
terminating programs 239
testing costs 19, 308
text compression 137
text editors 262
ThemePark 161
Thoelke, A. 100
Thomas, D. 31
Thompson, K. 46, 104, 152
thrashing 124
thread creation 37
threshold switch pattern 170
throw statement 52
TIFF image files 159
time performance 19, 297–8
Timex Sinclair TS-1000 266
Tofte, M. 250
tracing garbage collection *see* garbage
  collection
transient objects 239–40, 247
transparent pools 254–6
traversals 203–4

Ungar, D. 250, 283
Unicode 152
UNIX
  application switching 90
  data files 99
  directory trees 277
  file system call 46
  master programs 87
  memory limit 35, 37
  program chaining 89
unloading packages 113
usability 296–7
UTF8 encoding 148

variable allocation 3, 21, 220, 224,
    236–43
    avoiding fragmentation 239–40
    consequences 237
    deleting objects 238
    implementation 238–41
    implementing a heap 241
    known uses 242
    signalling allocation failure 238–9
    standard allocation sizes 240–1
variable-sized objects 253
variable-sized pools 254
vector class 28–9
vector tables *see* hooks
version control 70, 113
Vinoski, S. 110
virtual memory 35
    see also paging
Vlissides, J. 12, 172, 291
VMS 257–8

Waite, W. 208
Wall, L. 90

Ward, B. 166
weak references 281
Weir, C. 13, 31, 186
Wheeler, D.J. 166
Wills, A.C. 211
Wilson, P.R. 243, 288
Witten, I. 140, 142, 145, 147, 152, 159,
    166
Woods, R.E. 139, 159
working set size 124
worms 223
writable iterators 45–6
writing to objects in ROM 194

Xanalys Corporation 288
X Window System 29
Xt Window System Toolkit 29

Yellin, F. 37, 118, 141, 152
Yoder, J. 25
Yourdon, E. 40

Ziv, J. 141, 162, 165